Surviving post-socialism

The disintegration of the socialist states of eastern Europe in 1989 and the subsequent collapse of the Soviet Union in 1991 marked the beginning of what was hailed both East and West as a period of transformation to liberal democracy. Yet in the years that have followed, the peoples of this vast region have found themselves dealing with new tensions, insecurities and the chaos of the new order.

This wide-ranging study comprises a set of case studies drawn from the former USSR and eastern European socialist countries. Centring on the theme of survival strategies developed in response to changing cultural, political and economic structures, the contributors consider the problems implicit in these changing economies at all levels, from household strategy to state and policy formation. As well as covering a broad geographical area, the study takes an interdisciplinary approach, exploring a complex set of themes including: gender, ethnicity, migration, employment and labour patterns, changing family structures, and nationalism.

By emphasising local level experience, regional difference and the use that actors make of local knowledge in developing survival strategies the authors of this book argue that local-level research enhances macro-level analysis and is essential to an understanding of the transformation process.

Sue Bridger is Senior Lecturer in Russian Studies at the University of Bradford. **Frances Pine** is Research Associate of the Social Anthropology Department, University of Cambridge.

Routledge studies of societies in transition

Surviving post-socialism

Local strategies and regional responses in eastern Europe and the former Soviet Union

Edited by Sue Bridger and Frances Pine

London and New York

First published 1998
by Routledge
11 New Fetter Lane, London EC4P 4EE

Simultaneously published in the USA and Canada
by Routledge
29 West 35th Street, New York, NY 10001

Typeset in Times by
Ponting–Green Publishing Services, Chesham, Buckinghamshire

Printed and bound in Great Britain by
T.J. International Ltd, Padstow, Cornwall

British Library Cataloguing in Publication Data
A catalogue record for this book is available from the
British Library

Library of Congress Cataloging in Publication Data
Surviving post-socialism: local strategies and regional responses /
edited by Frances Pine and Sue Bridger.
        Includes bibliographical references and index.
    1. Europe, Eastern – Social conditions from 1989 – Case studies.
    2. Former Soviet republics – Social conditions – Case studies.
    3. Post-communism – Europe, Eastern – Case studies.
    4. Post-communism – Former Soviet republics – Case studies.
    5. Europe, Eastern – Economic conditions from 1989 – Case studies.
    6. Former Soviet republics – Economic conditions – Case studies.
    7. Europe, Eastern – Rural conditions – Case studies.
    8. Former Soviet republics – Rural conditions – Case studies.
    9. Decentralization in government – Europe, Eastern – Case studies.
    10. Decentralization in government – Former Soviet republics – Case studies.
    I. Bridger, Susan.   II. Pine, Frances.
    HN380.7.A8S87   1998
    306'.0947–dc21   97–8843

ISBN 0–415–15850–8

Contents

Illustrations

TABLES

MAPS

Contributors

David G. Anderson is Visiting Assistant Professor of Anthropology at the University of Alberta. He lectures on circumpolar ethnology, aboriginal rights and ecological anthropology. His ongoing research is on identity and ecological relationships in several sites in the circumpolar Arctic including Evenki, Athapaskan and Altaic landscapes.

Sue Bridger teaches Russian language and politics at the University of Bradford. She is the author of *Women in the Soviet Countryside*, the co-author of *No More Heroines: Russia, Women and the Market*, and the author of numerous articles on women in Russia.

Marta Bruno is Research Fellow in Russian Politics at the Russian and East European Research Centre at the University of Wolverhampton. Her current research interests include gender and rural development, and ongoing research on urban labour markets.

Sarah Green lectures in Social Anthropology at the University of Manchester. She is the author of various articles on the construction of gender. Her most recent research has been on the Greek–Albanian border.

Chris Hann is Professor of Anthropology at the University of Kent. He has done extensive research in Hungary and Poland, both during and since the socialist period, and has also worked in Turkey and China. His publications include *Tazlar: A Village in Hungary, A Village without Solidarity: Polish Peasants in the Years of Crisis* and, most recently, *The Skeleton at the Feast*, as well as several edited volumes and numerous articles.

Myriam Hivon received her PhD in Social Anthropology from the University of Cambridge in 1996. She carried out field work in the Russian countryside, and is the author of several articles based on this research. Her main area of interest is the rural domestic economy. She is currently working as a consultant in international development for the Canadian firm APOR International in Montreal.

Deema Kaneff is a Research Associate of the Department of Social Anthropology at the University of Cambridge. She has done extensive field research in Bulgaria, both during the socialist period and since, and has published several articles on her work.

Martin Kovats is completing a PhD on Roma politics at the University of Portsmouth, which is based on research with Roma in Hungary.

Louise Perrotta received her PhD from the London School of Economics and is currently working as a consultant to international organisations operating in Russia and Ukraine.

Frances Pine lectures in Social Anthropology at the University of Cambridge. She began doing research in the Polish countryside in 1977, and has continued to work on family farms, kinship and gender, and more recently on female work and unemployment, in different regions of Poland. She has published numerous articles on this work.

Michael Stewart is a Research Fellow in the Department of Social Anthropology at the London School of Economics. He has carried out research in Hungary, the Czech Republic and Romania. He is the author of *The Time of the Gypsies*, as well as many articles on Hungarian Gypsies, and is the director of the documentary *What Magdalena Said* and other ethnographic films.

Michael Walker lectures in Sociology at the University of Wales at Cardiff. He has been involved in research in Ukraine since 1993 and has published several articles based on this.

Foreword

C.M. Hann

In the latter part of the eighteenth century many areas of England, then still a predominantly rural society, experienced great changes in economic organisation and property relationships. As historians such as Karl Polanyi and E.P. Thompson have shown, the implications for established concepts of morality and community were far reaching. The rural societies of much of the so-called Third World have undergone a comparable transformation in the course of the twentieth century, perhaps with greatest intensity during the last decades of European colonialism. Their impact at local level was richly documented by anthropologists such as Paul Bohannan and Richard Salisbury. Now, in the last decade of this century, Polanyi's 'Great Transformation' has been extended to the Second World, that is, to those countries which set out to construct societies on a foundation other than that of market capitalism and private property. How has this latest extension of the market principle been achieved? Given that most of the societies affected were already industrial societies to some degree, to what extent can it legitimately be compared to earlier extensions?

These questions are surely among the most important facing contemporary social scientists. There has been no shortage of commentators ready to present the end of socialist power in the former Soviet bloc in general and abstract terms. Even where analysts and politicians have refrained from making explicit historical comparisons, the models they have applied have usually been driven by their understandings of what happened in 'the West'. It was assumed that liberal democracies as they have evolved in North America and western Europe provide the optimum political framework for post-communist societies, a framework within which 'free markets', 'rule of law' and 'civil society' will emerge as a coherent package to replace the evils of totalitarianism.

It did not take long for some observers to realise that the transition in eastern Europe was likely to be a more complex process than the simple models allowed, and that all talk of the 'end of history' was premature.

Privatisation has not been easy to implement, and even where vouchers have been finally distributed this has not been sufficient to induce a sense of ownership conducive to promoting investment, as in classical models of entrepreneurship. It has proved more conducive to speculation, and widespread allegations of corruption and 'mafia'. New flows of people and of goods have had sordid spinoffs and created a climate in which social identities, of gender as well as of ethnicity, region and nation, have been refashioned by prejudice. Instead of the flowering of pluralist societies old hatreds have been revived, leading in some places to extreme violence. In a development that hardly anyone predicted in 1989–91 when the Soviet system collapsed so dramatically, communists have been voted back into power in many countries of the region.

The contributions to this volume will help readers in western countries to understand these unexpected developments from a new angle – the perspective of ordinary people in the region, the people who were supposed to be the empowered citizens of post-communist societies, but who have more often come to perceive themselves as victims. The authors have each conducted first-hand research in the countries they write about. Most of them are social anthropologists, and the anthropologist's preference for qualitative methods seems to have rubbed off on other contributors who do not, formally speaking, carry this label. What this means is that they have spent a considerable time with relatively small groups of people, observing them in action and above all talking to them, in their own language, in order to elicit their own understandings of their own new social worlds. The precise tools used vary from chapter to chapter. Some authors rely mainly on their personal interviews and observations, others supplement telling anecdotes with rigorous statistical data. Sometimes the simplest methods can produce the most satisfying results, guiding the reader through the clouds of rhetoric to perceive the concrete life experiences of real human beings.

The emphasis of the collection is on survival strategies, on how people have coped in their new situations. It is perhaps best read as a counterblast to the pervasive influence of western development models which, at the macro level, predict the superiority of competitive market systems, and which have as their micro foundations notions of rational, utility maximising, individual actors. While no one doubts that eastern Europe needs good economists and accountants, it seems to me that the current transition in eastern Europe presents orthodox economists with formidable challenges, at both macro and micro levels. Their market models are fundamentally static and unhelpful in grasping the dynamic realities of economies undergoing massive dislocation, where the institutional context is crucial. At the micro level, the economists' models might at first sight seem more useful. It is true that a great deal of what is described in this book can be seen in terms of rational choices. People may join the *mafia* as a very deliberate calculation, and an old lady may 'rationally' choose to go hungry in order to ensure that she leaves enough money at her death to pay for a decent funeral. But what does the imposition of a model of *femina oeconomica* actually tell us about the predicament of this lady? Do we understand her circumstances any better as a result of having said that she has maximised her utility, given her perception of the constraints upon her in a city in eastern Ukraine in the 1990s?

The contributors to this collection take the view that it is more valuable to explore the contexts in which individuals make their decisions, as members of families and larger collectivities. They show how people draw upon old and deeply held cultural beliefs and values as they try to manage change. They show how, when material conditions deteriorate, people tend to take refuge in those groups. People may exaggerate previously understated ethnic loyalties in order to exclude others from scarce resources in conditions of increased uncertainty. Groups that were scapegoated in the past, notably the Roma, are the first to suffer. But people may also invest in an elaborate and idealised reappraisal of the history of their own group as a symbolic strategy, with no obvious material payoff for those who participate in the new rituals. There is now a solid body of anthropological work on eastern Europe which shows the enormous symbolic importance of the land to personal, familial and ethnic identities. Of course some villagers are capable of making rational choices about whether to buy the land that is now available for purchase in terms of sober assessments of their labour resources and the general economic prospects of the agrarian sector. But for many others the acquisition of land is an emotional imperative which does not seem to be influenced by any process of rational calculation.

When anthropologists emphasise the importance of culture, they seldom mean to argue that it poses insuperable barriers to change. Rather, they too make use of the idea of constraints. Cultures, the evolved beliefs and practices of particular groups, set real constraints on the implementation of a process such as the decollectivisation of agricultural land. It is possible for a new private farmer in Russia to prosper and to win the respect of his less successful neighbours – if he is sensible enough to devote a slice of his profits to the restoration of the village church, a cause that expresses the moral unity of his community. On the other hand, an individual in the same community who ignores traditional moral obligations, which include the obligation not to let good land go untilled, will attract censure. He may attract even greater opprobrium and suffer arson attacks from his neighbours if he uses his government credits not for growing crops but to finance his activities as a *spekuliant*. Similar stories were widely repeated when agricultural credits were made available to private farmers in the latter decades of the British empire. The parallels can be extended. Superficial legal changes in title in themselves seldom suffice to create a new 'feeling of ownership' among the natives or to supersede older ideas of reciprocity. It is possible to recognise here, alongside constellations of power that are the specific legacy of the socialist period, embedded customs that bear similarities to those that were eliminated in England two centuries ago with the arrival of the first industrial society, and then later on in her colonial territories.

It is, then, a relatively straightforward task to describe the problems of millions of people in the former Soviet bloc, and to tease out historical parallels. But it is not so easy to know what to do about these problems. Several chapters in this collection explore the effects of western interventions. These have taken many forms, with private foundations playing as prominent a role as governmental development aid. The agenda has often been explicitly political. For example, support for the rural sector has been solely directed towards private farmers; no matter how strongly villagers show their support for innovative forms of cooperative, these have not been eligible for support. Priority has often been given to supporting non-governmental organisations, but this focus has tended to restrict funding to fairly narrow groups, typically intellectual elites concentrated in capital cities. Those who succeed in establishing good relations with a western organisation manoeuvre to retain the tremendous advantage this gives them. The effect of many foreign interventions is therefore to accentuate previous hierarchies, where almost everything depends on patronage and personal connections. Even the well-intentioned initiatives of western feminists have not always succeeded in addressing the needs of the majority of disadvantaged women.

It is difficult to read through this book without sometimes giving way to feelings of despair and cynicism. Some of the westerners newly involved with the region are only there in search of a sensuous personal experience, while those with other motivations and deeper commitments find their work frustrated at every step by stifling bureaucracy – both local and in the hierarchies of the donor organisations. It is tempting to conclude, as others have done for the Third World, that a great deal of intervention has actually had negative consequences, and that no outsiders can do anything constructive to help ease the pain of the capitalist revolution in eastern Europe.

On the other hand, these studies do not all point to a counsel of despair. Some point to signs of hope – not so much in beneficial linkages with the West, though these do undoubtedly exist, but in the talents and energies of East Europeans themselves. From a sophisticated fashion designer in Moscow who teaches urban women about self-development to a Romanian farmer who is trying to establish an association for independent farmers from his attic, there are plenty of examples here of worthwhile personal initiatives that do not seem to be receiving the support they are crying out for. Anthropologists and others prepared to work like them can surely play a constructive role not merely in exposing the bias of existing aid programmes, but in helping to ensure that support is better, more efficiently directed in future. Often this can be achieved by a correct understanding of the appropriate cultural contexts, for example the values of Roma communities and of their neighbours' attitudes to them. Anthropological advice can mitigate the consequences of the ethnocentric assumption that English terms such as 'employment' and 'ownership' have ready equivalents in other languages. This is not in fact the case, and a better understanding of the different meanings of key terms in the eastern European context might in itself go some way to improving policy outcomes.

Local and regional studies also have a role to play in exposing the limitations of the most influential scholarly models of the post-communist transition. They suggest that ideas such as 'market equilibrium' and 'civil society' are themselves best approached as symbols or slogans, rather than as value-free, descriptive terms for the new forms of economy and society that have emerged in the region. The inadequacies of the dominant liberal paradigm, increasingly shaky in its western homelands, are now being fully exposed in the East. Perhaps the greatest challenge facing the scholars of this transformation is to use studies such as these as the foundation for building a new paradigm, capable of grasping the true significance of recent world-historical changes.

Not long ago I was the only social anthropologist at an interdisciplinary meeting on eastern Europe's transition, held in London. I was asked by a distinguished local scholar, why was an anthropologist working on eastern Europe? What sort of work could we possibly be doing there, and wasn't our real speciality the study of 'primitive peoples' such as the Trobriand Islanders of Melanesia? People in Budapest and Warsaw regularly ask me similar questions. This volume provides excellent material to answer such questions.

Canterbury, January 1997

Acknowledgements

The editors would like to thank many people who have, over several years, helped the ideas behind this volume take shape. First of these must be the contributors to the Birmingham group in its various incarnations, most recently as the ESRC Seminar on Women and Gender Relations in Russia, the Former Soviet Union and Eastern Europe, for their discussions and support. Most of all, thanks go to Linda Edmondson and Hilary Pilkington for their invitations, their welcome and their much appreciated organisational efforts.

Secondly, we are most grateful to everyone who took part in the Ilkley workshop, especially to Lydia Morris and Nigel Swain who acted as informal discussants, and to the Warsaw panellists, particularly Chris Hann and Hilary Pilkington. Several people gave presentations at Ilkley which greatly contributed to discussion but which we have not been able to include here, either because they have been published elsewhere or due to space constraints. We would like to thank all of these contributors for their interest and involvement. Louise Perrotta and Michael Stewart were unable to attend the Ilkley workshop as they were carrying out research elsewhere; we are grateful to them both for providing us with the papers published here.

We are indebted to the Department of Modern Languages, University of Bradford, for the initial financial and practical support of the workshop. Above all, heartfelt thanks go to Anne Croasdell for her quietly brilliant organisational efficiency over the last two years. We would also like to express our warmest thanks to Bernard Bickers and the staff of Myddelton Lodge for all their hard work in providing such a peaceful and inspiring atmosphere in which to work.

On a more personal note, Frances would like to thank Helen Watson and Dai Jenkins for being with Ania while she was away. Both editors would also like to express their appreciation of the time and patience of everyone who helped them survive the technology: the staff of Cambridge computing services, Andre Czegledy and Deema Kaneff in Cambridge, Rebecca Kay in Bradford and Baz Hampshire at the Flower in Hand, Scarborough. Many thanks to you all.

1 Introduction: transitions to post-socialism and cultures of survival

Frances Pine and Sue Bridger

'You wonder when it's all going to end. There's no end in sight at present. No doubt our children will grow up and live out their lives during the period of transition to the market. We'll still be on our way, crawling there. It doesn't exist, this market transition.'

(Irina, unemployed engineer, Moscow)

The period between the Polish elections of June 1989, which ended over forty years of communist rule, and the Russian coup of August 1991, which set into motion the disintegration of the Soviet Union, was for many 'the best of times and the worst of times'. The Berlin Wall fell, Wenceslas Square was stormed and reclaimed, the White House was 'defended by the people'. – these images are the heady stuff that popular myths are made of. The political events for which they have become shorthand, however, had enormous and often unanticipated repercussions for entire populations in the old states. Many of these were people who were far removed from the centres of power, played no part in the glorious revolutions, and yet for years to come would have to deal with the debris left over from communism as well as the chaos of the new order. This book is about the initial period of post-socialism, and about some of the strategies that people developed in order to survive the social, political and economic upheaval of those years.

The idea for a volume of articles dealing with local consequences of macro-level political and economic change evolved from a series of discussions and meetings between the editors throughout 1993 and 1994. Both of us were working on research projects dealing directly with the 'transitional' period, Sue on women and unemployment in Moscow region, Frances on responses to unemployment in two regions of Poland. The way in which our perceptions overlapped, and at times paralleled each other, was striking, even though we were working in quite different geographical regions, and Poland was arguably well ahead of Russia on the road to capitalism. It became clear to us that many of the women we were talking to in Poland and Russia were experiencing the same sorts of pressures, and were responding to the new economic orders in markedly similar ways. As we spoke to others involved in research in the former socialist countries, particularly to those colleagues and research students carrying out intensive field research, it became apparent that in spite of regional and historical differences, certain processes of adaptation were repeating themselves and were almost becoming predictable. Equally striking, however, was our growing impression that the world we were witnessing and our colleagues were reporting did not fit easily into the model of transitional economics which was most dominant in western press and academic writings at the time. Local history, experience and memory were being ignored in the grand narratives.

Believing it would be fruitful to explore the local perspective further, we invited a small group of colleagues, both from social anthropology and from Russian and East European studies, to participate in an interdisciplinary workshop. In April 1995 about thirty of us met for a weekend in Ilkley, Yorkshire. The following August a small group from the workshop – Anderson, Bridger, Kaneff, Pilkington and Pine – formed a panel on 'transforming local economies' at the Fifth World Congress of Central and East European Studies in Warsaw, where these ideas were pursued further before a wider audience. Chris Hann, who had been unable to attend the Ilkley workshop, was also in Warsaw and acted as discussant for the panel (Hann 1995: 216–19).

Most of the chapters in this book have their roots in papers presented at the Ilkley workshop. We asked participants initially to concentrate on ethnicity, gender and 'underclass', in terms of survival strategies developed to cope with the 'transitional' period. Although we ourselves found both 'transition' and 'underclass' deeply problematic concepts, they were being used as analytic shorthand in much of the social science literature on post-socialist societies, and we felt that as such they had to be considered carefully. During the workshop it became clear that most participants shared our unease about the terms. 'Underclass' particularly emerged as a term with such dubious political implications that most of us felt it could be of only the most limited use in analysing the experience of the former socialist countries. 'Transition', on the other hand, while also highly problematic, was so central to the emerging literature and so commonly used in both public and academic discourse that we felt it merited further serious and critical discussion. It is clear from the range of approaches taken to the concept of 'transition' that the implications of the term for post-socialism are obscured by the lack of clarity in social, political and economic definitions. The notions which underpin the concept reflect this theoretical confusion, precisely because, as various commentators have recently pointed out, reliance on any ill-defined blanket term obfuscates the range and variation of issues involved (Hann 1994; Verdery 1991, 1996; Watson 1994; but see also Humphrey 1995a for a view which balances regional and historical diversity against the shared experience of 'lived socialism' within a centrally planned command economy).

A transition implies a temporary state between two fixed positions, a movement between the point of departure and that of arrival. Many of the economists, politicians and management consultants involved in the process of restructuring appeared initially to place a somewhat unwarranted faith in the inevitability of a transformation to a capitalist demand economy, arguing that given the correct and economically rational conditions, ideals of standard liberal democracy would eventually take root. In a way reminiscent of development thinking of the post-war period, these assumptions hinge on the idea of a lineal progression, in which, if the correct procedure is followed, the desired outcome can be assured. Theorists of the post-war period assumed that development would lead automatically to modernity if local peoples could only be persuaded to abandon the constraints and chains of traditional culture; in a similar fashion, post-socialist planners have emphasised the economic freedom which will result as the antiquated machinery of state socialism is shed and the principles of free-market capitalism embraced (Aslund 1992; Winiecki 1993).

To some extent, this assumption of a logical progression towards capitalism must be seen as the result of mutual misunderstandings between East and West. The scope for misunderstanding was apparent from the onset of the changes. In the latter part of 1989, television screens, newspapers and magazines worldwide were saturated with images of popular protest throughout the socialist bloc: film crews avidly recorded the demonstrations in Wenceslas Square and the lines of Trabis jamming the roads out of East Germany. If the most powerful image of successful popular protest was the demolition of the Berlin Wall, the execution of the Ceaucescus offered a stark portent of power politics yet to come. Above all, this latter event reflected the wider political agenda which could underpin apparently spontaneous eruptions of popular sentiment. This raises the question whether the events of 1989 and the subsequent process of change can also be viewed in terms of a deliberate destabilising, or undermining, of the socialist regimes by interest groups in both East and West.

The fact that these images of change were carried on domestic network television within the socialist bloc itself both legitimated popular protest and gave impetus to a continuing wave of demands for change both in eastern Europe and in the Soviet Union. In this sense, it is impossible to see any of the political events as occurring in isolation; the instantaneous portrayal of history unfolding not only recorded but generated change. The important point here is that what was originally represented as grass-roots political protest sweeping across East-Central Europe and onwards into the USSR could in fact only have taken place with the explicit consent or, at least, the covert encouragement of the Gorbachev administration. The message that foreign adventurism was no longer part of the USSR's plan – powerfully conveyed by Gorbachev's withdrawal of troops from Afghanistan – clearly could be applied directly and much earlier to the satellite countries: there would be no Hungary of '56, no Prague of '68 in the 1980s. When Gorbachev made his famous walkabouts in the GDR in 1989, and essentially told the surging crowds that if they wanted their freedom they must take it, he appeared at the time to be acting in a way which was both spontaneous and dramatic. In fact, however, he demonstrated a marked continuity from the early 1980s; Russian troops, contrary to popular expectation, had not been sent into action against Poles during the Solidarity period, nor indeed against protestors in any of the Warsaw Pact countries during the sporadic but repeated periods of unrest.

Equally, this period of unrest and uneasy internal negotiations could be interpreted in terms of a highly cynical promotion of western economic and political interests in eastern Europe. It could be argued for example that the Cold War years of the 1970s and 1980s were marked by well-orchestrated attempts by western government and financial institutions to destabilise the eastern bloc, particularly through the medium of vast hard currency loans. In order to understand either the period leading up to the highly visible political protest against the socialist regimes in 1989, or the more recent and to some even more puzzling re-election of former communists to power, the long-term if hidden agendas of both western/American and Soviet administrations must be taken into consideration. While the images produced for general consumption suggested spontaneous outbursts of populist dissent, closer examination of the events of 1989 called into question not only their spontaneity, but the very extent of grass-roots participation itself.

Widespread local participation in political protest has become part of the mythology which has grown up around the demise of the socialist regimes. Closer scrutiny, however, casts serious doubt on assumptions of orchestrated popular participation in and even support of radical dissent outside urban or industrial centres. Few if any of the groups or peoples which form the focus of this book were involved in mass demonstrations of protest against the socialist regimes. We would argue that it is the experience of these people, rather than that of the more high-profile architects of public change, which was the more typical of the initial months of upheaval. When seen in this way, 1989 represents one defining moment, or particularly focused snapshot, in a much longer and more intricate process of political and economic disintegration. The acts of protest themselves can be interpreted not as the total catalyst of change, but as ritual acts or symbolic expressions of a much longer process. Throughout the Soviet bloc, the socialist state was dismantled in public, in an extremely ritualistic way. It is undeniable that crowds of protestors spontaneously pulled down statues of Lenin, destroyed party slogans and replaced flags and other communist iconography with national or western symbols. This was the dramatic face of change, captured on camera throughout eastern Europe. What the TV crews were less likely to record was the unchanging pattern of daily life, which went on much as before in many of the less central, off-camera regions.

After 1989, the language and symbols of socialism were replaced by those of free-market democracy. The free elections and the burgeoning of civil groups of every description lent validity to claims that the foundations of democracy were being established. As imported consumer goods filled the shops it was easy to believe that the prosperity associated with free-market capitalism was just around the corner. With the passage of time, however, it became increasingly apparent that the rhetoric of transformation did not accurately reflect the experience of most ordinary people. The new economies, rather than being incorporated into stable market capitalism, were suspended in a kind of limbo: while the structures of socialist polity had been removed, it was by no means clear what, if anything, could be salvaged which would be capable of replacing them.

Within the boundaries of the socialist bloc, the countries shared a common experience of a planned economy and Marxist–Leninist ideology, implemented through an extraordinarily powerful and ubiquitous bureaucracy. There was, however, an enormous diversity of history and culture; since 1989, each country's particular path towards free-market economy and civil society has been different. Despite the uniformity of experience created by the principles of centralised distribution and a command economy, these countries were not all at the same level of economic and industrial development.

The disparity between them arose from both geographical factors – their location and their natural resources – and politico-economic ones – their existing infrastructure prior to socialism. Even more importantly, it was also mirrored in the position of each in relation to western Europe, particularly during the latter socialist period. Thus, for example, Poland and Hungary by the 1970s were regarded by western Europe as 'central European' in terms of a shared culture, and were 'encouraged' both by hard-currency loans and inclusion in joint ventures. Romania and Bulgaria, on the other hand, were for quite different reasons associated with southern Europe, if with Europe at all; they were regarded as culturally different and economically underdeveloped, both of which justified their exclusion from the core of the European community. After 1989, these differences have been exacerbated by the pace of each country's programme of market reform and the extent to which each has been accorded status by the European Union. Furthermore, they continue to be reflected in actual standards of living, quality of life, and levels of economic development in the more and the less 'European' countries.

In social terms, since 1989, the significance of existing regional, ethnic and other historical differences has become increasingly apparent. The actual process of lived change, and the strategies which people have been able to develop at the local level for dealing with it, have arisen largely from the specificities of local histories, cultural experience, environment and landscape; and, of course, the particular economic position of each at the precise moment of change. Diversity has been a significant factor not only between individual countries, but between communities and regions within each country. The economic prospects of villagers living in beautiful mountain areas near western borders may be very different from those of industrial workers in areas highly polluted by crumbling and archaic factories. For the former, the new order may open opportunities for local developments such as tourism and cross-border trade; for the latter, unemployment and increasing privation has been a more common experience (Green, Pine, Stewart and Walker, this volume; Pine 1996).

This brings us back to the complexity of the concept of transition. Initially, with the disintegration of the socialist states, the point of departure at least appeared to be clear. However, as the disparity between the anticipated and the actual outcome of reforms and restructuring grew increasingly obvious, the lack of consensus about both the direction the reforms *should* take, and the ways in which socialism should be evaluated, became apparent. In retrospect, the memory of the socialist past itself has come to be obscured by differing interpretations. As the present becomes more difficult, and expectations of the future increasingly bleak and uncertain, those affected by the reforms have shown an ever greater capacity for reinventing the socialist past (Anderson, Stewart, this volume; Pine, forthcoming).

In a context of growing privation, people understandably re-evaluate their past, emphasising positive aspects of experiences which formerly they may have taken for granted or even opposed. This process of reinterpretation, as it is occurring in the former socialist countries, is further complicated by the fact that it is situated within a wider international discourse which represents the Cold War as a battle in which the 'good' forces of western democracy and capitalism defeated the 'evil' forces of communism. This triumphalism both underpins the idea of a logical transition and inhibits any coherent discussion of how the stability of post-war capitalism itself was eroded during the Cold War period.

The idea of a logical transition is rooted in the age of Fordism and the concepts of lineal development and modernity; the advanced capitalism of the late twentieth century, however, belongs more to the fragmented economic order of post-modernity. In this new global economy the old models are proving insufficient to cope with the complexities of an increasingly international labour force and a disrupted and dispersed labour process. Neither class analysis based on the appropriation of labour nor theories of the free market based on supply and demand can adequately explain the far more amorphous social relations of globalisation (see Featherstone 1990; Miller 1995). To a great extent, under both socialism and capitalism until the late 1980s, work was seen as the main source of economic and social value. In the last fifteen years the coherence of that position has been lost (see Lampland 1995). The problem with the terminology of 'transition' is that it assumes that coherence still remains and hence that the move from socialism to capitalism has continuity at this level at least. This model of transition presupposes – and here we would argue that it is aimed as much at the western as at the eastern audience – that capitalism is still fully functioning; it fails to acknowledge the fundamental shift in patterns of production and consumption.

The articles in this book reflect the complexity of the relationship between state and local-level change, concentrating primarily on local knowledge and practice. A dominant theme recurring throughout the book is that of loss and change: loss, in terms of past certainty, economic stability and moral order, and change, in terms of strategies developed and employed to cope with this loss. Many of the articles contain stories of people who have dealt with change with some measure of success. Yet this success is, on the whole, individualistic and set against a wider framework of uncertainty and instability. The demise of the socialist regimes in the Soviet satellite states, followed quickly by the collapse of the Soviet Union itself, set into motion a remarkable process of social, political, economic and physical upheaval with consequences extending far beyond the most obvious issues of unemployment and falling living standards.

While the most brutal confrontations have taken place within the former Soviet Union and the former Yugoslavia, throughout the region generally ethnic tensions have heightened, and local disputes may have unpredicted outcomes. As borders are being redrawn, and as competition for local resources is further complicated by the climate of scarcity, the absence of the levelling function of the socialist state allows a new emphasis on ethnic identity and incipient nationalism to emerge. The 'velvet divorce' between the Czech Republic and Slovakia, for instance, was effected relatively peacefully, but the forcible 'repatriation' of Slovakian Gypsies from the Czech side of the border has been both ruthless and violent (Stewart 1994).

In this case the losses and uncertainties generated by changing economic and social conditions are projected on to a scapegoat or 'other'. Similarly, the rise of anti-Semitism throughout the former socialist states can be seen in this light. On a rather different level, the influx of 'economic tourists' from Ukraine into Poland has generated ill feeling among those who feel that their own market territory is being usurped by outsiders. These 'Russian' women may be labelled as sexually promiscuous, or portrayed as selling sexual favours to local men, while 'Russian' males are represented as dangerous and threatening to the purity of local women. In Germany, meanwhile, it is likely to be Polish migrants who are labelled as encroaching 'others'. Here and elsewhere, complicated new discourses of identity and nationalism focused on images of race, sex and gender are emerging at the points where symbolic or political boundaries are crossed (Bridger *et al.* 1996; Hann and Hann 1992). On yet another level, ideas about ethnic identity may take on political dimensions revolving around claims of economic entitlement and resulting in rising tensions among a previously stable population; this has occurred most dramatically and tragically in Bosnia (Bringa 1995; Sorabji 1995), but it is a pattern identifiable on a lesser scale from Siberia to Bulgaria to the former GDR (see Kovats, Kaneff, this volume).

A major consequence of economic change through the former socialist bloc has been the renegotiation of status and identity, both of individuals and of groups. The combination of policies of full employment, ideologies of collective ownership, and social construction of identity through productive work meant that a job conferred not only a wage but also mediated a set of social, economic and cultural relations between the individual and the wider community. Job losses, workplace closures and changing relations between managers and workers as a result of privatisation all have an immediate impact on the individual's sense of personhood and status. This is not of course exclusive to the former socialist countries but can be observed wherever a dominant industry has collapsed. In Britain, for example, permanent closure of steelworks and mines and the consequent destruction of personal life and local community spring readily to mind. The dismantling of manufacturing in Britain, however, has taken place over an extended period and the concept of terminal unemployment has been introduced gradually. The experience of sudden and massive redundancies may be remarkably similar in communities in Poland, Russia or Britain. The difference lies in the pace at which the national picture has changed. In the case of the former socialist bloc the change from a state policy of full employment to one which allowed the introduction of mass unemployment was no sooner discussed than it happened. The situation was without recent local precedent: eastern Europeans, unlike westerners who found themselves unemployed, had neither any preparation for long-term unemployment nor any concept of what it might entail. In so far as safety nets, such as unemployment benefit, existed, they were on the whole inadequate and underdeveloped. Furthermore, in the centrally planned economies, specific industries tended to be concentrated in key areas, and there was rarely much diversification within one region. Given this fact, the loss of status entailed by individual unemployment has often been exacerbated by a community-wide deprivation of working identity and status (Nagengast 1991). Several of the articles in this volume examine ways in which the very powerful connection between labour and entitlement which was fostered by socialist ideology is moulding people's responses to new private owners and entrepreneurs; particularly in rural areas, it seems, people continue to adhere to a strong moral principle that land and its products should not be owned by those who do not work it (Hivon, Kaneff and Stewart, this volume). This 'old' association between labour and entitlement is seen as diametrically opposed to new opportunities for entrepreneurial investment and development, and new styles of consumption.

As Humphrey and others have pointed out, the work environment of the collective farm or factory was one of a 'total social institution' (Goffman 1962; Clarke 1992; Humphrey 1995a). Loss of employment and income was compounded by the breakdown of attached services such as childcare, health, subsidised shops, access to housing, and even to electricity, gas and water. Often these repercussions were quite unanticipated: local workers might well have been unaware of the significance of the interdependence between housing, utilities and continuing employment. Or, indeed, the collapse of the enterprise itself could result in the liquidation of all its ancillary services. Obviously, there is no one pattern here. Differences between levels of collectivisation, for example, during socialism, and between policies redefining private property and the processes of privatisation and restitution themselves in the post-socialist period, are enormous (see, for example, Hann 1993; Kaneff 1996; Swain 1996; Verdery 1996). National approaches to lack of work, welfare benefits and training, and development of local initiative and foreign aid vary, and each local landscape has its own stories to tell. There is certainly an overall pattern of traumatic change, resulting from the breakdown of the socialised sector, which can be observed throughout the entire region. The precise articulation between economic restructuring and local response, however, can best be demonstrated through examination of locally specific survival strategies, at the level of the individual, household, or community or interest group.

The impact of trauma has not been uniform. In many instances, old power structures have reappeared under new names and the same individuals may well wield influence under new guises. The privatisation of a collective farm in Poland, for example, may result in a former manager or new director leasing the best land and buying up the newest machinery for knockdown prices, primarily on the basis of inside knowledge, and setting up something resembling a latifundia, employing former farm workers on low pay (Swain 1996: 197–200). In Russia, the transformation of collective farms into joint stock companies has turned farm managers into company directors, with the potential for creating new and even more oppressive hierarchical relations with workers (see Bridger 1997; Perrotta, this volume). It must be kept in mind, however, that even these national differences by no means represent the entire spectrum. In Poland no more than a quarter of arable land was ever collectivised, and the privatisation process varies significantly from region to region (Pine, this volume; Swain 1996). Throughout Russia, where virtually the whole of agriculture was state controlled, there is far greater uniformity, and private farms have had to be set up from scratch (Hivon 1995, this volume). In other countries there is further variation (Swain 1996): Hungary, for instance, had already embarked on a mixed programme in agriculture well before 1989 (Hann 1980); in Bulgaria and Romania, even within individual villages different kinds of new co-operatives are emerging (Kaneff 1996; Stewart, this volume). With the exception of Russia, local restitution has played an important part in the discussion of land ownership in all of these countries. This has resurrected memories of economic inequality and raised new issues of contention concerning use and entitlement (Hann 1993, 1995; Kaneff 1996; Swain 1996). In Russia as well, the relationship between land use and entitlement to property has been made explicit through the process of privatisation. (Hivon, this volume).

Each of these situations has a different potential for the re-establishment of old power relations. What they have in common, and this is also observable in urban areas, is an exacerbation of established patterns of inequality. In the case studies presented in this volume, inequalities are shown to arise from age, gender and ethnic difference, and to be concerned with new patterns of power. One of the immediate effects of restructuring in all of the post-socialist countries has been, as already mentioned, the rapid rise of unemployment. This has particular and specific implications for certain sectors of the population. Women, for example, are most likely to be among the first victims of structural adjustment, as extensive cuts are made in light industry and the service sectors, both traditional locations of female labour. Equally significantly, there has been specific and overt sexual discrimination in patterns both of redundancies and of recruitment.

Finally, throughout the former socialist countries, pro-natalist policies and attitudes have gained momentum from the growth of ideologies of nationalism. In practical terms, economic rationalisation of social services, in conjunction with unemployment, has the effect of channelling women's labour into family obligations and caring activities often located within the home and the domestic sphere (Einhorn 1993; Corrin 1994; Bridger *et al.* 1996; Pine 1996). As well as gender, age is proving to be a significant factor in exclusion from long-term employment, with both men and women over 40 finding it increasingly difficult to obtain new work (Pilkington 1996; Corrin 1994). Finally, members of distinct ethnic groups have been disproportionately affected by the development of a hostile labour market (Kovats, this volume).

These patterns can be understood at least partly in terms of the distribution of resources, and can be analysed with reference to competition for position, influence, and material wealth in the new order. The studies in this volume focus on people who are on the whole excluded from the significant power structures, with neither the economic means nor the political influence necessary for the consolidation of power. They also show, however, the creative responses upon which even the most apparently powerless people can draw.

All the authors writing here focus on survival strategies which, to a greater or lesser extent, are being developed by local actors and interest groups within the context of displacement, dispossession and exclusion. Survival strategies are not necessarily 'economically rational' according to models of supply, demand and efficient self-interest. However, in terms of cultural meaning, local knowledge and understanding, and within the context of social relationships and networks, they are often the best and most sensible responses people can make. By stressing local-level survival strategies we do not for a moment intend to minimise the very real power exercised by the dominant structures of state and market economy; rather, we wish to show that individuals respond to those external structures, and are neither the passive victims of outside forces nor themselves totally in control of their own fates. The articles in this volume deal with local responses to macro-level change. They look at the displacement and dispossession caused by change – particularly privatisation – but also at the creative responses people develop from their repertoire of resources to deal with the new situations.

The authors share a strong commitment to writing about people with 'hidden histories' (see Watson 1994; Scott 1990; Kligman 1988) – people on the margins, or excluded in one way or another from the centre – and to shifting the emphasis of the academic narrative from the macro level to the micro level. These are political as well as academic issues which, in a period of rapid change such as this, are inevitably highly polemical. It is interesting to note that in many ways our assessments of the changing economic and political conditions of the post-socialist states coincide with those of economic analysts looking at the second phase of the macro picture (EBRD

1996; OECD 1996; Independent Strategy 1996). Where we diverge is in our understanding of what an acceptable cost of change might be. Many of those looking at the macro level and applying classic market models believe that progress can only be made, and the situation of the population at large improved, after severe and drastic measures of restraint have been implemented and followed. According to this line of thought, it is inevitable that there will be casualties, as the socialist system was, on the one hand, too benign and, on the other, simply too corrupt and too inefficient for too long. Now belts must be tightened and some people, or some sectors of the population, must be discounted or even discarded. A more liberal approach to take would be that this is in fact too high a price to pay for rapid change; here the premise is that the pace of change cannot justify the social costs. This leads to a further and equally significant point of difference, which is highlighted in several of the articles in this volume: what is to be considered the correct and proper role of the state. Some economists and policy makers may believe that the state should run its national economy like a business, aiming towards profit, abandoning hangers-on and abolishing the 'free lunch'. An alternate view taken by many social scientists is that the national economy should not be run in this way because the basic morality and economic premises underpinning government and business are quite different. Here it would be argued that the obligation of the state is to provide services for its citizens, and to protect their civil and social rights; through this it fosters social cohesion rather than divisive policies aimed at supporting individualist interest.

It is not the intention of the authors in the collection to present only a bleak and negative picture of the situation in the post-socialist states. The people described have survived a great deal already, throughout the socialist period and before it. They have become skilled at activating local networks, making use of local knowledge and resisting authority through their informal activities, their rituals, and above all their humour. Nevertheless, this is not to say that local populations will cheerfully endure whatever is thrown at them. From the very beginning of the process of reform, some western analysts warned of the undesirable political consequences which could potentially arise from too rapid or extreme an embrace of the market (Wapenhans 1991; Holzmann 1991; Standing 1991; Fischer 1993; World Bank 1990; Przeworski 1991).

If the social costs were to prove too high, as some were from the beginning anticipating, there could well be a popular rejection not merely of 'shock therapy' but of the very concept of liberal democracy and of market reform itself. Societies such as Russia, where the economy remains in a parlous condition, have already demonstrated through the ballot box their disenchantment with western-oriented prescriptions for change. What is more surprising, perhaps, is that in economies which are considered to be the great success stories of market reform, such as Poland and Hungary, the same phenomenon can be observed. Populations throughout the former socialist countries have disconcertingly failed to be grateful for the advent of consumerism and western-style consumption. Instead, the rise of erstwhile communist candidates and parties has reflected a mood in the electorate which tends almost towards protectionism. Hence we are witnessing disappointment at the failure to arrive at the new promised land, resentment at the promotion of an ideology of self-interest and distaste at the shift towards ever-increasing gulfs between rich and poor (see Humphrey 1995a; Pine 1996). On a more disturbing level, there has been throughout these states a growing nationalist sentiment which views the west with increasing mistrust and, at its most extreme, rejects it and all it stands for. Ironically, it might thus be concluded that, by its promotion of socially damaging economic policies and uncontrolled corporate self-interest, the West has inadvertently forfeited the right to uncritical emulation. It is in this context, not only of massive change but also of continuing internal tension and confusion within the former socialist states, that these articles have been written.

REFERENCES

Aslund, A. (1992) *The Post-Soviet Economy: Soviet and Western Perspectives*, London: Pinter.

Bridger, S. (1997) 'Rural women and the impact of market reform', in M. Buckley (ed.) *Post-Soviet Women: From the Baltic to Central Asia*, Cambridge: Cambridge University Press.

Bridger, S., Kay, R. and Pinnick, K. (1996) *No More Heroines? Russia, Women and the Market*, London: Routledge.

Bringa, T. (1995) *Being Muslim the Bosnian Way*, Princeton: Princeton University Press.

Clarke, S. (1992) 'The quagmire of privatisation', *New Left Review*, 196: 3–28.

Corrin, C. (1994) *Magyar Women: Hungarian Women's Lives, 1960s-1990s*, London: Macmillan.

EBRD (1996) *Transition Report Update*, London: European Bank for Reconstruction and Development.

Einhorn, B. (1993) *Cinderella Goes to Market: Citizenship, Gender and Women's Movements in East-Central Europe*, London: Verso.

Featherstone, M. (ed.) (1990) *Global Culture: Nationalism, Globalisation and Modernity*, London: Sage.

Fischer, G. (1993) 'Social Protection', in G. Fischer and G. Standing (eds) *Structural Change in Central and Eastern Europe: Labour Market and Social Policy Implications*, Paris: Organisation for Economic Cooperation and Development.

Goffman, E. (1962) *Asylums*, Chicago: Chicago University Press.

Hann, C.M. (1980) *Tazlar: A Village in Hungary*, Cambridge: Cambridge University Press.

—— (1993) 'From production to property: decollectivisation and the family–land relationship in contemporary Hungary', *Man*, 28, 3: 299–320.

—— (1994) 'After communism: reflections on East European anthropology and the transition', *Social Anthropology*, 2, 3: 239–49.

—— (1995) *The Skeleton at the Feast: Contributions to East European Anthropology*, Canterbury: University of Kent at Canterbury CSAC Monographs.

Hann, C. and Hann, I. (1992) 'Samovars and sex on Turkey's Russian markets', *Anthropology Today*, 8, 4: 3–6.

Hivon, M. (1995) 'Local resistance to privatisation in rural Russia', in D. Anderson and F. Pine (eds) *Surviving the Transition: Development Concerns in the Post-Socialist World*, *Cambridge Anthropology*, 18, 2: 13–22.

Holzmann, R. (1991) 'Safety nets in transition economies: concepts, recent developments, recommendations', in P. Marer and S. Zecchini (eds) *The Transition to a Market Economy: Special Issues*, Paris: Organisation for Economic Cooperation and Development.

Humphrey, C. (1995a) 'Introduction', in D. Anderson and F. Pine (eds) *Surviving the Transition: Development Concerns in the Post-Socialist World*, *Cambridge Anthropology*, 18, 2: 1–12.

—— (1995b) 'Creating a culture of disillusionment: consumption in Moscow, a chronicle of changing times', in D. Miller (ed.) *Worlds Apart: Modernity through the Prism of the Local*, London: Routledge, 43–68.

Independent Strategy (1996) *Emerging Markets: The Coming Crisis*, London: Independent Strategy.

Kaneff, D. (1996) 'Responses to "democratic" land reforms in a Bulgarian village', in R. Abrahams (ed.) *After Socialism: Land Reform and Social Change in Eastern Europe*, Oxford: Berghahn, 85–114.

Kligman, G. (1988) *The Wedding of the Dead: Ritual, Poetics and Popular Culture in Transylvania*, Berkeley: University of California Press.

Lampland, M. (1995) *The Object of Labor: Commodification in Socialist Hungary*, Chicago: University of Chicago Press.

Miller, D. (ed.) (1995) *Worlds Apart: Modernity through the Prism of the Local*, London: Routledge.

Nagengast, C. (1991) *Reluctant Socialists, Rural Entrepreneurs: Class, Culture and the Polish State*, Boulder: Westview Press.

OECD (1996) *Agricultural Policies, Markets and Trade in Transition Economies*, Paris: Organisation for Economic Cooperation and Development.

Pilkington, H. (1996) *Gender, Generation and Identity in Contemporary Russia*, London: Routledge.

Pine, F. (1996) 'Redefining women's work in rural Poland', in R. Abrahams (ed.) *After Socialism: Land Reform and Social Change in Eastern Europe*, Oxford: Berghahn, 133–56.

—— (1997) 'Pilfering identity: Gorale culture in post-socialist Poland and before', *Paragraph*, 20,1: 59–74.

Przeworski, A. (1991) *Democracy and the Market*, Cambridge: Cambridge University Press.

Scott, J.C. (1990) *Domination and the Arts of Resistance: Hidden Transcripts*, New Haven: Yale University Press.

Sorabji, C. (1995) 'A very modern war: terror and territory in Bosnia Herzegovina', in R. Hinde and H. Watson (eds) *War: A Cruel Necessity?*, London: Taurus Academic Press.

Standing, G. (ed.) (1991) *In Search of Flexibility: The New Soviet Labour Market*, Geneva: ILO.

Stewart, M. (1994) 'What Magdalena Said', *Everyman*, BBC1, Tx.3, January.

Swain, N. (1996) 'Getting land in Central Europe', in R. Abrahams (ed.) *After Socialism: Land Reform and Social Change in Eastern Europe*, Oxford: Berghahn, 193–216.

Verdery, K. (1991) 'Theorizing socialism: a prologue to the "transition"', *American Ethnologist*, 18, 3: 419–39.

—— (1996) *What Was Socialism and What Comes Next?*, Berkeley: University of California Press.

Wapenhans, W. (1991) 'The World Bank', in P. Marer and S. Zecchini (eds) *The Transition to a Market Economy: The Broad Issues*, Paris: Organisation for Economic Cooperation and Development.

Watson, R.S. (ed.) (1994) *Memory, History and Opposition under State Socialism*, Santa Fe: School of American Research Press.

Winiecki, J. (1993) *Post-Soviet Type Economies in Transition*, Aldershot: Avebury Press.

World Bank (1990) *World Bank Development Report 1990*, Oxford: Oxford University Press.

2 When 'land' becomes 'territory'

Land privatisation and ethnicity in rural Bulgaria

Deema Kaneff

'We were better before, in the other times [meaning the socialist period], when it didn't matter if we didn't have land.'

(Macedonian woman from Talpa)

In 1994 a Bulgarian politician of Turkish ethnic background, Ahmed Dogan, reportedly made some comments in a newspaper with respect to land privatisation. He was quoted as having said to the Turkish community in Bulgaria, 'remember it's not land you're buying but territory in this country'.[1] The remark went directly to the heart of Bulgarian fears, playing upon a continued perceived threat of Turkish domination. The 500 years during which Bulgaria was under Ottoman rule, with freedom being gained only in the latter part of the last century, has featured centrally in questions of Bulgarian nationalism. But it is not the continued historical relevance of perceived Turkish domination with which I am concerned here. The quote also indicates a strong association between land ownership and ethnicity. Dogan's comment implies that 'when Turks come to own Bulgarian land it becomes Turkish territory'. In speaking publicly to one sector of the Bulgarian population – the Turkish community – the veiled threat implied the importance of land ownership in the ethnic cause. It is this relationship between ethnicity, land and territory which is explored below.

My initial assumption is that 'territory' is a cultural construction, physical space burdened with socio-political significance. This has particular relevance in the context of the renewed importance of land ownership brought about by the emerging capitalist agenda of the Bulgarian state. Land ownership is becoming another important basis of ethnic differentiation (along with other more 'usual' criteria such as religion and language). While the Communist Party's 'broadly homogenizing goals' were designed to eliminate differences of various forms (Verdery 1994a: 225), post-socialist restitution of land is leading to the (re)creation of various divisions

– including ones of an ethnic nature. This is not to say that ethnic distinctions did not exist before 1989, but rather that privatisation is giving ethnic differentiation a new impetus. The particular way in which the Bulgarian state has carried out privatisation – that is, through restitution to pre-1944 landowners – is central to the ethnic divisions that have become evident in the last few years. Below I examine one instance where ethnic tensions between villagers are a local-level consequence of the state-enforced privatisation programme. At the same time, these emerging divisions may also be viewed in terms of strategy; with those disadvantaged by land restitution finding solidarity with others in similar circumstances.

The topic is explored by focusing on the situation in one village in central-northern Bulgaria which I call Talpa. Fieldwork was first conducted in 1986–88 during the final years of socialism. Regular trips since then provide data for the more recent period, the descriptions below being largely based on the latter stages of 1994.[2] While the comments made with respect to this village do not necessarily reflect the situation throughout the country, the association between privatisation laws and increasing divisions along ethnic lines has relevance in the numerous Bulgarian villages where resettlement during the socialist period had taken place.[3]

BACKGROUND

The association between land and descent is not new. Indeed the notion of 'spilling blood' to gain freedom from Turkish domination abounds in Bulgarian history. Land is significant as a metaphor, uniting all those who share blood and have spilt it, in the name of freeing Bulgaria from its historical oppressors. If Dogan's comment associating land ownership with Bulgarian–Turkish relations has general relevance within the country, it also has specific significance in the case of Talpa. In Talpian history, land and its transference of ownership between Bulgarians and Turks have been portrayed – by the Bulgarian inhabitants – as having central importance. In a history of the village written by a retired (now deceased) school principal, it is noted that the earliest records of settlement in Talpa date back to 1618, when documents indicate that the village was populated by a purely Bulgarian population. However, the same history notes that later documents reveal the gradual increase in Turkish population so that by the time Bulgaria attained freedom from the Ottoman empire in 1878, Talpa was inhabited solely by Turks. The Bulgarians were attracted to the fertile lands and resettled the area after the Turkish inhabitants had fled. The latter returned briefly after outright defeat to sell their properties to Bulgarian families (Naymov, cited in Kaneff 1992). According to Talpian stories, the few Turkish families who remained were driven out by the Bulgarians who placed pig fat in the village water supply. The Bulgarian settlers levelled all existing structures, the mosque included, and constructed Bulgarian-style buildings including a church, a school and later a cultural centre located around a central square.

The village remained 'purely Bulgarian' until after the Second World War, when the industrialisation policy of the socialist government led to a number of demographic changes throughout the country. Most importantly, there was a huge out-migration of village youth to the cities. For example, in 1934 Talpa's population was 1,969; this had declined to 615 by 1994 (predominantly elderly, two-thirds of whom are pensioners). To some extent this was a consequence of socialist ideology which placed greatest value on the urban-based working class, who were assigned the historically most important position in realising the goal of communism, while the contribution of agricultural workers was devalued. The out-migration of Bulgarian youth to the cities in search of higher education, more comfortable lifestyles and non-agricultural occupations resulted in a shortage of rural labour. This was partly redressed through the movement of people from other areas within the country.

In 1994 the village population comprised 11 Pomaks[4] who immigrated in the late 1940s, 28 Macedonians who immigrated in the 1960s, 24 Turks and 47 Gypsies, who immigrated in the 1970s. Although all are Bulgarian citizens, there are contexts such as restitution in which these villagers (about one-sixth of the permanent Talpian population) do not define themselves as Bulgarian.[5] It is worth emphasising that all the immigrants arrived after 1944, that is, during the socialist period. Before 1944 the village was occupied entirely by Bulgarians. This becomes particularly significant when considering land restitution.

Reasons for migration to Talpa varied, but a combination of forcible relocation by the socialist government and the more attractive living conditions existing in northern Bulgaria provided the major elements. In the case of the Pomaks, the families were forcibly resettled. One Pomak family with whom I am acquainted had been moved to Talpa from southern Bulgaria after the husband had been sent to a concentration camp in 1948 for his alleged pro-fascist activities during the war. The wife and children were given the minimal amount of land necessary for their household's farming needs, 25 decares (2.5 hectares), and were rejoined by the husband after his two-year imprisonment was over. Since 1989 they have received monetary compensation. The forced relocation of one Macedonian family in Talpa led to the immigration of a number of other Macedonian families from southern Bulgaria who learnt from this first family about the greater wealth of the Talpian area and decided to move. The Turks were also immigrants from southern Bulgaria. The greater poverty of the southern region (in part due to the difficult mountainous terrain and in part to larger sizes of families) forced them to look elsewhere for a better life. The agricultural labour shortage in northern-central Bulgaria provided a further reason for choosing Talpa, where they have lived since the 1970s. Many of the Turkish families, unlike the Macedonians, intended their moves to be temporary. They planned to return to southern Bulgaria (or even Turkey) after saving enough money. This explains why to date only one Turkish family has bought a house in the village while all the others rent.

The most recent post-1944 settlers, the Gypsies, are the only ones who have not participated to any significant extent in village agriculture either during the socialist period or since. The one Gypsy family with whom I am acquainted moved to Talpa from Varna, after their (illegal gold-trading?) activities forced them to escape police observation in that region. Their many 'business' enterprises distinguish them from the other villagers and help to explain, in part, why they have shown little interest in present land restitution claims.[6]

One final demographic point worthy of note is that with one or two exceptions, the only families with children in the village are non-Bulgarian. The influx of new settlers since 1944 meant that a minimal supply of younger workers to the agricultural co-operative has been maintained, while during the same period the majority of Bulgarian youth was leaving Talpa – initially to continue their higher education and following this for greater employment opportunities. Industrialisation, resulting in the high levels of out-migration of Talpian (Bulgarian) youth to the cities, has been accompanied by a numerically less significant arrival of larger and poorer Turkish, Macedonian, Pomak and Gypsy families (Bates 1995: 149). Given the fact that two-thirds of the Talpian population are pensioners, young Pomak, Turkish and Macedonian families make up a sizeable proportion of the working-age inhabitants in the village, the majority being employed in the agricultural co-operative. Even some of these latter groups – primarily the Macedonians and Pomaks, but to a lesser degree the Turks – having reaped the benefits of greater opportunities and wealth, are sending their children to receive higher education in the cities, thus imitating the trends set by the Bulgarian inhabitants one generation before them.

An implication of socialist industrialisation is that family structure has changed dramatically over the past fifty years. Before 1944 patrilineal and patrilocal organisation, exemplified in the *zadruga* which continued until the 1880s (Sanders 1949: 65), was the norm. By the late 1930s there was some evidence of the breakdown of male-dominated inheritance. For example, Sanders wrote that both daughters and sons inherited land, with sons usually inheriting twice as much as the daughters (Sanders 1949: 55). After the Second World War industrialisation led to a transformation of this traditional structure, not only through progressive laws for equality but also because the accompanying demographic changes noted above – especially a massive migration to the cities – resulted in a shift away from the traditional patrilineal and patrilocal structure of the pre-1944 era. One-child families, and youth living away from the older village-based generations, have become common phenomena. For example, my landlady, as the sole survivor and inheritor of her in-laws' property, has in turn one beneficiary, her only child, a daughter who lives in the regional capital. The latter was educated away from the village and married a chemistry graduate who is himself from another village in the region (where his parents still live). The couple have one child, a teenage son. Among the Macedonians, Pomaks and Turks in Talpa – who by the very nature of their immigrant status have clearly broken traditional kinship arrangements – similar patterns (of leaving the villages, declining family size) are emerging. Only the Gypsies are outside this framework, at least when considering factors such as education and family size.

LAND PRIVATISATION AND ETHNICITY

The particular way in which land privatisation has been carried out in eastern Europe has varied between countries, with some – for example, Romania, Bulgaria, Slovakia and the Czech Republic – placing greater importance on restitution to pre-Second World War owners, while others – for example, Hungary, Albania and Russia – combine this with some consideration of who works and lives on the land (Verdery 1994b: 1074; Swain 1993). In Bulgaria the Land Privatisation Bill, passed in 1991 and amended in 1992, involved the restitution of the land to its 'rightful' owners, that is, those who owned the land before the Communist Party attained power in 1944.

Restitution involved the liquidation of the previous socialist co-operative – its assets, including the land, animals and buildings. Two separate organisations were given responsibility for the liquidation of the co-operative – one dealt with returning ownership rights to the land, the other with distribution of all co-operative wealth. In the latter case, wealth was returned as shares which were worked out in terms of villagers' original contribution to the co-operative, that is, the total amount of assets with which they entered the co-operative (land, machines, animals) as well as the amount of labour invested in the co-operative since its foundation in 1947. The shares were expressed in monetary value, dependent on villagers' proportion of work and land contributions calculated in terms of the total co-operative wealth. Clearly, the shares received by the post-1944 settlers were of less value than the shares allocated to those who had made both labour and material contributions to the co-operative.

The law was viewed by the anti-communist party, the Union of Democratic Forces (in power at the time of the amended law), as an important way to eliminate all remnants of socialist agricultural policy based on the collective ownership and working of the land. Despite many problems (Kaneff 1995), the process had been almost completed in Talpa by late 1994, unlike many other rural areas where restitution was still under way. As was the case across the region, new private co-operatives were formed; in Talpa, two new co-operatives were established. The rejection of private individual farming is just one of the unanticipated consequences of the land privatisation laws. Another consequence has been the increasing tension within Talpa between those with rights to ownership and those without. For restitution has in effect emphasised the importance of kinship (since it demands the highlighting of present ancestral ties to pre-1944 ownership rights) and at the same time de-emphasises the importance of work as a valid criterion for land ownership (since labour contributions are only a part of the way of attaining shares and do not grant automatic entitlement to land). The clear weighting given to one above the other sits at the core of village discontent.

INCREASING IMPORTANCE OF KINSHIP AS A DETERMINANT OF LAND OWNERSHIP

Land restitution has meant that villagers have had to examine their kinship ties in a detailed and thorough manner in order to determine the amount and location of land to which they are entitled. It has raised an awareness among villagers of the connection between their kin and the land. My landlady, for example, has gone to considerable effort to determine the land rights to which she is entitled. Being a widow, Maria has land claims to both her own family's lands and those of her late husband's family. Her activities have thus included approaching her own kin over inheritance matters as well as the more problematic issue of attempting to acquaint herself with the estate of her late husband's family. As she explained, she married into the family in the early 1950s when, because of the already established collectivised working of the land, she had paid little attention to the land holdings of the family. However, Maria had known them to be wealthy, with 49 decares, including vines and forested land (both particularly valued). Maria has thus had to seek the help of her deceased husband's cousins (he was an only child, making my landlady the sole inheritor) in order to ascertain details necessary for dealing with the officials assigned the responsibility of restitution.

Consulting official documents in archives and searching at home for documents filed away twenty years earlier by her father-in-law were other activities which sharpened her knowledge of inheritance dues and, by implication, kinship ties. But the rising awareness of the relationship between kinship and land has also resulted in conflict both between and within families. An example of the latter was the disagreement between 60-year-old Maria and her 78-year-old mother. Their once close relationship was jeopardised by the issue of land. Maria had a rightful claim to one-half of the land from her parents' estate. Having inherited her deceased husband's residence, she had relinquished her rights to any joint ownership in her family home, willingly signing them away to her brother. However, the other lands had not been discussed. The assumption made by Maria's mother, that her daughter would relinquish all land claims to her brother, was a sore point. In justifying her position, Maria pointed out to me that Radka, her cousin who had married before 1944, had received a dowry of 10 decares (1 hectare) which had come out of the joint family holdings. But she herself had received nothing because her marriage had taken place after 1944. 'So now, it's proper for my mother to give me some land – the family at least owes it to me to sit down and discuss the matter.' The dispute continued over a number of months during which time they spoke little to each other, despite the fact that they lived in the same village and until this point had always had a close relationship, visiting frequently and helping each other out in the numerous agricultural tasks. On another occasion Maria said to me with respect to her mother, 'as a mother you'd think she would look after both her children, but no. Now I've decided that I am not going to sign away my share of the land to them – why don't they give me 10 decares, as it is now, my brother has more land than me?' Interestingly, behind Maria's decision to fight out the issue with her brother and mother, was her own daughter. Maria confessed to me that her daughter was demanding her mother receive her rightful land claims. 'I didn't get my land from my family at the time and so now I should – that is how Tanya [the daughter] feels about it.'

Such estrangement between kin over land divides siblings and cousins, parents and children. Those who for years have been on amicable terms are now embroiled in unpleasant legal battles. Others have experienced a deterioration of their relationships as quarrels split their once close links.

That my landlady was seeking the land in the name of her husband's family became clear one afternoon when we were returning from a visit to her cousin by marriage, who was able to inform us of details concerning the land which my landlady had not known. On our way home we met a villager from our neighbourhood. My landlady told her what we had been doing and added jokingly, 'with all these headaches over the land I'll end up there [nodding towards the cemetery] before my time and my [deceased] father-in-law will meet me and be angry that I haven't been able to sort out the family wealth.'

Validation of land ownership in the case of the Bulgarian villagers was expressed in terms of their obligations to family members – both dead and living. The use of inheritance and the argument that 'people deserve land because it belonged to their ancestors' (Verdery 1994b: 1105) is clearly evident from the above. Rights to possession based on inheritance re-inforces, as pointed out by Verdery, a kinship ideology which is 'honoured less in the observance than in the breach' (1994b: 1106). Despite the mobilisation of kinship ties in terms of conflict and contention, the law serves to exclude all those who can make no kinship claims to land. Kinship is a means of defining who is and is not a property owner and therefore a village 'native'. The fact that such claims are carried out in an atmosphere of contention does not reduce the significance of the activity in creating a boundary, rather it heightens awareness of the limits. Shared descent and the bonds of ancestry to the land have now become criteria which separate the 'insiders' from the 'outsiders' on the basis of kinship, which in turn is given 'real' spatial boundaries through land ownership.

Economic restructuring in the post-1989 period has served to strengthen the renewed awareness of the association between kinship and the land. The concern to keep up the 'connection to the village' emphasises the dependency of kin (those both in the village and outside it) on the land. Food production necessitated the return of pensioned city inhabitants to their parents' homes to take over the growing of fruit and vegetables and the raising of animals. It was viewed as a central survival strategy in a period of economic uncertainty. The production of preserves, fresh food and meat is carried out usually for several households. For example, my next-door neighbours were producing food for themselves, their two married children in the cities and their ailing parents who had taken on the less arduous task of house-sitting the family home in the nearby township. The concerned grandparents living down the street from my landlady told me that they regularly send bottled meats, fruit and vegetables to their granddaughter studying medicine in Sofia. 'If we didn't there would be no way that she could afford to live there. She would have to give up her studies', the grandmother told me. It is not only the transference – or on occasions exchange – of food that binds kin, for the increasing demand on village-produced food demands greater participation between kin sharing in its joint preparation. The return of city-dwelling family to help with agricultural work over the summer months provides a means by which kin strengthen their associations. The village population swells from 615 in winter to approximately 750 in the summer. Such patterns of movement and dependency between kin have not been confined to the post-1989 period, as food sharing and production have always had symbolic importance in maintaining kinship (Smollett discusses the importance of kinship in socialist society, precisely through, for example, the production and exchange of food[7]). However, the economic hardships of the past six years have given a new impetus to this relationship.[8] The importance of land ownership in the context of new survival concerns cannot be overestimated. Kinship is being tied to food production and by implication to property interests, while during the socialist period and collectivisation, land ownership was not a concern in food-production activities.

Thus while kinship relations have apparently maintained an important position in both political-economic systems (socialist and post-socialist), the content of the relationship has changed, according to ideologically based policies on property ownership. The restitution process requiring villagers to take a renewed interest in their kinship connections (sometimes after a lapse of thirty to forty years), the tensions over property ownership arising from renewed contact between kin and the harsh economic environment have all served to strengthen the ties between kin and land. Kinship is being used in new ways, to construct bonds of closeness between people and the land. This is also a means to exclude others with no blood ties to the land – namely those who have immigrated to Talpa after 1944.

Land restitution has served to highlight a genealogy within the village; one which grounds descent both spatially, through land restitution, and also temporally, since validation of land ownership in terms of ancestral links implicates the importance of the past. Possession of land founded on past ownership not only unites kinship in the present, but also serves to extend it into the past and the perceived future. History binds all those who own land. Those without land are those with no extensive temporal connections to the village. New property relations establish village boundaries via kinship, acting to locate persons temporally as well as spatially within boundaries of what now constitutes 'the village'. Those with limited kinship ties and land ownership rights are therefore excluded from 'the village'. If 'village' is constituted as both a temporal and spatial entity, then kinship serves as a criterion by which to include or exclude people as village natives. Land becomes a concrete symbol of kinship – bonds which in turn have spatial and temporal significance in defining village boundaries. The land privatisation law serves to discriminate between who is and is not a native of the village, which is, in essence, an issue of who is and is not Bulgarian. Ultimately Talpa is a Bulgarian village because its lands are owned by Bulgarians.

DE-EMPHASIS OF WORK AS A DETERMINANT FOR RIGHTS OVER LAND

A vital effect of the law, which established land restitution through inheritance rights, is a reduction in the importance of work as defining rights over land ownership. Post-1944 settlers do not own land in the village despite the fact that many have worked at the village agricultural co-operative for many years and are presently working in the newly formed private co-operative.

In arguing the unfairness of the privatisation law a new solidarity is becoming evident within each ethnic group in the village. Villagers themselves make a connection between the issue of land and ethnicity. For example, when I visited one Macedonian household, a Bulgarian neighbour was coincidentally also present. The Macedonian woman explained my interest in the issue of land to her puzzled Bulgarian neighbour by saying 'we [the Macedonians] are fifteen households with no land'. On another occasion when I approached a Turkish woman and told her I wished to speak to people in the village who were without land, she clearly saw it as an issue associated with the problem of ethnicity and immediately launched into a discussion about 'being a Turk'. At the intra-ethnic level the lack of land has become a binding force, solidifying relations within each different ethnic group. Thus a Macedonian informed me that they had made a 'group' decision not to cash in the shares that every worker and landowner of the previous socialist co-operative was given at the time of its liquidation. 'We decided to keep it all in the co-operative and hopefully get land . . . That's what all us Macedonians decided to do, not to take a thing so we have more shares.' A Turkish woman told me the same with respect to the Turks, that 'we purposely left our shares and took no animals because we want land'. Joint action took the form of discussion which to my knowledge did not occur through the formal organisation of meetings, but through casual gatherings such as social occasions or chats over the backyard fence. The decision was not to sell the shares or to use them to claim animals, but rather to hold on to them and eventually buy land, once this was made available. (The village mayoress informed me, in late 1994, that the council plans to sell them common village land. But as one Macedonian pointed out on a different occasion, it is unlikely it will be at an affordable price, even if/when the government officials do actually release the land for sale. In September 1996 when I was last in Talpa, land had not yet been given a monetary value, let alone made available for sale to non-landowners.)

Of the four ethnic groups cited above, only the Pomaks and Macedonians have (limited) ownership rights. The Pomaks, it may be recalled, had been granted some land by the socialist government at the time of their forced resettlement in Talpa. For very different reasons, some Macedonians also own land. (In a few cases Bulgarian men have married Macedonian women; through marriage these Macedonian women have indirect ownership rights to Talpian land.) All Macedonian families own the house in which they live and the yard surrounding it. However, it is not sufficient for the agricultural needs of the household. This is very different from the situation of the Turks who, except for one family, do not own their houses but prefer to rent instead. They are thus, more than the other two groups, dependent on having to pay extra money to the co-operative in order to rent some land. Another option is the rental of land directly from landowners in privately arranged deals (the Macedonians rather than Turks prefer this option). Pomaks, Macedonians and Turks all have inheritance rights in their native villages in southern Bulgaria which, however, they relinquished long ago. As members from all groups informed me, the large families from which they came meant that their land claims were small, thus their entitlement would have been a trivial amount, often less than 1 hectare. Without exception they had chosen to give up inheritance rights to their siblings who had remained in the region.

The economic disadvantage of being landless is evident to Pomaks, Macedonians and Turks in the village. This has become especially true since the hard economic times of the post-socialist period. An issue of concern to both groups has been meat production. Villagers produce most of their own fruit, vegetables and meat. Household production of meat is especially important to the predominantly elderly population which cannot meet sky-rocketing costs while living on pensions which are below the poverty line. Animal raising for meat production requires a sizeable amount of fodder to be grown and household plots are not large enough for this purpose. Landowners who have other plots apart from those surrounding their houses have been at an advantage in the newly formed co-operative. Co-operative organisation has meant that village members who own land in the co-operative are able to obtain cost-price animal fodder – they pay only for the services provided in growing the crop – sowing, ploughing and so on. Further, co-operative members who are landowners receive an annual rental for the land they placed in the co-operative. Non-landowning co-operative members must pay not only for the basic production costs of the fodder but also the annual rental payment on the land. Essentially this means that while all co-operative members are able to raise animals, and therefore have meat, the (Bulgarian) landowning members pay less for their meat than the non-landowning members.[9]

In their growing anger, members from all three groups have pointed out that they can work the land because they are young, while most of the Bulgarians – the landowners – are too old to do so. In fact it is the

Macedonians, Turks and Pomaks who have provided and still do provide a large proportion of the labour force in the co-operative, although importantly Bulgarians hold most of the administrative, managerial positions (an inequality inherited from the socialist period). Thus one Macedonian commented with respect to the landowners, 'They're old, they can't work the land, they don't even want the land, yet they are given it. I've worked thirty years in the agricultural co-operative and so has my wife, but we don't have any land.' A Turkish woman told me a similar thing when she said, 'it's not fair, these old people have land and get money, we who are young and work in the co-operative get nothing. You'd think they could strike some deal with the co-operative and receive a discount on the fodder, on the basis that they work there, but no.' Another Turkish woman, who had worked sixteen years in the cattle section of the co-operative, said, 'We [the Turks] don't have any land and it's not only us, the Macedonians are in the same position. Is this fair that everyone else has land except for us? Let there be some allocated to us too, so we too can feed our animals.' Notably, when the new settlers complained that landowners were too old to work their land, they were clearly referring to Bulgarian owners who, almost without exception, are pensioners.

In pointing out the unfairness of the restitution system whereby those who work the land do not own it, the post-socialist settlers are emphasising the importance of work as the best criterion for justifying land ownership. Indeed 'work' was the reason that all these groups (save the Gypsies) left behind their native homes and any inheritance rights associated with them, for the promise of greater employment opportunities in northern-central Bulgaria. It is thus not surprising that their basis for claims to land are now expressed in such terms. It is because Pomaks, Turks and Macedonians clearly feel that the land privatisation law disadvantages them – the very people who both want and can work the land – that all three groups have become vocal in expressing their nostalgia for the pre-1989 period when state-run co-operatives made private land ownership a non-issue. Such a view is expressed in the comment by the Macedonian woman, reproduced at the very beginning of the paper. The pro-socialist view also explains why all post-1944 settlers give vocal support to the Bulgarian Socialist Party (previously the Bulgarian Communist Party) who have been more cautious in their pursuit of land privatisation than the anti-communist party. Further, at the national level, the largely Turkish-dominated political party, the Movement for Rights and Freedoms, has been aligned with the Bulgarian Socialist Party for much of the contemporary period. The two political parties share similar views concerning post-socialist agricultural development (Bates 1995: 1138).

Yet, despite the unified objection to land ownership by post-1944 settlers, the landless are not acting in unity against landowners; rather the issue of the landless has been fragmented in terms of different ethnic groups. While the Macedonians, Turks and Pomaks are all in the position of being landless, they are not all equally positioned. Kinship reinforces a hierarchy between Talpa's new settlers, as some post-1944 settlers have limited access to the land. Thus both Macedonians and Pomaks have some access to village land via kinship; the former through marriage, the latter via the first-generation children who are the first generation of landowners in the village (after the resettlement of their parents in the 1940s). The Turks, on the other hand, have no claims to land ownership in the village on the basis of kinship, reflecting their greater level of 'outsiderness'. Indeed, it is only the fact that the Turks desire to possess land, and are willing to cultivate it, that makes their position different from that of the Gypsies who appear to have shown no interest in land. These groups are further disadvantaged in that they are removed from their own kinship networks in other areas of Bulgaria (or Turkey as in the case of a few of the Turkish families).

We therefore see a 'ranking' among the new settlers which is now being cemented via land ownership, based on their claims of kinship rights over the land. Macedonians and Pomaks are both accepted to varying degrees as 'Bulgarian'. Turks and Gypsies remain as 'outsiders' in a village defined along kinship–land lines.[10] These differing types of 'Bulgarianness' grant Pomaks and Macedonians a degree of acceptance not given to the Turks or Gypsies. Generally speaking, the result of the privatisation law, with its emphasis on ownership based on kinship, is that in Talpa (and presumably in other villages in northern Bulgaria where there are landless post-1944 settlers), land ownership and ethnicity converge, as land is returned to the Bulgarians and denied to the Turks, Gypsies and, to a lesser degree, to the Macedonians and Pomaks. In turn, the evident location of different groups on the basis of kinship must be understood in terms of more general historical and social considerations. For example, the resistance to the Ottoman empire, which is a significant feature against which Bulgarian nationalism is defined, contributed to locating the Turks in a position of greater exclusion than the Pomaks and Macedonians.

CONCLUSION

Local-level research reveals problems that arise in the building of a new state, problems that cannot be understood by simply paying attention to initiatives and policies which are formed at the national level. Indeed, from the perspective of the macro level, Talpa would appear to be one of the few 'success' stories of land restitution – for at least in this village restitution occurred relatively quickly, with little open resistance and few charges of corruption against the officials. But local-level research points to the complexity of the matter. Present processes geared to restoring greater democracy – in part through land restitution – are serving to strengthen ethnic differences in rural Bulgaria.[11] Restitution has reinforced the already existing ethnic boundaries in the village, acting as a determinant of ethnic divisions. This was not presumably an intended consequence of urban-located government initiatives, which nevertheless have paid little attention to the political and economic interests of the rural sector. Privatisation has led to the contesting of the meanings of land. De-emphasising the importance of work on the land has had the (unforeseen?) effect of denying access to land to non-Bulgarians; heightening the importance of kinship ties as the determinant factor in ownership has resulted in sole Bulgarian ownership. A local-level response has been that those left landless have found solidarity with those of a similar position. By virtue of their disqualification from land ownership, post-1944 settlers have found themselves excluded from 'the village'. The division is essentially between those accepting inheritance as a valid means of legitimating property ownership and those who argue for ownership on the basis of including 'work' as a legitimate consideration. Forming or reinforcing bonds between ethnic groups has become one way some villagers 'survive' the new state-induced changes. The survival strategy of falling back on support from those also temporally and spatially excluded from 'the village' has resulted in the renewed importance of ethnicity. Bourdieu's concept of strategy – with respect to marriage – is of some relevance here, since ethnicity in the situation described above is a means of minimising the economic and social cost of being landless. As a strategy, the mobilisation of ethnic boundaries has involved some degree of intentionality although it was not an organised movement in any formal sense. As O'Brien (1986: 906) writes in a very different context, 'ethnicity represents an organising principle articulated by the Sudanese people through their creative struggles to respond to the challenges of colonial capitalist encroachment'. While the situation is very different in Bulgaria, the activation of ethnicity as a response to capitalist development is not.

In such a context it is notable that a united front of all the landless has not occurred, but rather solidarity has been fragmented in terms of different ethnic groups. It is not simply a matter of 'Bulgarians' versus 'the rest' or landowners versus non-landowners, but various degrees of acceptance, with only the Turks (and in a different sense the Gypsies) remaining totally outside the boundary. The different histories of the groups as well as other ethnic markers of differentiation, such as language and religion, provide some indication as to why a unified response by the landless has not been sought.

Such ethnic differentiation is being accompanied by the creation of a hierarchical class society with Bulgarian landowners and non-Bulgarians as the landless. The apparent result is the asymmetric incorporation of the population into the new political economy. Thus the ethnic majority – the Bulgarians – are becoming a propertied 'class' while the others remain landless, at least in the region of Bulgaria I have been discussing here. In this way ethnicity is being linked to the creation of a new class structure, with the Bulgarians rising above the other ethnic groups on the basis of land ownership. Despite the cushioning effects of this via the (re)formation of co-operatives, the consequence of the land privatisation law is both to elevate ethnicity to greater prominence and attribute to it a class dimension.[12] Such an ethnic–class differentiation not only creates differences in terms of property ownership, but also in terms of wealth (recall the example of meat production).

The importance of land ownership is much more than simply economic. The relatively 'neutral' term of 'land' attains political, historical and social significance far beyond its immediate economic functions. The term 'territory' resonates such significances. Land has become a highly politicised symbol; when land becomes an 'instrument' of ethnicity, as I have suggested it has in the above case, then it takes on importance as 'territory'. When Ahmed Dogan remarked that 'remember it's not land you are buying but territory in this country', he was, implicitly, raising the matter of ethnicity as fundamental to the transformation of 'land' into an issue of 'territory'. Further, he was rejecting the relationship between land ownership and kinship (descent) which has occurred as a consequence of the current privatisation laws. His statement denies the present legitimation of land ownership in terms of kinship. Instead, once the process of privatisation has been completed, he reminds us, land will become a marketable commodity removed from the domain of kinship, and when it does, Dogan threatens, Turks can own Bulgarian land. At this point the land will become Turkish territory.[13] It is precisely this symbolic importance of land which through its ethnic significance attains relevance as 'territory'. When land is politicised through state intervention and local battles over meanings of land ensue – as either kinship or work determined – it becomes 'territory' and is raised as an issue of ethnicity.

ACKNOWLEDGEMENTS

This paper has been presented – in earlier versions – at an interdisciplinary workshop on Survival Strategies in Post-communist Societies: Gender, Ethnicity and 'Underclass', held at Ilkley, Yorkshire, April 1995, and at a panel on Transforming Local Economies: Gender, Survival Strategies and the New Underclass in Post-communist Societies for the Fifth World

Congress of Central and East European Studies, Warsaw, August 1995. I would like to thank the participants at both meetings for their helpful questions and discussion, and express my gratitude to Sue Bridger and Frances Pine for giving me the opportunity to participate. Special thanks to Frances Pine for her support and critical comments.

NOTES

1 This quote was given during a paper presentation at the International Seminar on 'Relations of Compatibility and Incompatibility between Christians and Muslims in Bulgaria', Sofia, 9–10 September 1994. I have not been able to follow up the original newspaper report from which the quote was reportedly taken.
2 Fieldwork for this paper was carried out with the generous support of a Social Science Small Grant from the Nuffield Foundation.
3 It should be noted that my own position within the village, that is, an outsider but with Bulgarian ancestry, influenced the nature of my relations and in turn the data that I have collected. While I socialised freely with Macedonian families and to a lesser degree with the Pomaks and Turks, I have very little data on the Gypsies, whose marginalised position with respect to the other village ethnic groups, and especially the Bulgarians, made close contact with them difficult.
4 Pomaks are Bulgarian Muslims, distinguished from Turks who have ancestral connections with Turkey and speak the Turkish language.
5 Since officially all inhabitants are classified as 'Bulgarian', the figures provided above were calculated by the village mayoress. I confirmed her statistics with a number of other villagers.
6 The disinterest of Talpian Gypsies towards land ownership is not reflected nationally, where some lobbying by Gypsies for land rights has occurred.
7 She mentions the importance of the separation of kin from productive property as significant in understanding socialist kin ties, especially their considerable 'nurturing-supportive functions' (1989: 133).
8 That the dependency on kinship networks is associated with economic position is explored in a very different context by Stack, who shows how the mobilisation of kinship ties is fundamental to the survival of poor urban black families in the USA.
9 There are two co-operatives in Talpa. The situation described above relates to members of the large co-operative. The position of the landless was even worse when considering the second co-operative which would not accept landless members. Exclusion occurred because the smaller co-operative was organised on very different principles, whereby landowners rented out their property to two men who worked the land, pocketing all profits save an annual rental fee which they paid to their landowning members. Clearly, there was no place for landless members in such an organisation.
10 Evidence of this is through the way they are spoken about. For example, the Macedonians are always referred to as 'from the south (of Bulgaria)'. The Pomaks, like the Macedonians, are rarely distinguished in conversations and only if the issue of religion arises are the former described as 'Muslims but nevertheless Bulgarians'. It is only the Turks who are explicitly distanced from

the Bulgarians since they are always referred to as 'the Turks'. The same is true of the Gypsies who are so peripheral that they are the only group with whom the Bulgarians (and others) do not share the same social space. For example, there are no usual neighbourly bonds between them and the Bulgarians. Also, Gypsy kinship practices such as first-cousin marriages are identified by Bulgarians as beyond the bounds of acceptability.

11 Developing a different interest, Creed also comes to a similar conclusion about ethnicity, namely that the political-economic changes 'may have actually generated and intensified conflicts' (1990: 17).

12 There is a wide literature on ethnicity, including its class dimensions as well as its associations to resources and the economy. For a summary see Williams.

13 In the same way that O'Brien describes the breakdown of the ethnic structure of the Sudanese labour force (1986: 904), I suspect that in the Bulgarian context Dogan is correct. Access to land ownership serving to create ethnic differentiation in Talpa will also have a relatively short lifespan, as initial land restitution is overtaken by the sale of land on the market.

REFERENCES

Bates, D. (1995) 'Uneasy accommodation: ethnicity and politics in rural Bulgaria', in *East European Communities: The Struggle for Balance in Turbulent Times*, ed. D.A. Kideckel, Boulder: Westview Press.

Bourdieu, P. (1976) 'Marriage strategies as strategies of social reproduction', in *Family and Society*, ed. R. Forster and O. Ranum, trans. E. Forster and P.M. Ranum, Baltimore: The Johns Hopkins University Press.

Creed, G. (1990) 'The bases of Bulgaria's ethnic policies', in *The Anthropology of East Europe Review*, 9, 2, fall: 12–17.

Kaneff, D. (1992) *Social Constructions of the Past and their Political Significance in the Bulgarian Socialist State*, PhD thesis, University of Adelaide.

—— (1995) 'Developing rural Bulgaria', in *Cambridge Anthropology*, 18, 2: 23–34.

O'Brien, J. (1986) 'Toward a reconstitution of ethnicity: capitalist expansion and cultural dynamics in Sudan', in *American Anthropologist*, 88, 4: 898–907.

Sanders, I.T. (1949) *Balkan Village*, Lexington: The University of Kentucky Press.

Smollett, E. (1989) 'The economy of jars: kindred relationships in Bulgaria – an exploration', in *Ethnologia Europea*, XIX, 2: 125–40.

Stack, C.B. (1974) *All Our Kin: Strategies for Survival in a Black Community*, New York: Harper and Row.

Swain, N. (1993) 'Agricultural transformation in Hungary: the context', paper presented at Budapest Workshop on 'Transitions to Family Farming in Post-socialist Central Europe', 25–28 March.

Todorova, M. (1993) 'Ethnicity, nationalism and the communist legacy in Eastern Europe', *East European Politics and Societies*, 7, 1, winter: 135–54.

Verdery, K. (1994a) 'From parent-state to family patriarchs: gender and nation in contemporary Eastern Europe', in *East European Politics and Societies*, 8, 2, spring: 225–55.

—— (1994b) 'The elasticity of land: problems of property restitution in Transylvania', in *Slavic Review*, 53, 4, winter: 1071–109.

Williams, B.F. (1989) 'A class act: anthropology and the race to nation across ethnic terrain', in *Annual Review of Anthropology*, 18: 401–44.

3 The bullied farmer

Social pressure as a survival strategy?

Myriam Hivon

Better a hundred friends than a hundred roubles.

(Old Russian proverb)

Since the beginning of the 1990s, the Russian countryside has been undergoing radical transformations. Following Yeltsin's decrees at the end of 1991, most collective farms (*kolkhozy*) and state farms (*sovkhozy*) were privatised and the establishment of small individual or family farms (*krest'ianskie khoziaistva*) was strongly encouraged. New private farmers encountered many practical difficulties in the establishment of their small enterprises, but more strikingly, they also faced the resentment of a large part of the local population. This resentment sometimes took dramatic forms. For instance, in the province of Omsk, a farmer was told: 'If you become a private farmer, we will fire your wife!' (FBIS 1992a: 42). In the district of Veliki Ustiug, where I conducted fieldwork, some new private farmers had their harvests destroyed and their tractors or combines burned by other villagers. The violence towards new private farmers[1] had become such a tangible reality in the Russian countryside that the government was considering granting them the right to use firearms. 'After all, peasants today have found themselves virtually unprotected in the face of a crime wave. Their farms are being burned down, their cattle slaughtered and equipment stolen' (FBIS 1992b: 43).

At the time of my fieldwork in 1993, these forms of 'bullying' had slightly calmed down. Nevertheless, most people I met in the district of Veliki Ustiug continued to express negative feelings towards private farmers. The latter remained the focus of many attacks in the local press. These attacks did not only come from local authorities or farm authorities who, at the beginning of the reforms, had felt their power threatened by new private farmers (Abrahams 1994; Humphrey 1989; Pryor 1991). They also came from 'ordinary villagers' who had decided to remain in state and collective farms or other rural enterprises, instead of taking the opportunity of starting a farm on their own, and who were opposed to anyone who dared to try.

In this article, I examine the reasons behind these forms of community opposition. I aim to demonstrate that the various types of social pressure used by villagers against private farmers can be viewed as strategies to gain control over, or access to, the natural and technical resources monopolized by the latter. The following analysis is based on fieldwork carried out in the district of Veliki Ustiug, in the province of Vologda, from October 1992 to October 1993.[2] I start with the examination of western and Russian views on community opposition. This first section is followed by an analysis of rural dwellers' former categories of 'private property' and 'private farming'. I conclude with the examination of 'private farming' as implemented by the recent agrarian reforms.

CURRENT VIEWS ON COMMUNITY OPPOSITION

Community opposition to private farmers is a phenomenon which is stressed in the literature on Russian agrarian reforms, but not adequately explained (Pallot 1991; Pryor 1991; Van Atta 1993a). According to Van Atta, 'individual peasants (private farmers) are often not accepted by their neighbours, who tend to resent anyone who attempts to pull himself above the general level by individual efforts' (1993b: 83). He continues: 'To an unknown extent, such popular resistance grows from acceptance of the ethic of lowest common denominator egalitarianism ... consciously fostered by the State during the past sixty years' (1993b: 87). Thus, according to him, community opposition towards private farmers resulted from a 'culture of envy' and a 'tradition of egalitarianism'. Although anyone who has spent some time in Russia cannot deny the existence of these characteristics,[3] they must not only be identified but also explained. Contrary to Van Atta's assumptions, these characteristics have not been engendered by the socialist state in Russia. They existed before the October Revolution (Shanin 1972). Furthermore, the 'culture of envy' and 'tradition of egalitarianism' are not specific to the Russian rural population, but have been noted in other rural societies (Foster 1965). Although views like those of Foster are in some ways problematic (relying too heavily on psychological reductionism), they do suggest that the reasons behind villagers' resentment towards private farmers are more complex than those recognized by western pro-reformers such as Van Atta.

On the other hand, Russian pro-reformers such as Linin, the Vice-President of the Association of Private Farmers of Russia (AKKOR), have argued that 'the main reason [for the difficulties in establishing peasant farms] is that a significant part of the population, especially *the rural one,* has not accepted the principle of private ownership and private entre-preneurship' (Wegren 1993: 140). Similarly, Russian specialists such as Nikol'skii (1993) stress that the concept of private property has never existed in the Russian countryside as far as peasants are concerned, and therefore is alien to the rural population. Nikol'skii explains that land ownership was first vested in the commune[4] after which it was transferred to collective and state farms. He concludes that more than a hundred years of 'collective ownership' speak for themselves. The concept of private property goes against the 'Russian peasant character', and that is why the rural population will never recognize it.

Nikol'skii's argument is rooted in a deep knowledge of Russian rural history. However, it ignores the fact that collective farming was not the only *[too very variation]* type of farming existing in the former USSR. Each *kolkhoz* and *sovkhoz* worker's family (and, indeed, workers of many other types of rural enterprise) retained the rights to cultivate a small piece of land and keep a limited number of livestock to fulfil its own consumption needs. This small piece of land and livestock holding is referred to in the literature as the 'personal plot', 'private plot', or 'subsidiary farm'. The property rights over the personal plots were vested in the household itself, and in this sense subsidiary farms represented the form of property which was the closest to any form of 'private property' under the former regime.[5] Moreover, subsidiary farms have always played a significant role in the domestic economy of rural households as well as in the national economy, producing an important part of the overall agricultural production of the former USSR (Hedlund 1989; Shmelev 1986; Wadekin 1973). Therefore, in order to understand community opposition, it is perhaps more appropriate to compare the new private farms to these subsidiary farms than simply to conclude that private farming goes against collective farming principles. My hypothesis is that rural dwellers did have an experience of 'private ownership' and 'private farming' under the former regime, but that this previous experience is not compatible with the type of private farming the government aimed to establish in the countryside: hence their dis-contentment towards those who embrace this new form of farming.

I shall summarize briefly the practice of subsidiary farming in the village of Borovinka, where I lived for twelve months. At the time of fieldwork, it was a small village of 100 households, demographically, spatially and politically similar to any other village in the area. Economically, however, it differed in the sense that the main institution of the village was not a state or collective farm, but a *dom otdykha* or rest house. This rest house was designed to allow pensioners and veterans to come for twelve-day holidays. They were provided with a room and meals. A wide range of cultural and sports activities was organized to entertain them. They could also benefit from a medical centre which offered a variety of services such as dental care, alternative medicines, massages and so on. The rest house employed approximately ninety workers. It had its own land on which were grown potatoes and vegetables to feed holidaymakers. It also had a pig unit to provide its employees with piglets and pork. As a state or collective farm, the rest house fulfilled various social functions such as supplying its employees with accommodation, land and services (transportation, kindergarten, library, cultural club, etc.). As in state and collective farms, every family of the village owned a plot of land on which it cultivated potatoes, vegetables and berries. Most of them also kept livestock.

THE SUBSIDIARY FARM

In Borovinka, as in the district of Veliki Ustiug as a whole, the subsidiary farms usually consisted of at least three distinct types of plot: the garden, the potato land, and hay land. The garden (*ogorod*) was usually fenced and located near the house. It was used to grow vegetables, some herbs and a variety of berries.

Potatoes constituted villagers' main food. They grew them in huge quantities for their own consumption, but also to feed their livestock, especially pigs. Thus, potatoes were an important link in the meat production chain. The land on which potatoes were cultivated was distinct from the gardens, since it was generally not fenced and was located on large, open areas, at some distance from the house, sometimes even outside residential zones. Most families cultivated more than one potato plot. Although these were not demarcated by fences, each family knew where its plot started and ended, and cultivated it independently.

Hay land (*senokos*) was allocated exclusively to households keeping livestock and was situated a few kilometres from the village. The size of the field was not dependent upon the number of head of livestock one household had, but on the availability of such fields. In the whole district, hay land rights could be granted over an area not exceeding 3 hectares. In general, 2 hectares were granted to households holding cows and 1 to those keeping goats. Therefore, householders who wished to expand their livestock holdings could not rely on being granted a larger field and had to develop other strategies to feed their animals. One important strategy is for villagers to gather grass wherever they can find it, that is, from the banks of rivers, from the borders of footpaths, roads or woods and from remote fields left unused by state farms. This practice of gathering hay wherever one can find it is neither new nor peculiar to Borovinka. Research conducted by Soviet specialists shows that, at the beginning of the 1960s, as much as 5 million hectares of land such as public footpaths and unused *sovkhoz* and *kolkhoz* land were cut to feed livestock privately owned by members of *kolkhozy*, and workers on *sovkhozy* and in non-agricultural enterprises (Wadekin 1973: 222).

Finally, it must be stressed that in Borovinka, there was no communal pasture: again, villagers grazed their livestock near the river or on unused state farm land. In this sense, workers of state farms were privileged over those of Borovinka, since they could use the pastures of their enterprise to graze their own livestock. In the state farms of the district, this was generally done without payment.

In Borovinka, most families kept one or two pigs, and while a couple of years earlier almost none had cows, more and more were acquiring one at the time of my fieldwork in order to cope with the increasing prices on dairy products. Goats, sheep, chicken, rabbits and bees were also kept privately in a significant number of households. Nevertheless, the villagers of Borovinka (and those of the district of Veliki Ustiug) still kept privately a relatively small number of livestock, despite the fact that limits on the size of livestock holdings had been abolished in 1988.

Property rights over subsidiary plots

Under the Soviet regime, the allocation of subsidiary plots to rural households was performed by the Land Committee of their respective enterprise, whether it was a state or a collective farm, or another type of rural enterprise such as the rest house. Land was not allocated to *individuals* but to *households*. This means that it did not belong to one member in particular, although it was registered under the name of only one person, usually the head of the household. As will become clear below, this had important implications.

It is generally argued that in *kolkhozy*, the size of the subsidiary plot depended upon the number of household members working in the socialized sector. For instance, households with three members employed full time in the collective farm were entitled to larger plots than households with only one member employed in the *kolkhoz* (Abrahams and Kahk 1994: 358; Dunn and Dunn 1967: 41). However, the norms regulating the plot size of *sovkhoz* workers and non-agricultural workers were more fixed and depended less upon the number of household members employed in the socialized sector (Wadekin 1973: 35–6). In Borovinka, I was explicitly told that the size of the plot was determined according to *the needs* of the household and its *ability to cultivate*. No mention was made about the number of household members employed in the rest house as a determinant criteria in the size of the plot, and, indeed, the material collected in the village shows no correlation between these two elements. The needs and ability of a household to cultivate were determined by taking into account factors such as the amount of land available for subsidiary farming and the number and type of consumers and workers (that is, whether they were children, adults, pensioners) within the household.

Under the Soviet regime, the subsidiary plots of land were held in *vladenie*. That is, villagers had a *right to work* the land, but could not buy, sell, mortgage or lease it. To some extent, these rights were inheritable. In principle, the land tenure on allotment allocated by rural enterprises expired on the 'termination of the working relationship' and therefore was granted only for a *limited period of time* (Wadekin 1973: 38). However, data gathered in Borovinka showed a different situation. Firstly, it showed that villagers retained their plots of land even when they were no longer employed by the enterprise. Secondly, it revealed that the only time villagers were really threatened with losing their rights over land was when they were not considered to be making 'proper use' of it. These threats did not necessarily only come from the authorities of the enterprise, but from other villagers. As the following material reveals, the *rights to use* the subsidiary plots were secured by membership in the enterprise; by membership in a household; and by the use villagers made of their land.

The agronomist in charge of allocating land in Borovinka explained to me that a household could not be deprived of its subsidiary plot as long as at least one of its members was employed in the rest house. If villagers secured their property rights over their land by committing themselves to work in the enterprise, the latter could not deprive them of land. It was the enterprise's obligation to provide land to its employees, and if its land fund was insufficient to do so, additional allotments were taken from the State Land Fund or Forest Fund managed by the local soviet.[6] In addition, if for some reason the enterprise had to take back land already allocated (to build new houses for instance), it was obliged to provide the residential groups affected with new allotments. Thus, households did not necessarily have rights over a *particular plot of land*, but they certainly had an undeniable *right to some land*. Clearly, property rights over land were secured by the reciprocal obligations between villagers and enterprises.

Villagers who had retired from the enterprise by virtue of age or illness retained their plot of land for life. Moreover, if, for instance, the only member of the household employed by the enterprise died, his or her co-residents retained their rights to use the plot. This was possible because the plot was not granted to one individual only, but to the household as a whole, as I mentioned earlier. Therefore, as long as there were members in the residential group to which the plot had been allocated, the enterprise could not, in principle, take that land back without providing a new plot or some compensation. Thus, householders' property rights over land did not depend solely upon their involvement as members in the enterprise, but also upon membership in the household.

The following anecdote shows that further considerations must be taken into account to understand fully the rights which linked residential groups to their subsidiary plot of land. A young couple had recently moved into the village when I arrived in Borovinka. When summer came, they asked to be given a plot of land to cultivate potatoes. They were living in a semi-detached house that was divided between three families, A, B and the couple C. One half of the house belonged to family A, while the other half was divided into two to accommodate families B and C. The garden was also divided into three unequal shares: family A owned half of it while families B and C shared the second half. Behind the backyard, outside the fenced area, there should have been three strips of land for potatoes, but in fact there were only two, because the tenant living previously in the flat of the young couple had declined the use of his piece of land and had given it to family B. Family B was using it, although none of its members was working for the enterprise any more. Although couple C maintained very good relations with family B, they felt strongly that they could not ask for this plot of land. The woman told me: 'If we ask them to give us that land, we'll probably never be invited again to their house. We don't want to lose their friendship.' It is clear, in this instance, that the young couple felt that this piece of land now belonged to family B even though, in principle, they could have asked them to hand it over. By enforcing their right over this particular plot of land, family C would have deprived family B of resources that the latter used and obviously needed. This would have caused resentment on the part of family B and probably that of some other villagers as well. To avoid general discontent, the young couple opted to find a piece of land elsewhere. Finally, an elderly couple, living in the house next to theirs, decided they did not need one of their plots any more, and gave it up to the young couple. Knowing that the young couple needed land, other villagers would have looked askance at the elderly couple keeping a plot of land without using it.

This example illustrates two important principles in understanding property rights over land at the subsidiary farming level in Borovinka. First, the land belonged to *those who worked it*. As long as a residential group used a plot of land for the purpose of fulfilling its consumption needs, no one deprived it of its land. On the other hand, and this is the second principle, *land was never left untilled*. If a household, like that of the elderly couple, did not make a profitable use of its parcel any more, it had the social obligation to surrender it. *This obligation was not enforced by a written law, but through social relations often expressed in terms of social pressure.*

A conflict which arose between two households in the village highlights this second principle. One of my informants told me how her family had cleared 2 hectares of hay land many years ago. For four years they did not touch it, since they had stopped keeping cows. One day, they learned that a villager had gone to the local soviet to get the permission to use this parcel of land. He argued that the parcel had been left unused for many years, and concluded that the previous 'owners' obviously did not need it any longer. Hence, villagers were aware of what others did with their land, and when they believed that people did not use their plots of land 'properly', they could ask for the right to use it. This family finally managed to keep the land it had cleared, by starting to use it again the next summer.

Ultimately, it is the effective use of land expressed through 'work' which secured villagers' rights over their land. Cultivating an allotment represented a clear statement informing the whole village community that a given household needed the produce of that land. Consequently, no villagers would be supported if they attempted to deprive a given residential group of its land. On the other hand, leaving a piece of land uncultivated meant depriving others who might need it, and this was unacceptable. To some extent, villagers viewed land as belonging to everybody. It was there for all to use. These views were well expressed by the way they made use of public spaces to graze their livestock. They took what they needed without asking permission from anyone and no one expressed concern when they did. A woman living in the town of Veliki Ustiug told me how twenty years ago her parents cleared by themselves a small plot of land at the limit of the town and had been using it ever since for their subsidiary farming. She said: 'The land does not belong to anybody. It's there. All you have to do is to take it.' They never registered it or paid any taxes over it and no one ever challenged their ownership. According to her, had they needed more land, they would only have had to clear an additional area. Tima, a villager of Borovinka, had a similar experience. The house of his family was located on the bank of the river, at some distance from the village centre. He had no immediate neighbours. He told me that if he needed more land, he only had to clear a bit of the forest behind his house and expand it. In this respect, he was happy to live in a site remote from the village since he did not have to take into account the limit of other villagers' plots.

This emphasis on 'needs' and 'work' rather than on the legal 'proprietor-ship' of land also provides information on the 'meaning of land'. It stresses the fact that for the villagers of Borovinka, land was first a productive resource, that is, where production was determined in terms of needs and work rather than in terms of economic efficiency. Land was there to feed them, not to be possessed. Shanin traces this idea of the land as mainly *kormitel'*, that is, 'serving essentially consumption purposes', back to pre-revolutionary times (Shanin 1972: 40). Data gathered in Borovinka suggest that this meaning had been maintained ever since.

The examination of the land distribution in Borovinka emphasizes all the more the idea of land as a productive resource. Interestingly, the material gathered reveals that the size of the subsidiary plots, which in the literature is usually presented as static and fixed, fluctuated following the development of the household itself. It shows that unmarried individuals or newly settled couples with pre-school children cultivated less land, but as the family grew, the demand for produce and workforce increased and so did the parcel of land. As the second generation married and left the parental home, the residential group was reduced once more and so often was the household plot.[7] The size of the household personal plot was thus *flexible*. This flexibility was without doubt linked to the very nature of the property rights held over the household plot. The fact that householders' property rights over land were secured by the work they put into it implied that the land could not be concentrated in the hands of those who did not need it or could not work it. According to the principle that land should not remain untilled, those who did not use their plots any more were encouraged or sometimes urged to transfer it to those who had greater needs. These principles allowed, to some extent, a circulation of land among the households of the village following everyone's needs.

Thus, the analysis of property rights over subsidiary plots reveals a specific pattern of land management where rights over land were distributed according to households' needs and production capacities. Importantly, these rights were not secured by law, but regulated by the whole community through social relations and social pressure. When people were believed to make improper use of their land, they were strongly encouraged by their neighbours to dispose of it. Let us now examine whether this pattern of land management fits in with the organization of private farms as implemented by the recent reforms.

THE NEW PRIVATE FARMS

As in the case of subsidiary plots, the size of the household was taken into account to determine the size of the plots allocated to new private farmers. However, other factors were also considered. The most important was probably the type of farm intended: whether it was a dairy farm, a pig unit or simply the cultivation of grains or vegetables (Kulikov and Smolentsev 1992: 12). In comparison to subsidiary farm holders, private farmers were allocated plots of land much larger than they needed to feed their own family. The average private farm in the district of Veliki Ustiug covered approximately 39 hectares of land while the average subsidiary plot amounted to 0.15 hectare. This difference was normal, however, since private farms fulfilled a function different from that of subsidiary farms. They were expected to provide foodstuff to feed not only the family, but the population. On a long-term basis, private farms were called upon to replace state and collective farms.

Thus, in order to facilitate their establishment, the Russian government had put forward a number of incentives including various mechanisms of land distribution giving private farmers easier access to land and securing their property rights over it, freedom from some taxes in the first five years of their establishment, and loans with preferential interest rates (Hivon 1995a; Perrotta 1995; Van Atta 1993a).[8] As a result, 148 private farmers were officially registered in the district of Veliki Ustiug at the time of fieldwork. They were granted 19 per cent of the farming land of the district. With the help of loans at low interest rates, they were able to purchase 150 tractors and 58 lorries (*kamaz*); some of them had also acquired hay balers and combines to plant and lift potatoes (Bushmanov 1993).

This preferential treatment of private farmers placed them in a privileged position compared to other villagers, and to state and collective farms. While the creation of small, private farms was strongly encouraged, very few measures were undertaken to help collective and state farms to become more efficient, and at the time of fieldwork, many of them were struggling to make ends meet (Hivon 1995b). Some were not even able to pay their workers. Yet they still produced most of the food available on the market, while private farmers produced approximately 1 per cent of the district's total agricultural production (Bushmanov 1993). This position, clearly in favour of the development of private farming, was deeply resented by most people I met. No matter whether I spoke with state farmworkers, officials from the local soviet or villagers of Borovinka, I was repeatedly told: 'The government has abandoned state and collective farms. All the resources are forwarded to private farmers who are not producing anything.'

But this was not the only reason for rural dwellers' discontent. According to Bushmanov (1993), in 1992 and 1993, less than half of the farming land allocated to private farmers in the district of Veliki Ustiug had been cultivated. In many cases, problems such as the location of land far away from settlements, the lack of suitable roads, electricity, water supplies, fertilizers and building materials prevented private farmers from cultivating their land properly. Land left uncultivated went directly against the pattern of land management familiar to most villagers (as elaborated in the previous section). In the eyes of villagers, private farmers monopolized land resources which they were unable to use, depriving, by the same token, potential users from the benefit of them. This idea was further reinforced by the fact that a large percentage of farmers[9] in the district were engaged in other types of economic activity (mainly commercial). For instance, they would use their lorries to carry products from the district to other areas of the country. These activities were very profitable. A twenty-four-hour trip from Vologda to Veliki Ustiug to transport sugar provided one farmer with a profit of 50,000 rubles at a time when the average monthly salary in his village was 3,000 rubles. These kinds of side activity led to the assumption that farmers were busier with commercial activities than with agricultural ones and that they were taking advantage of their privileged access to resources (such as technology and machinery) to enrich themselves. Here again, such complaints against private farmers emphasize the fact that they were not using 'properly' (as defined by other villagers) the resources put at their disposal. They used resources intended for agricultural purposes for commercial gain.

Such attitudes often led to such accusations as, 'The government gives them *our* money [meaning public funds otherwise used for other social services] and what do they do with it? They buy *kamaz* [lorries] and sell them for more money! They're not cultivators, they're speculators [*spekuliant*]'. Unfortunately, accusations of speculation towards some farmers were well founded. Many farmers were serious about their enterprises, but it was obvious that others were simply taking advantage of a system which favoured those interested in making money. For example, the government granted farmers (at the beginning of the reforms) loans at 8 per cent interest rate instead of the 28 per cent for collective enterprises. This was very favourable in the context of hyperinflation prevailing at the time. A private farmer I met bought himself a *kamaz* (lorry) for 1 million rubles. By the time he received it, the cost of such a lorry had risen to 7 million rubles. He could have sold it immediately and made a huge profit, but he was committed to private farming, so he did not. He told me, however, that many of his acquaintances had sold their lorries and bought new combines out of the profits, and then in turn, had sold these new combines and so on. One of them was now comfortably installed in a flat in town and was not cultivating at all.

Finally, because private farmers were not yet well established, many were able to produce enough food for their family's consumption requirements, but little surplus. I met a few private farmers who did not intend to sell anything on the market. In the end, these enterprises served the same function as subsidiary farms. Their primary goal was to feed the family. These farmers were in a peculiar position. On the one hand, they had been granted privileged access to 'public resources' (land and governmental loans), while, on the other, they ended up using them for private purposes (feeding their family).

Of course, accusations against private farmers often resulted from ignorance of their real situation. The local population with whom I worked was not always aware of all the obstacles private farmers had to overcome in order to establish a viable enterprise. None the less, discontent arose mainly because private farmers had obtained privileged access to natural and technical resources and were not believed to make 'proper' use of them. These attitudes ran directly against the previous pattern of land management.

As I mentioned above, the principles regulating the use of land at the subsidiary farm level under the former regime were not enforced by law, but by various forms of social relations and social pressure. Let us remember the young couple who, in order to avoid their neighbours' disapproval, did not enforce their rights over a piece of land, or the family who had to make use of an unused plot in order to avoid being dispossessed by another villager. Thus, the pattern of control of land resources was unwritten and governed through social relations. It was a *common understanding* that land should not be left untilled and that no one should be deprived as long as they were making proper use of it. Given this, it was therefore predictable that villagers would react to the 'unfairness' of the new situation by relying on a pattern of control already familiar to them, that is, social pressure. And, indeed, the expression of their discontent towards private farmers bore some fruit. It actually shaped private farmers' economic and political behaviours as the following two case studies demonstrate.

Case one

Fedor, the private farmer of Borovinka, had a cow, a calf, a pig and six sheep in addition to his 15 hectares of land. Sheep were kept essentially for meat and the wool with which Fedor's wife made clothes for the family. Apart from milk, all the remaining products provided from this livestock holding were consumed by the family. Fedor's livestock holding was in every way comparable to that of a few other families in the village who, however, only had subsidiary farms. On his 15 hectares of land, Fedor grew some hectares of grain and had converted a few hectares of hay field in order to feed his own cattle. Only potatoes, cabbages and carrots were grown to be sold to the population. Nevertheless, priority in the purchase of these products was given to the rest house which had leased him its land. Thus, the largest part of Fedor's farm was primarily used to feed his own family. For this reason, many villagers felt that Fedor's farm fulfilled the same function of subsistence as their own subsidiary farm. They did not understand why, then, Fedor should be entitled to 15 hectares of land, while they had to struggle to find hay for their cattle and grow enough potatoes to feed their families and livestock on less than 3 hectares of land. Furthermore, since

Fedor was registered as a private farmer, he had been able to purchase with the help of government loans a tractor, a lorry, a haybaler as well as two combines to plant and dig potatoes. Here again, some of his neighbours did not understand why he should be encouraged to purchase all this machinery to put solely at the disposal of his family. One villager once said:'What is the difference between his holding [*khoziaistvo*] and mine? We both have a cow, a calf, a pig, and we both cultivate potatoes for our family. Why does he have a tractor and me, a horse? What makes him more important than me?'

Although many villagers recognized that Fedor was a hard worker and that his farm was, in agricultural terms, quite successful, many others thought his activities did not justify him having more land than other villagers. Fedor was very much aware of such griping against him. He frequently repeated to me that 'villagers' psychology' should never be ignored if one wanted to run a private farm successfully. For this reason, he worked very hard at maintaining peaceful relationships with the other villagers. For instance, he would use his machinery to plough the land or dig potatoes on the subsidiary plots of elderly people free of charge. He would do the same for other villagers in exchange for their help on his own land. He would show respect to those villagers whom, he knew, were more knowledgeable on agricultural matters by seeking advice from them. He kept a book in which he recorded all the hours villagers worked on his land and made sure they were compensated with produce. After having transplanted all the cabbage seedlings he needed on his field, he allowed other villagers to take the remaining ones for their own gardens.[10] He also made a good deal with a state farm of the district and obtained many tons of manure, some of which he sold to villagers at a better price than anyone else in the area could offer. Most importantly, he took upon his shoulders the renovation of the village church which had been converted into a warehouse after the Revolution. He hired two villagers, whom he paid very substantially to clean it, and he managed to organize a priest from town to come and bless the church, and to reopen it as a sacred place. This was appreciated by many villagers.

In short, although Fedor's rights over his land were legally secured, he felt compelled to maintain good relationships with other villagers in order to justify his privileged position. Since he had more than others, he had to do more for others to be accepted by the rest of the community. Fedor was encouraged, or felt compelled, to place his privileges (machinery, access to manure, seeds, etc.) at the disposal of the population in order to be accepted by them. By maintaining good relationships with the rest of the community and by placing some of his resources at the disposal of other villagers, Fedor was able to develop his private farm in relative peace.

Case two

The example of Nikita, another farmer living in a neighbouring village serves to emphasize further the importance of maintaining good relations with the rest of the community in managing a private farm.

Nikita came from another area of the country. He had been working for two years as a builder in a state farm of the district before the new legislation allowed him to ask for his share of land and agricultural assets and start farming on his own. He had been granted 20 hectares of land, most of which were located near the village of Kupalno at a distance of 1.5 kilometres from Borovinka and over 10 kilometres from the centre of the state farm which had granted him his land. Most of this land was sown with grain, the remainder being used as hay field. The land which he had been allocated was unused by the state farm, but had been exploited extensively by the villagers of Kupalno. An old man told me that for the past twelve years, he had been cutting hay for his cattle in the field now granted to Nikita. As a result, he was now prevented from using it. Other villagers also told me that they used to gather wild berries in this field, but could not do it any more for the same reason. Thus, Nikita was resented by a large part of this village community for having deprived them of this important land resource.

Before settling in Kupalno, Nikita had lived with his wife and two young daughters in another village closer to the state farm centre. After having had his tractor and haystack burned, he moved to Kupalno where his mother-in-law lived. There, he undertook the construction of a pig unit but soon encountered the opposition of most villagers who said it would smell. After having suffered many complaints from other villagers about his project, he changed his mind and started a dairy farm. When I met him he had seven cows and three calves. He also raised a pig for family consumption. He sold milk to a few villagers from Kupalno, but had more success with the villagers of Borovinka. Meanwhile, he had another tractor burned and the villagers of Kupalno continued to complain that he was damaging the village's single asphalt road with his tractor.

Like most private farmers, he was known in the whole district. Everyone I met, whether they lived in Kupalno, Borovinka or Veliki Ustiug, if they purchased milk from him or not, if they had ever met him or not, would gossip in the same way about him. Repeatedly, I was told that Nikita did not know anything about agriculture, that his farm was incredibly dirty, that he always had ten thousand projects in his mind but did not pursue any of them. Nikita was clearly the focus of much resentment. The last time I met him, he offered to give me milk free of charge every day because he was unable to sell it any more. Fewer and fewer people were buying milk from him. To prevent his surplus from spoiling, he used it to feed his calves and pig. This was far from being profitable and he was seriously considering liquidating his dairy farm. He had already sold a cow to a villager of Borovinka and two calves to the meat processing factory. At that time, he was also planning to build himself a house on one of his plots of land which was located in the middle of a forest at a reasonable distance from both Borovinka and Kupalno. Although he did not tell me this clearly, I was left with the impression that he was trying to isolate himself from the rest of the community by building a house in a place where he would not annoy or be annoyed by anybody.

Unlike Fedor, Nikita was an outsider to the community. He had come from far away and had been living there only two years before starting a private farm. His network of social relations was probably less developed than Fedor's. Moreover, again unlike Fedor, he had been allocated land which was exploited by other villagers before his arrival. Thus, many members of that community had concretely lost land resources and resented him for that. But also important was the fact that he showed no sign of participation in community life. He worked only on his own land with his own means. Instead of working on building relations with other villagers, he isolated himself constantly, and planned to do so even more by settling on remote land.

This case shows the continued importance of social relations and community control over the management of resources. Even though Nikita had legally acquired property rights over certain resources, he had never really been free to exploit them as he wanted. Not only had he deprived the community of tangible resources, but he had never tried to compensate for these losses, for instance by placing his privileges as a private farmer at the disposal of the rest of the community as Fedor did. As a result, he was the target of constant harassment from the local community and the viability of his farm was seriously challenged.

CONCLUSION: SOCIAL PRESSURE AS A SURVIVAL STRATEGY

The examination of property rights over the subsidiary plots of land and the various ways they could be enforced brings a new way of looking at villagers' negative attitudes towards private farmers. Property rights over the subsidiary plot of land were shaped around the household's needs and capacity to farm. This implied that land was first viewed as a productive resource, its main function being to serve consumption purposes. In order to fulfil its function, the previous system of land tenure made possible the concentration of land in the hands of those who needed it and could cultivate it. The land tenure was not so much secured legally as controlled socially.

Such social control allowed a greater flexibility in the management of resources without really threatening anyone's access to land and rights to work it. This tradition was particularly dear to the villagers I met given the overall economic context of the country, a context of complete insecurity which compelled them to rely more and more on their subsidiary plot of land to fulfil their most basic needs (Hivon 1995b). The control of resources, particularly of land resources, was, therefore, essential to their survival.

The establishment of private farms – as it took place in the district of Veliki Ustiug – ran completely against this previous pattern of land management. Private farmers were granted privileged access to natural and technical resources but were not believed to make proper use of them. Many used them primarily for their own personal benefit, while in the eyes of other villagers they should have been using these resources to feed the population. Consequently, they were seen as depriving other rural dwellers of important resources. By putting social pressure on private farmers, villagers tried to force them to redistribute these resources in one way or another, so that these would benefit them as well. The result of successful pressure was that the local community maintained a certain access to private farmers' resources (land, products and technology) and a certain control over their management. In this sense, the various forms of social pressure used against farmers constituted a survival strategy, especially in a context of complete economic chaos.

On the other hand, taking into consideration the communities' concerns also constituted a survival strategy for private farmers, since it was essential to the establishment of a successful enterprise. As Fedor's case shows, by taking account of other villagers' concerns, some private farmers succeeded in gaining their esteem and even their collaboration in the establishment of their farms. However, those like Nikita, who tried to ignore it, continued to be the target of constant harassment from which the viability of their farms suffered greatly.

I do not argue that the incompatibility of different patterns of resource management alone explains the local resistance to private farmers, but it certainly indicates that one cannot reduce its understanding to mere allegations of 'Russian culture of envy' or 'tradition of egalitarianism', as certain western pro-reformers have concluded. Nor can it be reduced to an ignorance of the principle of 'private ownership' and 'private entre-preneurship' as Russian pro-reformers have stressed. I have tried to demonstrate here that villagers had previous experience of 'private owner-ship' but that this experience differed significantly from the capitalist model of private property implemented in the Russian countryside by the recent agrarian reforms. More importantly, the new model tended to reduce rural dwellers' access to, and control over, essential resources. It is, therefore, not surprising that they made every possible effort to resist these changes. It will be very interesting to see whether these negative attitudes will change if private farmers get on their feet and start to supply foodstuffs of any significant quantity to the market.

NOTES

1 By new private farmers, I refer, throughout this chapter, to former state farmworkers and collective farm members who left their enterprise, asked for their share of land, technology and livestock and started a farm on their own; or to urban dwellers who were granted some hectares of land through the State Land Fund to start farming privately.

2 Readers should bear in mind that the present analysis refers to the material collected during this specific period. The economic reforms have brought rapid and radical transformations in the Russian countryside. It is quite possible that the situation depicted in this article has now changed significantly. However, the conclusions are relevant to understanding the important 'reshaping of mentality' that the present reforms imply.

3 One villager related to me the following anecdote which tends to support Van Atta's assumption. He asked me: 'Do you know the difference between a German and a Russian?' When I answered no, he said: 'A German will look at his neighbours' nice houses and gardens and ask himself: "What could I do to live as well as them?", while a Russian will look at his neighbour's nice house and garden and ask himself: "What could I do to make them live as badly as I do?"'

4 The commune (*obshchina*) was a peasant self-administrative body charged with distributing land among its members which consisted of several peasant households, each one represented in the administrative body (*mir*) by the head of the family. For more details on this complex pre-collectivization institution, see, among others, Atkinson 1983; Blum 1961; Dunn and Dunn 1967; Robinson 1932; Shanin 1972.

5 By 'private property', here, I refer to Macpherson's definition: 'private property is created by the guarantee that an individual [or a group] can exclude others from the use or benefit of something' (Macpherson 1978: 5). Once a plot was allocated to the household, no one else could use it. In this sense, the subsidiary plot was 'private' even though the household had only the usufruct of it.

6 The local soviet or *sel'sovet* is the elected organ of the local government.

7 This suggests a practice similar to the repartitional land tenure prevailing before collectivization (Atkinson 1983; Blum 1961; Dunn and Dunn 1967; Robinson 1932; Shanin 1972). A complete analysis of land distribution in Borovinka can be found in Hivon (1995b).

8 These privileges changed later.

9 Official figures reveal that approximately 80 per cent of new private farmers in the province of Vologda (which includes the district of Veliki Ustiug) derived the main part of their income from commercial activities (Berezhnoi 1993).

10 At the beginning of the summer, Fedor's wife planted thousands of cabbage seeds under glass. Once the seedlings were about 15 centimetres high, they were transplanted by hand in the field. Only a few hundred seedlings were necessary. The remainder were given to other villagers.

REFERENCES

Abrahams, R. (1994) 'The re-generation of family farming in Estonia'. *Sociologia Ruralis XXXIV*, 4: 354–68.

Abrahams, R. and Kahk, J. (1994) *Barons and farmers: continuity and transformation in rural Estonia, 1816–1994*. Göteborg: University of Göteborg.

Atkinson, D. (1983) *The end of the Russian land commune 1905–1930*. Stanford: Stanford University Press.

Berezhnoi, N. (1993) 'Putei v kommunizm – net'. *Sovetskaia Mysl'*, 16 February.

Blum, J. (1961) *Lord and peasant in Russia from the ninth to the nineteenth century*. New York: Princeton University Press.

Bushmanov, V. (1993) 'Budushchee – za mezhfermerskimi khoziaistvami'. *Sovetskaia Mysl'*, 2 March.

Dunn, S.P. and E. Dunn (1967) *The peasants of Central Russia*. New York: Rinehart and Winston.

FBIS (Foreign Broadcast Information Service) (1992a) *Conference notes local resistance to reform*, 4 March.

FBIS (1992b) *Gaydar addresses Congress*, 5 February.

Foster, George M. (1965) 'Peasant society and the image of limited good'. *American Anthropologist*, 67: 293–315.

Hedlund, Stefan (1989) *Private agriculture in the Soviet Union*. London: Routledge.

Hivon, Myriam (1995a) 'Local resistance to privatization in rural Russia'. *Cambridge Anthropology*, 18, 2: 13–22.

—— (1995b) 'Ploughing through the reforms: the domestic economy of rural households in post-Soviet Russia'. PhD thesis, University of Cambridge.

Humphrey, C. (1989) 'Perestroika and the pastoralists: the example of Mongun-Taiga in Tuva ASSR'. *Anthropology Today*, 5, June: 6–10.

Kulikov, E.P. and B.P. Smolentsev (1992) '*Kak priobresti zemel'ayi nadel, sad ogorod?*' Vol. 10–12. *Press-Biulleten' Tsenovaia Politika*, Moscow: Meriia Pravitel'stvo Moskvy Upravlenie Tsen.

Macpherson, C.B. (ed.) (1978) *Property: mainstream and critical positions*. Oxford: Basil Blackwell.

Nikol'skii, S. (1993) 'Agrarnaia reforma i krest'ianskii fundamentalizm'. *Krest'ianskie Vedomosti*, 22–28 March.

Pallot, J. (1991) 'The countryside under Gorbachev'. In *The Soviet Union: a new regional geography*, ed. Michael J. Bradshaw. London: Belhaven Press.

Perrotta, L. (1995) 'Aid agencies, bureaucrats and farmers: divergent perceptions of rural development in Russia'. *Cambridge Anthropology*, 18, 2: 59–72.

Pryor, F.L. (1991) 'When is decollectivization reversible?' *Studies in Comparative Communism*, XXIV, 1: 3–24.

Robinson, G.T. (1932) *Rural Russia under the old regime*. New York: Macmillan Company.

Shanin, T. (1972) *The awkward class: political sociology of peasantry in a developing society: Russia 1910–1925*. Oxford: Clarendon Press.

Shmelev, G.I. (1986) *Personal subsidiary farming under socialism*. Moscow: Progress Publishers.

Van Atta, D. (ed.) (1993a) *The 'Farmer Threat': the political economy of agrarian reform in post-Soviet Russia*. Boulder: Westview Press.

—— (1993b) 'The return of individual farming in Russia'. In *The 'Farmer Threat': the political economy of agrarian reform in post-Soviet Russia*, ed. Don Van Atta. Boulder: Westview Press.

Wadekin, K. (1973) *The private sector in Soviet agriculture*. Berkeley: University of California Press.

Wegren, S.K. (1993) 'Political institutions and agrarian reform in Russia'. in *The 'Farmer Threat': the political economy of agrarian reform in post-Soviet Russia*, ed. Don Van Atta. Boulder: Westview Press.

4 Living in a subterranean landscape

Identity politics in post-Soviet Khakassia

David G. Anderson

For the past month the politicians have been drilling us like woodpeckers with their promises about a heavenly future. Recently we have been voting more often than we have been paid.

(letter from Abakon, December 1996)

The residents of Abakan, like those in many provincial cities of the Russian Federation during the summer of 1996, invested their waking hours in a wide range of survival activities. Pensioners anxiously minded their places in long queues at the post office to receive their overdue pensions while simultaneously trying to sell home-grown vegetables on the street corner. Employees of state enterprises creatively balanced their time between the workplace, where their wages had been unpaid for four months, and their wilting suburban potato plots, which suffered during this unusually hot summer. Some of the more fortunate wage-earners, such as the employees of the nationally renowned railway container manufacturing plant (Abakan-VagonMash), or of one of the nearby coal mines, had an even more complicated juggling act. Each of these enterprises, having long ceased to receive cash payments from their customers, had taken to paying their employees in objects that they had received as payment in kind. Thus, some coalminers received their income in salmon which had been sent from the Far East as 'payment' for coal. Other Khakassian coalminers had the choice of being paid in furniture or in special wage deductions/instalments which could be exchanged at the end of a year for a car. These more fortunate employees divided their day between producing coal, minding the potato plot, and trying to sell the objects that they received in kind in order to have some cash with which to purchase the other things needed for their families. The economic survival strategies of these city-dwellers were *ad hoc*, creative, but far from being accepted as natural. As televised debates for the presidency of the Russian Federation played out their course far away in central cities, Khakassians reflected upon the 'unorderliness' (*besporiadok*) of their current lives as compared to the stability of the past. What was surprising for me, as an ethnographer of post-Soviet culture, was the piercing depth of their memory. Although Khakassians, like many citizens of the Russian Federation, would commonly reflect that the 'past was better' (*ran'she bylo luchshe*), the most common remembered past was not the stable wages and cheap goods of Brezhnev's 'epoch of stagnation' but rather the ideals of a mythic past just beyond the reach of the written word. While travelling between the thresholds of rural kin and urban marketplaces, and juggling various subsistence strategies, many household heads also made time to make offerings at ritual stones, to participate in 'clan' gatherings and to engage in heated debates on how best to express their Khakassian national identity. It is impossible for me to give a statistical rendering of how general these small acts of ritual remembrance have become in this southern Siberian republic. However, I wish to show that, through reviving the prospect of a pre-Soviet and idyllic pre-Russian past, at least some urbanites have found a symbolic strategy with which to confront the instability of the post-Soviet present.

As Rubie Watson (1994b) remarks in the introduction to her recent collection on memory and resistance, the recollection of a lost past provides a powerful tool with which to imagine a different future. She writes, '[An] examination of memory and secret histories takes on an added significance when we consider that many of these unapproved rememberings are now the stuff of which new histories and new states are being created' (p.4). The remembered past which evokes a different future need not only be assembled from the murmured stories of persons or parties who had once dared openly to resist a regime. The images which spark political change can sit mutely but conspicuously in public monuments, such as the monument to the Iberian conqueror Santiago which has become a focus of peasant resistance in Mexico. Similarly, a pastoral landscape, which makes itself conspicuous merely through having escaped the razing blade of the bulldozer, may evoke powerful messages in people. As Caroline Humphrey (1994: 40–1, 349–50) has demonstrated for a number of contexts in inner and northern Asia, the land itself with its balanced vistas of sky and steppe dotted with ritual cairns provides a powerful image of social order. In her view, a majestic but fixed landscape, in that it commands the attention or awe of the observer, can actually be an active entity: 'the mountain's quality of "being" or "standing" is also conceived as a process – the process, if you like, of being the same' (1996: 88). In order for a landscape to become an actor in a political struggle, it must become the subject of a narrative or of a simple action. Just as certain covert histories might be recounted with a trickster's smile in order to evoke the multiple meanings of an 'evocative transcript' (Humphrey 1994: 22–7), making offerings at ritual cairns or upon mountain passes transforms topographic maps into an evocative landscape. During the Soviet period, the architecture of special places such as Red Square (or one of the hundreds of Lenin Squares in front of the Party headquarters of every province) were designed to evoke a sense of power and hegemony over citizens (Arvidsson and Blomqvist 1987). In this chapter I wish to explore how spaces which have escaped refashioning on the state planner's drafting table have become symbols of power in a post-Soviet context.

THE CONTOURS OF THE KHAKASSIAN STATE

Khakassia is a recently created republic within the Russian Federation at the borderlands between the steppe and the Sayan Mountains in central-southern Siberia. Its eastern border follows the Yenisei River, here a narrow ribbon near its source (as opposed to its yawning majestic aspect at its Arctic mouth). To the south, Khakassia borders on the Tuvan republic and on the western frontier of Mongolia. To the west, it borders on the Gorno-Altai republic. On both of these frontiers the boundaries of the republic border as much on the sky as with the land as the boundary lines trace watersheds along the Altai and Sayan mountains. To the north the highlands give way to the agricultural steppe lands of the Minusinsk basin and the beginning of Krasnoiarsk Territory. The title 'Khakassia' comes from the official Russian designation of its native inhabitants – Khakassy – who are primarily a Turkic and Russian-speaking people. This makes the Khakassy a 'titular national-ity' according to the political science literature (Bremmer 1993). However, as we shall see below, this authorised ethnonym, congruent with the borders of the republic, is controversial and begs the question of exactly how this extensive steppe landscape is being remembered.

In the idealised version of their national history, Khakasses 'are' a semi-nomadic pastoral people with a shamanic religion and an ancient history of occupation in the steppes and foothills of the Sayan and Altai mountains. In contrast to other Turkic peoples, like the Kazakhs, Khakasses do not incorporate Muslim themes in their traditional culture. Nevertheless, the authors of the traditional culture draw many other rich parallels between Khakassian rites and those from other empires and culture areas such as Mongolia, Persia, and even the northern Samoieds (Butanaev 1994).

Leaving behind the idyllic picture of Khakassian identity, it is important to mention that within the territory of their titular republic Khakasses are a minority outnumbered by settlers from the European parts of the Russian empire and the former Soviet Union. In the wheat-growing lands of its northern steppes one can find Russian, Cossack and German communities.

In the highly industrialised cities of Khakassia there are a great number of Russian technicians as well as Khakassian urban intellectuals. The high degree of industrialisation perhaps best characterises the national and physical landscape of the republic of Khakassia. Having been the object of the intense developmental reforms of the Khrushchev administration, Khakassia boasts a huge hydro-electric dam, several mines producing coal, molybdenum and gold, and a number of military and civilian factories. Unlike the republics of Gorno-Altai and Tuva, the rural landscape of Khakassia has been transformed through the hasty amalgamation of grain-producing state farms out of a sparse network of small, pastoral households (*aal*). Thus although Khakassia takes much of its national image from its rural past, the architectural, economic, and spatial features of the contemporary rural landscape bear much more resemblance to the modern Russian heartland than to the diffuse collections of hexagonal yurts and unbounded horse pastures of living memory. To a great degree the contrast between idealised and built landscapes underscores the dynamics of post-socialist politics here. Are Khakasses a pastoral shamanic people or are they an urbanised, post-Soviet nation?

The transition between republican Khakassia and the Khakassia of mythic memory has been mediated by several layers of state building. The contemporary Khakassian republic traces its genealogy to the Kyrgyz state of the sixth century – a culture which today communicates its identity through archaeological digs and a few archival references (Kyzlasov 1993: 73–89). This state controlled the trade routes between the Persian, Chinese and Uigar empires and left a written trace in Chinese manuscripts which some scholars identify as the earliest use of the term *Khakas* (Koz'min 1925; Kyzlasov 1993: 59–61; and contra Butanaev 1995a: 74). After its fall to the Mongols at the end of the thirteenth century, the pastoralists of the Sayan-Altai depression controlled a much more modest regional economy of trade with surrounding peoples until the arrival of Russian Cossacks in the eighteenth century (Forsyth 1992: 123–30). The ethnographer Butanaev (1995a) makes a strong argument for the existence of the 'Khongorai ethnosocial union' during this period giving rise to a different and competing ethnonym: khorai.

The history of Khongorai/Khakassia from the eighteenth century onwards is read through the words of Russian scribes under the name Tatar. According to the records of Russian tribute takers, the nomads of this area were known as the 'Minusinsk and Askiz Tatars' – a name that still finds its echo today in the way Khakasses indentify themselves in their own language – as *Tadar* (Butanaev 1995a: 69–70). As political, economic and kin relations became more closely intertwined with the Russian frontiersmen, these borderlands took on many different institutional forms. Perhaps the most interesting formation was the creation in the middle of the nineteenth century of the 'Steppe Parliaments' (*stepnye dumy*). Based upon regional self-administration of four tribute-paying districts, the regional associations associated with the Kacha, Kyzyl, Sagai and Koibal Steppe Parliament today find their reflection in the 'ethnic' subdivisions of contemporary Khakasses: Kachintsy, Kyzyltsy, Sagaitsy and Tubalartsy. Following the Russian Revolution, Communist Party organisers searched for a new Soviet term which could capture the delicate combination of subservience and regional autonomy long practised in this steppe region. In 1927 the Khakassian Autonomous Province (*oblast'*) was created around the unified ethnonym Khakas, ratified by the Second Conference of Tribals (*inorodtsy*) in 1917. According to accounts of contemporary nationalists, the last three generations struggled steadily until August 1991 to re-establish Khakassia's long lost statehood .

The history of Khakassian statehood is much more nuanced than this overview will allow. For our argument it is sufficient to note that from the sixth century forward some scholars are able to imagine a series of bounded spaces within which a predominantly Turkic-speaking people reproduced a series of complementary identities which fit together harmoniously like the shards of a broken vase. There are a number of controversial debates between Khakassian scholars which none the less do not threaten the model of an overall national unity. In the pages of the Russian press a vicious argument has been raging between two scholars about whether the people inhabiting these spaces were proto-Khakassy or proto-Khoraitsy. Similarly, physical anthropologists and politicians have been publishing closely argued treatises on the genetic continuity between modern Khakasses and their Bronze Age neighbours who had once inhabited the same landscape. The debate here focuses upon the strength of an ancient Turkic culture to assimilate outsiders (Butanaev 1995a) as opposed to a model of one thousand years of homogeneity (Kyzlasov 1993: ch. 5). According to my cursory research in the summer of 1996, there are some seven or eight identifiers in circulation which signify fine regional and linguistic differences between people within the boundaries of the Khakassian republic.

The important insight for the argument at this point is that despite the diverse nature of identity between communities (and between families) and the very complex history of alliance and conquest with several great empires, all observers seem to agree that the sum total of all of these different identities is a single appellation as a common people with a common history. Whether one agrees that sixth-century Chinese scribes accurately rendered then existing identities as Khakas, Kyrgyz, or Xi Xsi, the bordered space which encapsulates this argument was established and authorised in the twentieth century by Soviet ethnographers and planners. The post-Soviet dilemma for contemporary residents of this republic is how to interpret their relationship to this single bounded landscape. It is interesting that instead of questioning the legitimacy or usefulness of imagining the steppe encapsulated by boundaries, the attention of many is diverted from the visible (and audible) landscape of place and ethnonyms to a subterranean landscape which holds great significance for the present. As with the impressive obelisks left by the Bronze Age Tagars, which are today the focus for offerings and ritual placings, the national imagination of contemporary Khakasses unites present observers with the symbols of a buried past.

KINSHIP PLACINGS AND THE KHAKASSIAN NATIONAL IDENTITY

Careering down a wide asphalt road in northern Khakassia, my host pointed out to me the shallow shores of Lake Shira. As well as their republic's industrial might, contemporary Khakasses take pride in the fact that the quality of their motorways is the best in the Russian Federation – and that these motorways can take you to some of the finest salt-water spas anywhere. As Motorway 21 descends over the crest of a hill, the blue-green waters of Lake Shira fill a wide horizon broken only by the jagged edges of dozens of Tagar *kurgany* (burial mounds). It was the latter that were pointed out to me first. 'You see,' says my host, 'the old-timers must have known that this is a good place. That's why they put their graves here. Khakasses live here to the present day.' This reference to the ancient culture served as much to underscore the quality of the water as to emphasise the antiquity of Khakassian tenure.

The positing of ancient genealogies is a common rhetorical device in inner Asia. Buriats and Mongols make similar deep connections (but not nearly as archaeological) in contested mountainous areas (Humphrey 1979). In Khakassia the expression of kinship to ancient Bronze Age peoples not only provides a national origin myth but also becomes a personal story which links a person to very specific places. This seems to have much to do with the pre-revolutionary geography of the present republic. Before collectivisation, and indeed before the widespread penetration of land-tilling peasants, Khakasses lived in sparse settlements of one or two households and were known simply by the surname of the patrilineage of the settlement. Each settlement was established in a 'special place'. Houses were not built at the bottom of valleys but always partway up an incline. Certain aspects in valleys were preferred. Generally, 'bad' places were avoided. All of these preferences were united by the consciousness that powerful entities tended to roam the mountain tops and interact either positively or negatively with the living. Many of these rules for placing dwellings are now folk-sayings. From the mid-1950s onward most of rural Khakassia was uprooted and resettled into new rationalised environments – often at the bottom of valleys or on top of levelled graveyards (Sheksheev 1994). Nevertheless, the predilection for locating identity in specific sites has not disappeared. This rich contextual history has meant that most Khakasses can instantly put a region to a surname (if not a particular valley or river confluence). In written form, this fact is represented by popular publications which give tables of surnames, clans, locations and toponyms (Butanaev 1994, 1995b). Interestingly, there are very few surname/patrilineages which overlap across regions despite three generations of urbanisation and the undoubted Slavic origin of some of the names. Thus, kinship in this republic can always be 'placed', and often kin members actively signify their connection to the landscape with ritual placings.

Today, there are few Khakasses who live in the exact site of their birth but most know where that site is. Those rural kin who live in the vicinity have long since been resettled into cramped collective villages. The sometimes wealthy, sometimes destitute, urban kin usually make frequent trips to their rural places of origin. Since the collapse of the one-party state, these periodic pilgrimages have taken on increasingly symbolic forms. Aleksandr Kostiukov, the leader of the Khakassian political Association 'Tun' ('First') conducts annual sacrifices at his lineage's 'clan stone'. This impressive grey monolith, sited in the middle of an alpine valley, is carved with a face oriented due south. Like many ritual sites of old, this stone is now annually fed the blood and meat of a goat which, after being guided three times (clockwise) around the monument, is slaughtered and prepared for the guests (the right side of the goat is consumed first). The only significant changes in this old ceremony are that the sacrificial procession is accompanied by a standard-bearer in national costume carrying the new national flag of the Khakassian republic and that the audience tends to be made up of young students from the city of Abakan instead of older locals. Although most Khakassians with whom I spoke affirmed that they 'have' a clan stone, many preferred instead to indicate their affinity to special places. These can be lakes or mountain glens. Each place is similarly fed when the person goes nearby (with milk, bread or vodka). These rituals, either garish or subtle, reinforce the kinship connection between person and place.

The fact that during the Soviet period such 'idol worshipping' was strictly forbidden probably accounts for both the subtle and elaborate forms of acknowledgement practised at these places today by different generations. For most Khakasses the exigencies of everyday life in a post-Soviet landscape mitigate a widespread reconstruction of traditional practice. Yet within urban environments the tie of place and kin is often very strong. One modest example comes from the realm of everyday conversation. When Khakassian strangers meet, rather than talk about the weather they will often enquire who their respective 'people' (*rod*) are. More often than not they will not identify a common patrilineal link (for if they did they would not be strangers) but rather a kinship trajectory by alternately exploring matrilineal and patrilineal lines. I often heard the phrase 'we are relatives somehow'. This common vehicle of establishing connections is used in contemporary Abakan to determine how to place one's trust in people. In an environment becoming increasingly ruled by informal survival strategies, negotiating the kinship landscape is an important orienteering technique. On the more elaborate side, kinship placings can often be found now on the boundaries between districts. On the Shira district border, westbound motorists stop to tie fabrics to birch trees. On the Azkiz border, a more dramatic 1.5-metre 'tether post' (*sarchyn*) has been constructed, draped with four long streamers of multicoloured cloth ribbons and covered with sweets and low-denomination paper money (metal coins long being a rarity). Both of these placings are traditional forms of paying respect to one's place of origin. What is new here is the convenient location next to major highways of sites where one can pay allegiance to one's territorial identity as a Kachinets or Sagaiets (but not as a member of a patriline). The nationalist significance of both types of placing is quite clear. My hosts often explained to me that it is always easier for Khakassians to buy goods at the markets from other Khakassians since 'we always help each other out'. The tether post at the gateway to the Sagai homeland has been doused twice in petrol (reputedly by Russians).

NATIONAL IDENTITY AND THE SUBTERRANEAN LANDSCAPE

The giant Salbytskii *kurgan* lies in the centre of a wide valley just to the north of Abakan. Until its excavation in the 1950s, it was the largest burial mound in Khakassia. The flat obelisks which mark its perimeter are between 4 and 5 metres high and 2 metres wide. The mound itself rose more than 30 metres, appearing like a small mountain in the midst of this plain. A lesser mound nearby, still unexcavated, acts as a surveying platform for the neighbouring collective farm. Aside from a stone plaque at the entrance to the excavated crater informing chance visitors that this spot is an archaeological site protected by the state, the Salbytskii *kurgan* has not been developed in any unique manner. The shallow ploughs of the Deviaty Khutor collective farm circle around it. The trail that leads to the mound is unmarked and consists of multiple sets of indentations in the soil that turn to muddy ruts when it rains. Nevertheless, it is this mound which has captured the imagination of many artists and political organisers in the nearby city of Abakan.

In July 1996 I was brought to the Salbytskii *kurgan* by charter bus in the company of four other foreign guests and a troupe of folklore artists. The expedition, led by Gavril Kotozhekov, was intended to impress on us the richness and ancientness of Khakassian culture. I learned later that the script to be followed had been rehearsed several times before – first as a political-cum-cultural festival shortly after independence in 1992, later in a series of smaller visits designed for foreign dignitaries. Prior to independence I understood that Muscovite dignitaries and foreign tourists would occasionally be brought here. However, in the four years since independence the 'tradition' of presenting the *kurgan* had rapidly evolved into a complex symbolic form.

Before approaching the mound, our bus was stopped about 1 kilometre away where the 'gateway' to the *kurgan* was displayed to us. Kotozhekov, the head of the Institute of History and Literature in Abakan, warned us against approaching the twin stone monoliths until he had climbed eastwards towards them to feed them milk. The image of this grey-haired man sprinkling milk before a dangerous-looking sky remains with me to this day. As this introductory ritual was completed, the tour guide from the local museum began to explain to us that we stood at the entrance of the 'valley of the dead' at the twin pillars of the gate through which spirits entered the 'central pyramid' of the revered land of the ancient Khakasses. Approaching the stones, men were advised to touch the southern pillar (thought to be the bearer of 'positive' energy) while women made small gifts to the northern pillar. An old woman hastily retreated from the site claiming that her head was spinning.

Having presented ourselves to the invisible gatekeepers, we continued in our bus towards the central attraction. A sudden cloudburst turned the path ahead into an instant marsh, forcing us (not for the first time that day) to dig our feet into the ground to push the bus. Arriving at the circular epicentre of this ethereal land was no less impressive than arriving at its gate. Four local actors, dressed in bright traditional costume, had positioned themselves upon various obelisks. A grim soldier in an ancient helmet held a bowl in which 'holy grass' (*shibr*) had already been set alight. Opposite him across the trench created by the archaeologists' bulldozer was a minstrel playing sombre songs. The head of the ensemble was dressed in a long flowing white robe with an immaculate beaded breast-plate (*poho*) and a long wooden staff. She led the group in a slow circuit around the mound (clockwise) while milk was offered, holy grass burned, and the minstrel sang appropriate prayers in Khakassian. In this manner the *kurgan* was 'opened' for our visit.

After the theatrical opening our excursion broke into small groups who climbed the perimeter stones and explored the barren interior. Kotozhekov called me over to point out a barren patch of earth. 'This is where the body was found,' he said sternly. He went on to explain that this graveside was a sort of porthole connecting this world with a stream of 'cosmic energy' which flowed through this spot (hence the lack of vegetation). Near by, a woman from Tuva swooned and she too complained that her head was spinning. Overhead the sky darkened once again. We were ushered into our bus while the theatrical ensemble quickly 'closed' the *kurgan* with more offerings of milk and burned grass. We all crowded into the bus as the heavens opened and the site was covered in a deep layer of mud through which we would plough our vehicles for the next three hours. Later, older members of the Institute of Literature and History would confess to me that such excursions to the *kurgan* would have to be curtailed since obviously the local spirits were demonstrating through the weather that they were losing patience with the living.

Over the next month, casual conversations with members of the Khakassian intelligentsia often turned to the giant Salbytskii *kurgan*. When people spoke of the streams of cosmic energy which invigorated Khakassia they would always mention the *kurgan*. Some would add that teams of western scientists had discovered 'cosmic anomalies emanating from the site'. With my curiosity stirred, I attempted to investigate these authoritative-sounding claims only to discover that not only accounts by western scientists but archaeological reports of the 1950s were difficult to locate. After excavation, the artefacts had all been removed to a warehouse in Moscow and the results of the dig were never published. It was rumoured that the Khakassian scholar Kyzlasov was hoarding in his flat in the city centre the controversial results discovered by his supervisor. Where authoritative knowledge was lacking, local initiatives had taken over. A woman in the employ of the Khakassian Archaeological Service showed me a detailed atlas of the burial mound where every perimeter stone was measured for its emanation of 'positive' or 'negative' bio-energy. Using a larger-scaled map, others pointed out to me the distinctive pattern which placed this *kurgan* at the centre of a collage of other mystical sites such as bottomless wells, alpine caves with ghostly voices, and holy mountains. It seemed that summer that as soon as one raised the topic of Khakassian identity in any of the multi-storeyed buildings of Abakan one would soon be guided outside of the urban environment of the capital city to explore the mystical wonders of the surrounding countryside.

It would seem that for urban Khakassians, not only is their native land invested with certain kinship placings, but it is also invigorated by a subterranean landscape from which they claim their origins. Like the kinship postulates negotiated by strangers in the Abakan marketplace, there is often no clearly established link between present-day Khakassians and the Bronze Age past: only an imputed trajectory in the end makes them heirs to a landscape dotted with burial mounds and spirit-filled valleys instead of one cluttered with power transmission lines and hydro-electric projects. For post-Soviet urban dwellers in this region, the buried past is always on the verge of welling up to present itself as a political imperative.

This point is best made by recounting a contemporary urban myth told to me three times on the streets of Abakan: first by a university lecturer, then by a police officer and finally by a young journalist. According to them, a few years after the end of a war (the Second World War – twice; the Afghan War – once), two young Khakassian soldiers returned home from the front. They were full of youthful vigour and their battle training made them confident in the face of any obstacles that life in their native province put their way. One evening towards nightfall, after drinking heavily, they declared that they would walk over the escarpment to the neighbouring village to find mutual friends. The local residents warned them away from their foolhardiness since at night, according to traditional lore, the tops of mountains become the domain of spirits and are forbidden to mortals. The young soldiers shrugged off these warnings as superstition. After all, they had fought at the front and returned home to inner Asia alive and well. Surely they could walk a few kilometres across a mountain! At dusk they set off up the road, alternately taking swigs from a bottle of vodka. On the trail, as the sun was setting, they encountered an old man with a long beard who was dressed in traditional costume. He hailed them in their native tongue and enquired as to their destination. The young men declared their intention to cross the mountain. The old man crossly warned them to return back to the valley – and then ominously added that they would not be warned again. He then continued along the road and disappeared into the dusk. The young soldiers laughed at the old man's suggestion and continued on their way. As the night fell and the temperature dropped they began to feel weary. The younger soldier suggested that they rest. Both immediately fell into a deep sleep. According to the younger, their sleep was a troubled one full of frightful visions. He remembered, in his dream, being awoken by three men on horseback dressed in the armour of ancient times. The old man whom they had encountered on the road at dusk was the leader of this ghostly trio. He declared that the two youths had been warned away from this territory and yet had dared to continue. He pointed out that this was the territory of these mounted protectors. He then pronounced that the penalty for violating this territory was death. His two companions grabbed the elder soldier and disappeared with him into the darkness. The old man then told the soldier that he would be released to warn others never again to violate this rule. The young soldier awoke in a sweat as the dawn was breaking on the mountaintop. His companion was still asleep. Try as he might, he could not awaken his friend and discovered to his horror that he was dead. In the days that followed, after the villagers had retrieved the body and an autopsy had been conducted, the doctors could find no apparent cause of death. It was concluded that the soldier's heart had stopped due to overconsumption of alcohol. However, to this day the locals do not cross the escarpment at night.

Variants of this myth remain in the memory of the urban residents of Abakan. In some stories, mountaineers descend into caverns to find a fully dressed Khakassian shaman tending a fire and warning people to mend their ways. In other stories, curious divers find underground settlements somehow suspended in an underwater air-bubble, with people going about their traditional ways. The explicit message of these contemporary myths, like that of many folk tales, is that elders and old things should be respected. However, what makes these myths evocative in a contemporary context is their common theme of a twentieth-century protagonist (soldier, diver, explorer) who discovers after embarking upon a relatively easy journey that the deep past of the Khakassian nation can be recovered. (For a similar modern myth in Mongolia see Humphrey 1994: 42–3.)

The dismissive rationalism of the traveller is no match for the moral strength and magical powers of the pre-Soviet past. The past generations are not buried so deeply in the collective consciousness that they cannot pass judgement on the failings of their modern descendants. The political message of these stories is that real Khakassia or real Khakassians can be discovered only through recovering what is known of the distant past.

THE PAST AND THE POST-SOVIET PRESENT

The most evocative symbol of how the subterranean past plays an important role in the present flies atop of every major government building in republican Khakassia. The republican flag of Khakassia is composed of a striking golden sun upon a dark green background. The solar emblem was adopted from a motif commonly found on Bronze Age petroglyphs and obelisks throughout the steppes of the republic: a set of three concentric rings from which four triangular rays emanate towards the four points of the compass. The green background, later to inspire great excitement among activists in other newly independent Turkic republics with an Islamic bent, was meant to symbolise the deep connection to nature felt by the Khakassian people. This bold design was discreetly consigned to the left edge of the Russian tricolour flag for official functions. At purely Khakassian functions, however, it often appears on its own.

As with the symbolism of the republic's flags, the interweaving of the deep past and the immediate present is a central element at most contemporary political events. When I first met Aleksandr Kostiukov, the president of the political association Tun, in Leningrad in 1987, he was nervously developing a network of Turkic student activists to raise public consciousness about the plight of the peoples of southern Siberia. Delicately steering our conversations away from politics then, he always focused on the idea of culture. Several times he spoke of the Sayan–Shushenskii Hydroelectric Station as a superior engineering achievement which was nevertheless weakening 'Khakassian culture' by flooding local gravesites and burial mounds. Aleksandr would publicise cases of the destruction of cultural monuments in his local newsletter, *Tun*, which he and his wife Yulya would patiently type out on manual typewriters with triplicate carbon copies. After completing his degree in journalism in 1990, Kostiukov attracted new members to Tun by focusing on the need to preserve the ecology and culture of Khakassians. The first 'political' meetings were held at ritual sites such as his 'clan stone' in Azkiz district or at the giant Salbytskii *kurgan*. Almost ten years after our first meeting, Aleksandr gave me a tour of Tun's most recent hotspot: a construction site in the centre of Abakan. Here the city authorities wished to rehabilitate Russian Christianity by building a church. However, Tun argued that this spot (like most of the territory of Abakan) was a traditional ritual site. To prove his point Aleksandr indicated that the foundations of the surrounding apartment blocks were built upon flagstones robbed from local burial mounds. To assert the Khakassian presence at this spot, Tun activists had erected a stylised tether post around which they conducted yearly sacrifices. At the time of writing, the construction project for the church has been delayed for a full year.

Remembering the past for contemporary Khakassians seems like a project for recovering the submerged landscape of a pre-Soviet and pre-Russian collectivity. Tun activists ask us to remember urban Abakan as a series of windswept rises covered with sacred burial mounds. By paying respects to special archaeological sites like the Salbytskii *kurgan*, people make the political argument that a better future is possible since the visible markers of the recent Soviet past are only epiphenomena hastily superimposed upon a much deeper tradition. An active agent in this argument is the landscape: an evocative landscape of burial mounds and tether posts untouched by the industrial rationalism of the Soviet period.

REFERENCES

Arvidsson, C. and L.E. Blomqvist (1987) *Symbols of Power: The Esthetics of Political Legitimation in the SovUnion and Eastern Europe*, Stockholm: Almqvist & Wiksell.

Bremmer, I. (1993) 'Reassessing Soviet Nationalities Theory', in I. Bremmer and R. Taras (eds) *Nations and Politics in the Soviet Successor States*, Cambridge: Cambridge University Press, 3–26.

Butanaev, V.Ia. (1994) *Proiskhozhdenie khakasskikh rodov i familii*, Abakan: Laboratorii etnografii NIS AGPI.

—— (1995a) 'The Khakass Ethnonym', in M.M. Balzer (ed.) *Culture Incarnate: Native Anthropology from Russia*, Armonk: ME Sharpe, 70–9

—— (1995b) *Toponimicheskii slovar' Khakassko-Minusinskogo kraia*, Abakan: Laboratorii etnografii KhGU.

—— (1996) *Traditsionnaia kul'tura i byt khakassov*, Abakan: Khakasskoe kn. izd-vo.

Butanaev, V.Ia. and A.A. Abdykalykov (1995) *Materialy po istorii Khakasii XVII–nachalo XVIII vv*, Abakan: Laboratorii etnografii KhGU.

Forsyth, J. (1992) *A History of the Peoples of Siberia: Russia's North Asian Colony 1581–1990*, New York: Cambridge University Press.

Humphrey, C. (1979) 'The Uses of Genealogy: A Historical Study of the Nomadic and Sedentarised Buryat', in Equipe Ecologie et anthropologie des sociétés pastorales, *Pastoral Production and Society*, Cambridge: Cambridge University Press, 235–60.

—— (1994) 'Remembering an "Enemy": The Bogd Khaan in Twentieth-century Mongolia', in R. Watson (ed.) *Memory, History, and Opposition under State Socialism*, Santa Fe: School of American Research Press, 21–44.

Humphrey, C. and U. Onon (1996) *Shamans and Elders: Experience, Knowledge, and Power among the Daur Mongols*, Oxford: Oxford University Press.

Koz'min, N.N. (1925) *Khakasy. Istoriko-etnograficheskii i khoziaistvennyi ocherk Minusinskogo kraia*, Irkutsk.

Kyzlasov, L.P. (1993) *Istoriia Khakasii s drevneishikh vremen do 1917 goda*, Moscow: Nauka.

Sheksheev, A.P. (1994) 'K voprosu o sselenii "neperspektivnykh" dereven' v Khakasii', in D.M. Karachakov *et al.* (eds) *Problemy sokhraneniia prirody i kul'turno-istoricheskogo naslediia Khakasii*, Abakan: Khakasskii Respublikanskii Kraevedcheskii Muzei, 84–93.

Watson, R.S. (1994a) *Memory, History and Opposition under State Socialism*, Santa Fe: School of American Research Press.

—— (1994b) 'Memory, History, and Opposition under State Socialism: An Introduction', in R. Watson (ed.) *Memory, History, and Opposition under State Socialism*, Santa Fe: School of American Research Press, 1–20.

5 'We should build a statue to Ceaucescu here'

The trauma of de-collectivisation in two Romanian villages

Michael Stewart

Two neighbours (women) from Jina meet 8 kilometres from the village at Sugag.
'Where are you going?'
'Oh, just over here.'
A while later they meet at Sebes, 20 kilometres further and the same conversation takes place. Then again 30 kilometres further. Finally they meet at the border town of Timisoara.
Where are you going? they each ask each other.
Oh, just over here.

Two shepherds from the village of Jina go to the zoo for the first time. They spend a lot of time looking at the elephants. Then they stand staring at the rhinoceros enclosure. Finally they end up at the giraffes, where they sit still until one says to another, 'No! Such an animal does not exist', gets up and walks off.

(Romanian shepherd's stories, 1996)

The process of de-collectivisation in Romania has not followed a single, straightforward path. Not only in different regions, but also in different villages in the same region, the rapid institutional and structural change which characterises the 1990s has progressed in quite distinct and diverse ways, both at the level of economic arrangements and in terms of altering social relationships among villagers and between villagers and outsiders. This article describes some of these variants. There are, however, some constants and it is to one of these that this article is also addressed. One of the noted features of Ceaucescuite socialism was the more or less deliberate cultivation of distrust between citizens (Sampson 1981: 172–5). This lack of 'trust' was not just a matter of economic co-operation, but involved ideas and practices rooted in notions of the family, the person and the house. In a number of ways, the spectacular forms of such distrust were more tangible in the rapidly growing cities than in the villages: I remember Romanian visitors to Hungary in 1982 whispering to me in the metro, unable to shrug off their local habits. The cities were sites and sources of wild rumours, and in them the state security apparatus was believed to be especially active. In the countryside, either the system of denunciation seems to have been less well established, or there were better means of avoiding neighbourly detection. In some rural areas at least, it appears that state policies only re-enforced the closed individualism of peasant households. Indeed, the ability to survive without putting one's trust in anyone seems to have benefited some villagers. As the first story (*bancu*) above suggests, in a mountain village like Jina there was a cultivated habit of not letting others know what one was up to. Though not designed as a means of resisting communist supervision, it functioned well as such. Today, however, it may be that generalised mistrust is a hindrance both to the development of the market economy to which villagers otherwise look forward and to the cultivation of open and democratic politics.

In this article I consider developments in two Transylvanian villages over the period 1992–6. The first village, Jina, lies high in the southern Carpathians above the town of Sibiu (also known by its German name, Hermannstadt). Since collectivisation had never succeeded in the villages in this immediate area, state control of land in communist times had largely been avoided. In this respect Jina is representative of other mountain communities in Romania. The second village, Apoldu de Sus, lies some 14 kilometres to the south of Jina in a region classified as 'mountainous' but where cereal and intensive animal farming has been traditional. There collectivisation took place in the early 1960s and came to an end shortly after January 1990.

The research on which this article is based was planned after a series of visits to Romania, both before and after the revolution-cum-*coup d'état* of December 1989. During this time I was struck by the extraordinarily diverse ethnographic and social character of Romanian village life. Contrary to all expectations, it seemed that Ceaucescuite socialism, far from levelling the distinctions of the past and turning everyone into 'little grey men', had allowed them to flourish in all kinds of unexpected ways. This in turn gave rise to the question of how this past would shape the emerging democratic and free village life that was being promised.

I started out in 1992 with a series of hypotheses and assumptions, brought with me from earlier experience in Hungary (see, for instance, Szelenyi 1988). First, I imagined that the experience under the communist regime of families cultivating 'household plots' (around 0.15 hectares of land retained by the household year on year) might have prepared peasants for adaptation to some aspects of the new social order. Following this, I hypothesised that the 'cultural' or 'ideological' construction of labour, money and the market among these peasants would shape and influence their integration into a new social order. Furthermore, the experience of the black economy under socialism would differentiate between farmers, giving some an advantage arising from both their contacts and their attitudes to risk. Finally, I was interested to see how the cultural division of labour between various ecological niches in the Romanian countryside would generate different types of structural change.

Since this chapter is about transformation, so as not to mislead the reader it is worth stating that my most powerful sense living in Jina was how strong the continuities with the past have remained. As illustration, I would mention three features of the landscape. First, the notion of what a Jinar (the collective term[1]) is, the *gospodar* ('householder') or *crescrator de oi* ('sheep rearer'), can only be understood in a much deeper historical context than that of either the communist or post-communist periods. Second, the representation of these villagers as *ciobani* ('shepherds') in relation to outsiders has, I suspect, barely altered over the last few decades; one aspect of this is encapsulated in the second story cited above, which both mocks the ignorant shepherd and celebrates his remarkable self-confidence. It is a feature of this continuity that a village like Jina still has a remarkably autonomous rhythm of life in relation to that of plain villages and to the calendar of the state. It is as if the isolation and closedness of the place is not just lived as brute fact, but also elaborated into a sense of personhood. Third, though I make little further reference to the role of the Church, my experience is that religion structures and influences all aspects of social and economic life in the most profound way. The raising and caring of sheep, for instance, is represented and experienced in intimately religious terms, and the annual cycle of shepherding is intertwined with a religious calendar that is largely, but not wholly, determined by the Church. Special 'saints' days' (*sarbatoare*) are celebrated by the shepherds alone to protect their flocks; they borrow from the rhetoric and symbolism of the Church for their own quasi-independent rituals. Or again, the annual pig-sticking, a common eastern European custom, is here imbued with intense religious symbolism and launches a very specific Christian calendrical ritual.

JINA: THE VILLAGE THAT CEAUCESCU BLESSED

Jina provides an excellent example of the ways in which the experience of economic activity in the socialist period prepared some peasants for the post-1989 order and placed others at a disadvantage. Jina is in one sense an exceptional village, being one of a small number of hill villages which continued to prosper economically under socialism. In fact, together with a handful of other villages in this area which are collectively known as the 'outlying villages of Sibiu' (Margineni Sibiului), Jina is one of the richest villages in the whole country.

Despite being the highest-lying settlement in the country Jina is a large village, both physically and demographically. It has 4,000 ethnic Romanian inhabitants and 2,000 ethnic Rom (so-called Boyash Gypsies). Of all Romanian villages, Jina's surface area is also the greatest: some 135,000 hectares of land – a situation deriving from the eighteenth century when the village, in exchange for extensive forest lands, garrisoned border guards for the Austro-Hungarian empire. Three-quarters of this land now consists of mountain pastures for sheep. Until 1945, the major activity of villagers revolved around forestry and its by-products. Jina was, in local parlance, a village of oxen – animals which were used to transport the wood for sale down in the plains of Wallachia – though nearly half the inhabitants also kept some sheep. Nationalisation of the forests at the end of the 1940s pushed most Jinar into adapting the transhumant pastoralism practised in all the villages lower down the hillside that were less well endowed with land. This adaptation proved particularly viable since efforts throughout the region to nationalise the sheep flocks by confiscation in the early 1950s proved unsuccessful. Jina may have been particularly fortunate in this regard thanks in part to the sheer isolation of the village at this time, 15 kilometres off the main road, and the ease with which villagers could take flight into the hills. From the oral histories I recorded in lower-lying villages, it seems they suffered worse depredation of the animal stock.

In the early 1960s there was a renewed effort to establish a co-operative in Jina, but within eighteen months this had foundered, with its members, who had in any case been coerced into joining, concealing their animals from the authorities. The chair of the farm at this time was a Gypsy from the village, who was aided by teachers drafted in from outside: that is to say, the people in charge of the farm had neither the experience of farming nor the moral authority necessary to lead the proudly independent house-holders. The location of the farm offices, in the centre of the village on waterlogged land that had lain unused for nearly 200 years since a church had subsided there, is indicative of the attitude of the Jinar. By the mid-1960s the local authorities had abandoned the collectivisation project and the Jinar were again paying quotas (taxes in effect) to the state, rather than submitting themselves to direct control over their time and labour.

This kind of restriction of state influence was not the only advantage conferred on the inhabitants of Jina by their ecological setting. The 'corruption' – networking would be as good a term, and more neutral[2] – engendered and even encouraged by the socialist economy created a niche which the shepherds were able to exploit. At 3,000 feet the land around Jina is insufficiently fertile to provide the quantity and quality of grass needed for the sheep through the year. While they are able to use land near the village for milking sheep and the high pastures for milkless animals in the summer, an 'average' shepherd with 300 sheep is constrained to transport them to the plains several hundred kilometres away where he can obtain abundant fodder. After the collectivisation of land in the plains (1959–62), transhumant shepherding involved the Jinar in establishing black-market, *de facto* trading relationships with local authorities, especially with the leaders of collective farms. Since the majority of collective farm (CAP) officials had little interest in maximising their profits it was possible while transporting sheep by land to bribe farm officials and local police to allow the passage of sheep at minimal cost. Likewise during the winter sojourn in one of the low-lying plain areas where payment to the CAP or state farm was by head of sheep, it was standard practice to pay for merely one-quarter of sheep actually kept. In return the shepherd would care for the sheep of the farm and, more importantly perhaps, would provide the occasional dead sheep, sack of wool or tub of cheese to the CAP leaders.

Back in the village the state tried to tax the animals but with little success. There was, for instance, a quota system for skins of animals but since, for a certain price, the local vet was willing to provide certificates that wolves had killed these animals, the Jinar ensured that pay-outs from the state insurance covered the cost of the quota! The effects of other quotas, like that for wool, were circumvented by providing the worst wool from the legs and tails, rather than that of better quality from the back of the animal. Again a bribe at the appropriate moment eased the passage of the transaction. At the same time, because of Ceaucescu's policy of economic autarchy and refusal to purchase agricultural goods on the world market, it was possible to sell the meat, the wool and the cheese – in a country increasingly bereft of fresh natural produce – on the controlled but open markets at what amounted to 'monopoly' prices. In practice what this meant was that each sheep paid for its entire annual cost with a single kilogramme of its (washed) wool – a minimum of 3 kilogrammes might be produced. So great was the demand for wool and meat that a good 'householder' would aim to own 600 sheep or more. It is perhaps worth stressing the enormity of scale. Pine reports, for instance, that in the 1980s individual farmers in southern Poland rarely kept more than ten or fifteen sheep (personal communication)!

The result of these extraordinary arrangements was an unprecedented wealth. In the neighbouring village, for instance, some stables were walled with black marble. And every young family aimed to build itself a new two- or even three-storey house. At the end of the 1980s I heard a rumour in the industrial town of Cluj, some 200 kilometres away, that one of these shepherds from Sibiu had been to see 'The Leader' (people rarely uttered Ceaucescu's name) to ask permission to buy a helicopter to make his shepherding easier. And after the revolution, in the neighbouring village of Poiana, one family installed a lift to service its three-storey house – so much spare cash did they have. It is therefore hardly surprising that when people came up from the valleys to work for the Jinar at this time they would say they were 'going to America'; or that there are Jinar who now joke that a statue to the old leader should be put up in the middle of the village to celebrate all that he did for them.

More important however, in the long run, has been the training which socialist negotiation and the rigours of transhumance have provided for the new economic order. For, since 1990, the economic basis of transhumant shepherding has been rapidly undone and massive inflation has wiped out the value of any savings shepherds may have had. And yet the shepherds of Jina and their neighbouring villages have continued to flourish.

The first challenge the shepherds faced derived from a still much resented governmental decree. An early act of the Petre Roman cabinet allowed the import of wool (mostly from New Zealand) at world market prices. This wool was, moreover, the softer, better-quality Merino sort, which contrasts favourably with that of the coarse, local Tsurcana breed (technically, the hairy Zackel type). The second problem was that, due to the partial privatisation of land, and the development in the valley of commercial farms which had an interest in retaining all their produce for use, shepherds say that 'one can no longer find a compromise with the engineer' (that is the head of the new associations which organise most agriculture in the plains). What this typically terse expression means is that all the old arrangements for cheating the CAPs have collapsed. As a result, in 1996 the sale of wool (at just over one US dollar per kilogramme) paid for less than half the cost of keeping a sheep through the winter. Finally, the continuing chaos in much of the country over land title has meant that it can prove hard to establish transhumant routes, especially on the slow return (spring) journey when the flock moves at the pace of the newborn lambs.

The broader importance of the Jina experience, however, lies in the way that Jinar have proved able to adapt to these straitened circumstances, in ways that peasants in more traditional cereal farming in former collectivised areas have not. While at the outset of this research (1992) many shepherds were reducing their flocks, over the ensuing four years they found alternative forms of income which sustained them until new markets for sheep produce were found. The most important factor for the continuing prosperity of Jina has been external: the war in Yugoslavia, and more specifically the embargo on trade with Serbia since May 1992. First of all, the embargo opened a lucrative market just across the Danube for smuggled petrol and other contraband. In Ceaucescu's time petrol had been severely rationed and since the shepherds were dependent on their four-wheel drives (locally produced 'AROs'), they had cultivated networks to supply themselves with petrol as well as means of storing it. These they simply revived in 1992. The trade into Serbia became increasingly risky (some Jinar were imprisoned in late 1995), but the income it generated easily replaced earnings lost from the declining sheep profits. The second effect of the war was on the international travel routes taken by Turkish long-distance lorry drivers. Passing through Romania and trading as they did on the street-side informal markets that had sprung up, they came in contact with Gypsies who themselves were well aware of the wool surpluses accumulating in the mountain villages. As far as I could gather it was in 1993 that the first significant sales of wool were made to Turkish buyers, and by 1996 Turks provided the main market. As a result shepherds in Jina no longer had three years' supply of wool in their lofts. Though a small number of shepherds had meanwhile moved full time into the petrol trade, opening garages on trunkroutes, and others had taken up alternative forms of long-distance trade, the overwhelming majority have retained their traditional occupation.

Though there is no space to develop the argument here, my suggestion would be that the experience of transhumant shepherding has provided a particularly fertile ground for the kind of calculative, individualised and risk-taking disposition so essential to the 'spirit of capitalism'. In these mountain villages, transhumance is organised around a pair of shepherds who are wholly responsible for the flock, often throughout eight months of the year. The whole economy of transhumance relies on the wit, cunning and negotiating skills, as well as on the physical strength, of the men. And unlike many twentieth-century shepherds throughout the Balkans (see Campbell 1964), but like earlier Alpine pastoralists (see Fontaine 1993), these shepherds have not been indebted to lowland money-lenders. On the contrary, using their extended kin networks they have expanded their activities from the mountains into the plains, using the home base as a sort of bank, secure from the depredations of the state and outsiders.

Indeed, it is striking that since 1989 the biggest demographic change in Jina has been the descent of some 200 families to the lowland villages around the regional capital, Sibiu, where they acquire houses from Saxon families who have left, and often take their former jobs as well. Such families may continue to farm sheep transhumantly besides engaging in other forms of trade (both long distance and local, for example, small village shops). It should be stressed that this is but the latest such extension of the mountain into the plain: from the eighteenth century onwards Jinar migrated into border towns in the then Romanian principality of Wallachia, providing a base for a kind of colonisation of the valleys.[3]

The idea that the particular developments of the Jina local economy during the socialist period provided a kind of training ground for the new capitalism also proved rather fertile in understanding the efflorescence and collapse of a spectacular pyramid banking scheme, Caritas, between April

1992 and spring 1994.[4] In Jina there was a clear pattern of shepherds with trading experience entering this 'circuit' or 'game' (no one referred to it as a bank) to advantage. Since the shepherding families were more or less constantly on the move they became aware of the possibilities offered by Caritas earlier than others and joined in good time. Many Jina foresters and carpenters, like the peasants in Apoldu, resisted and then entered too late – losing their money. Among the latter families, Caritas, in which money appeared to grow from money, was seen as the work of the devil and numerous were the stories of the sufferings of those who appeared to have benefited from this money: cows bought at market were discovered to be oxen when the householder got home; furniture bought with Caritas money creaked and moved during the night, and food bought with Caritas money bred cancer in its victims' bodies. Caritas inadvertently provided a means for villagers to experience and negotiate (albeit in a strange form) some of the most important elements of capitalism: luck, timing, risk-taking, the non-transparency (*sic*) of financial institutions, and their intimate implication in national and international politics.[5]

APOLDU DE SUS: GORBI AGAINST THE COLLECTIVE FARM

While in Jina the indirect consequences of de-collectivisation have been most apparent, in the farming settlement Apoldu and its linked village Singatin, the question of privatisation of and use of agricultural land has dominated villagers' lives since 1990. The evidence from Apoldu, it seems to me, refutes or at least shows the limitations of my first working hypothesis – that family-plot farming might provide a model for a more entrepreneurial agriculture – and suggests some surprising alternatives.

In Apoldu, many of the more negative features of Romanian economic and land reform have been visible, most importantly the chaotic fashion in which land has been restored to its former owners. However, although my findings support Verdery's observations (1996: 134) that restitution of former holdings will very rarely occur and that the whole process has been marred by political manipulation, the particular experience of Apoldu has proved rather more positive than elsewhere in Transylvania. In particular, the evidence from Apoldu suggests some of the conditions in which Verdery's most pessimistic prediction, that the privatisation of land might allow the rebuilding of state power and domination in rural areas (1996: 167), may not come to pass.

That Apoldu should stand out in this way is due in no small part to the efforts of one man, the former chief engineer of the village, Gheorghe Budrala. Mr Budrala, by chance a born and bred Jinar who then trained at agricultural college, has ensured not only that the state has been largely kept out of de-collectivisation (since disputes have been resolved locally) but also that on his land at least agricultural production has increased since 1989. As a (uniquely) respected CAP official, this man has been able to play a complicated, weaving game with local notions and practices in order to sustain one central project: the development of an intensive, industrialised farming practice in the village.

The challenge Gheorghe Budrala faced in 1990 was that the peasants of this village, as elsewhere right across Transylvania, were determined to break up the co-operative farm. This was, Mr Budrala said, 'the price of hatred', that is, the cost of all the suffering people had been put through. Gheorghe's concern was that if everyone received their original parcels of land, the subsequent parcelisation would be so great that no form of intensive farming could be maintained. At this stage, therefore, he seems to have manipulated local egalitarian ideas that had been fostered by the socialist regime among the small peasants and former landless of the village. In particular Gheorghe organised a classification of village lands into three categories, and the distribution of land within each category, proportionately, to former owners and landless workers, and to non-agricultural residents as well. Everyone who either lived in the village in 1990 or who had owned land there in 1960, when the co-operative was formed, was thus allowed to claim a portion of the total. Villagers were accorded quantities of land, shares, but not particular parcels. Because of the unresolved problems of division, in 1990 the land in Apoldu was still co-operatively farmed.

At the end of the year, however, Gheorghe faced an unexpected problem: the workers of the farm refused to allow non-labouring owners (residents in towns/the retired) to take a share of the produce. To cut a long story short, over the next three years several new forms of association were tried out, most working only just within the limits of the agricultural law or even without a 'true legal foundation'. Through this experience Gheorghe contrived a new solution to the villagers' problems: the creation of two forms of association. On the one hand, resident landowners who wished to work the land joined one of two farms constructed on the model of the old CAP and led by its former office staff. On the other hand, the engineer took all the land of non-residents and of those too old to work it and formed an association with employees to cultivate their land, approximately 450 hectares.[6] He named this association 'Gorbi' after one of his heroes. Under the cover of, or, less cynically, with the aid of, establishing and then protecting the idea of property rights this engineer was able to preserve a farm on which he could develop the kind of intensive, capitalised farming he believes is necessary to ensure the survival of Romanian agriculture.[7]

With seven workers he now farms 700 hectares (the growth is due to members leaving the other associations for his own) and owns all the ploughing and harvesting machinery he needs.

Meanwhile, the members of the two associations – which are modelled on the old CAP, and run by former officials less dynamic than Gheorghe – are paid in kind according to the quantity of land donated. Hence, there the link between labour, produce and profits is thus kept as it was in the past: broken. These farms provide at best an insurance and free food supply for those with employment elsewhere. It is also striking that neither of these associations keeps animals – the simplest way to increase the value of agricultural produce. In contrast, the former engineer has privately purchased a former CAP building and constructed a pig farm where at the time of my last visit (September 1996) 176 piglets were being prepared for Christmas sale. He has plans to add a poultry farm in the loft of this building in 1998. He is aided by his wife, who uses her chemistry degree to good effect. On behalf of the association he also rents out his farm machinery to the other two farms. Since the cash rent he pays to his members is of nearly equal value to the produce in kind provided by the other associations, without demanding any labour from members, had he the machinery to farm all the village land it is clear that all of Apoldu, with the exception of a few capitalist-oriented families, would join their land to his association.

Apoldu lies too far from any market to enable even small-scale marketing of vegetable and fruit produce. Here it seems that the experience of farming family plots under socialism has provided the basis for a practice of cost-cutting, subsistence farming, and not, as my first hypothesis suggested, a basis for independent market-oriented farming. It is, for instance, striking that whereas Gheorghe accurately assesses the cost of seed as 'very cheap', since he ends up using his grain to create added value via animal feed, the secretaries of the two other associations complain bitterly about the cost: for them all cash outgoings reduce the value of the produce they can distribute to their members.

Nearby villages which lack former CAP engineers with the dynamism and vision of Gheorghe Budrala in Apoldu have associations of the transformed CAP sort. An important exception, however, is Singatin, an administrative sub-village of Apoldu, where an alternative model of privatisation can be witnessed. There former 'boyars' ('nobles', but in reality families with between 20 and 50 hectares pre-war) have effected a *de facto* (strictly speaking illegal) privatisation of land ignoring the legal limit of 10-hectare ownership. Here, not through force but through their moral and social weight, a group of families has prevented the formation of any association so as to preserve their family farms. These individuals, who were often surprisingly successful and prominent 'peasants' by the late period of the old regime (having suffered terribly in the 1950s), are inventing a more classic form of capitalist family farming.

In contrast to the subjectivist trend in some recent economic anthropology, the biggest problem faced by these farmers is not cultural or ideological: there is no reluctance to rely on market forces, or to use the farm for more than family support. Problems stem rather from the attitude of the state and relevant ministries (rather as Chris Hann (1980) argued for the socialist period in Hungary). Throughout the period of research, it has been noticeable that, with one or two exceptions, raising loans has been an extremely fraught affair. Uncertainty over property and therefore collateral, and more generally over government policy, has made private banks shy away from agricultural investment. Moreover, since the titles to land have still not been distributed to 30 per cent of the families, the farmers themselves are left in a peculiar limbo. The privatisation of agricultural machinery complexes, which charged prohibitive rates for inefficient machinery, was too long delayed. Indeed, the farmers of Apoldu and Singatin believe that the whole focus of state policy has been towards helping the non-expansive associations and the bankrupt state farms that have never been privatised – farms which have 30 milliard lei (7.5 million US dollars) debts in the Sibiu county alone. In reality, though, even state farms and the CAP-type associations have problems dealing with the unpredictable and fickle state organs. Anecdotal though the evidence is, the fact that butter, milk and yoghurt in most shops in Sibiu is imported from Germany says much about the state of Romanian agriculture! The emergence in 1995–6 of three competing milk-marketing ventures in the area served by Apoldu indicates that this situation may at last be changing.

In terms of the economic transformation of Romanian villages, this study suggests a number of comparative points:

1 To talk of 'the transition' as if it were a single phenomenon is misleading since diverging ecological and historical starting points within one relatively small region of Romania have resulted in very different adaptations.
2 The primary problem for Romanian farming remains the attitudes of officials and state bodies still wedded to a modified socialist view of agricultural development (small-farm strategy to preserve egalitarian communities without a local bourgeoisie, continued state farms, etc.), which discourages investment and banking confidence. The example of Gheorghe Budrala's farm and others like it elsewhere in Transylvania offer a bright ray of hope for those who look to the transformation of Romanian agriculture from an extensive system aimed at self-sufficient, peasant farming into a force that might withstand entry to the European market.

3 Despite state impediment and structural inflexibility, there is an emerging 'class' of farmer–entrepreneurs formed primarily of former 'kulaks', the children of whom trained in agricultural college, and of mountain animal farmers. Agricultural development projects, especially those from outside Romania, might aim to target these groups specifically.

4 That the most successful adaptation to 'the market economy' may well be found among those previously marginal (often physically as well as socially) to the socialist economy. Those who were formerly central to the economy (industrial workers, employees of state and collective farms) find themselves lost in the new order. However, this finding must be tempered by the realisation that the vision of intensive, industrial farming, nurtured by such people as the engineer of the Apoldu farm, was also one cultivated by the socialist regime![8]

TRUST AND UNEVEN BOURGEOISIFICATION

In a sense the processes I have been describing in this paper can be subsumed under the rubric so neatly laid out by Ivan Szelenyi and his collaborators on processes of bourgeoisification in the socialist period (Szelenyi *et al.* 1988). The irony, in this material, seems to be that while – uniquely in the whole of Romania – the villagers of Jina and the surrounding mountain villages remained, in large measure, successful private capitalists throughout the communist period, they also remained locked within what, for want of a better term, one might call a deeply 'traditional', un-civil society. Let me give two examples of what I mean. One research interest which I had not anticipated at all beforehand was the experience and treatment of witchcraft in the village. Witches, it turned out, were an ever-present phenomenon, within both the village and the 'neighbourhood'. The primary activity of witches was the theft, by magic, of the fertility or productivity of other people's animals. Though the Church officially denies the existence of witches, the way the priest encourages the extension of ritual beyond the confines of the church into people's houses enables what one might define as good and bad magic to form a symbiotic whole, within a 'Christian' cosmology. Jinar thus live within a social world where those upon whom one is most reliant, one's neighbours, are also believed to harbour one's most dangerous enemies. It is hardly surprising that they are so reticent to let each other know the nature of their activities and movements.

It would be quite wrong to reduce witchcraft to any other feature of social structure, but the sheer force of these ideas, I am arguing, contributes to a sense of mistrust between villagers. Earlier this year, during electioneering for the mayorship of the village, this attitude of maintaining one's distance seemed to me to contribute to the failure of any normal campaign to get off

the ground: the processes by which reputations are established and challenged within the village do not allow the kind of parliamentary campaigning that I had expected to see.[9]

On the other hand I have described the case of Mr Budrala, the son of a
private forester from Jina who was educated within the socialist system.
Though he had no time for the politics of Ceaucescuite socialism, Gheorghe
had clearly absorbed its model of agricultural development: intensive
factory farming of land. The name he gave his association was a clear sign
of his sense of indebtedness to certain aspects of the communist past. And
unlike his shepherding brothers up in Jina, Gheorghe has sought to go
beyond the purely economic aspects of becoming a bourgeois. Since the
beginning of 1996, he has been active in laying the basis for a National
Union of Romanian Farmers. Since 1990 there have been two attempts to
construct such a professional association, but both have been driven from
the top, from within the Ministry of Agriculture, and both have failed to
involve the emergent class of farmers that includes Gheorghe Budrala.[10]
Gheorghe's idea is of an association that will grow bit by bit from his loft
(that is, without fancy offices), an association that will provide technical,
marketing and social advice. There will be entrance restrictions (a minimum
of 9 hectares, or so many pigs, or so many chicken) and recruitment will be
through nomination by other members. Though many of the technical and
legal details of such an association are yet to be worked out, what this effort
demonstrates clearly to me is the emergence of the kind of civic consciousness so characteristic of some of the urban bourgeoisie in earlier
periods in western Europe. This is a consciousness that slowly and
piecemeal creates trust-generating practices. It is, ironically, also an
expression of some of the ideals which Gheorghe and his generation heard
trumpeted during their education and saw flouted so grossly in the daily
practice of the old regime.

ACKNOWLEDGEMENT

I am grateful to the ESRC (Project R000233495) for funding the research
on which this article is based.

NOTES

1 I leave off the final, silent 'i' which is written in Romanian.
2 See Szelenyi 1988: 213.
3 The only negative consequence of this movement has been the collapse in school
   standards in Jina since twenty-three of thirty qualified teachers have been able
   to find work in more 'civilised' surroundings, that is, nearer the big town.

4 The developmental logic of such a scheme is largely like that of the chain letter. If you get in early returns can be great.
5 See Verdery 1996: 168–203.
6 See Kaneff 1996 for a parallel case in Bulgaria.
7 I think there are good grounds for not being cynical here, since Gheorghe came from the village of Jina, where, as he often proudly told me, 'people know the value of things because they owned them'. Thus, after buying a stable in Apoldu, he soon put a metal fence around it to mark out his property. He pointed out to me that it was only after he acted that other stable owners on the land of former CAPs did the same.
8 These findings neatly parallel some of those of Frances Pine's ESRC-funded study, 'Women's labour and kin networks: the social consequences of the Polish move to the market economy' (see Pine 1996, and this volume).
9 In fact the elections had to be held three times in Jina, as they were inquorate on the first two occasions. One factor contributing to the disillusionment with the whole process was the way the elections in Jina seem to be decided by 'the Gypsy minority' whom the incumbent mayor was prone to bribe with offers of land or development grants. The votes of the Jinar themselves (this is how they see it) would be split and then the Gypsies would have, in effect, the casting vote. This itself, it seems to me, is symptomatic of the problems in the village: that the fiercely independent shepherds have developed no fora within which they can align their interests.
10 I would estimate that there are at least 1,000 farmers such as him in the country.

REFERENCES

Campbell, J.K. (1964) *Honour, Family and Patronage*, Oxford: Oxford University Press.
Fontaine, L. (1993) *Histoire du Colportage en Europe (xv^e.–xix^e siecle)*, Paris: Albin Michel.
Hann, C.M (1980) *Tazlar: A Village in Hungary*, Cambridge: Cambridge University Press.
Kaneff, D. (1996) 'Responses to "democratic" land-reform in a Bulgarian village', in R. Abrahams (ed.) *After Socialism: Land Reform and Social Change in Eastern Europe*, Oxford: Berghahn Books.
Pine, F. (1996) 'Re-defining women's work in rural Poland', in R. Abrahams (ed.) *After Socialism: Land Reform and Social Change in Eastern Europe*, Oxford: Berghahn Books.
Sampson, S. (1981) 'Muddling through in Rumania (or: why the mamaliga doesn't explode)', *International Journal of Rumanian Studies*, vol. 3: pp. 165–85.
Szelenyi, I. (1988) *Socialist Entrepreneurs: Embourgeoisement in Rural Hungary*, London: Polity Press.
Verdery, K. (1996) *What Was Socialism, and What Comes Next?*, Princeton: Princeton University Press.

6 Post-communist neighbours

Relocating gender in a Greek–Albanian border community

Sarah Green

'Threspotia is in Greece, right? In the old days, Thesprotin was full of those goat thieves. Northern Epirus is in Albania, but that contained all our relatives and friends. What difference does it make to me where they drew their lines?'

(Pogoni woman, 1993)

In 1993–4, the border post between Albania and Greece was regularly clogged with traffic. The crossing point is at Kakavia, located in Epirus, the northwestern corner of mainland Greece, in Pogoni county (Map 6.1), and the southeastern corner of Albania. And other than this snaking line of people and vehicles leading to and from the border crossing, the area is sparsely populated and fairly ruggedly mountainous.

On the Greek side, the bustle of resigned travellers was added to by groups of Albanian kids selling cigarettes, the occasional caravan selling coffee and snacks, and a line of road workers and road-digging equipment improving the single, fairly narrow road. A couple of times a day, a Greek police bus would arrive, full of illegal Albanian immigrants who had been caught somewhere on their way south in Greece. Both the police and their captives knew there was not much point to this exercise, as most of those caught would be back again within twenty-four hours; but they also knew that this was a sad game that had to be played.

Nobody at the border talked very much; I would have expected a lot of shouting and tooting of horns and general noisy chaos, judging from my experience of ports and crossing points elsewhere in Greece, but things were relatively orderly and quiet, giving an air of subdued expectation. This place represented, almost more than anywhere else, the way things were for many ordinary people in the relations between ex-communist states and non-communist neighbours. In such a place, it was easy to allow a stream of simplistic statements to flow through my mind: those newspaper feature articles on the plight of illegal immigrants and refugees; the television specials on the state of economic, political and social chaos in Albania; the fear that this stream of often desperate people was engendering among many Greeks; the sheer inequity of the differences in living conditions on either side of the border. Everyone, on both sides, seemed to feel insecure and unsure about the situation; the only thing to do was to get on with day to day living and perhaps spend some time over a coffee or spirit cursing the behaviour of governments far beyond anyone's reach.

I first visited this border in 1993 – just out of interest, as I was intending to research changing attitudes towards landscape and space among the Greek villagers in the Pogoni county.[1] Unusually for an anthropologist, rather than spending most of my time in one village and making that the centre of my attention, my focus was on groups of villages within a landscape, and on regions separated by topographical, political, cultural and/or historical barriers. I visited the border because I knew the region from the early 1980s, while Albania was still an extremely secretive socialist state. In the end, the fact of the border – that it had opened again after almost fifty years – became a central part of the research. It proved impossible to study Pogoni concepts of space and place without the border, without the fact that Pogoni people had been the neighbours of a command-socialism state, and were now neighbours of a post-communist state. That was a central aspect to their existence, and to their understanding of the place in which they lived, not only because of the simple geographical proximity to the border, but also because many Pogoni villagers had been members of communities that straddled the border until it was closed in 1945.

This chapter explores how changes in the political, economic and social organisation of space can affect gender constructions, and can sometimes literally 'dislocate' people's gender, or 'relocate' it, both across time and space. Both an historical and spatial analysis of the way gender had been constructed in the past, and how it has changed with time since the border's closure, are necessary to understand what has happened since its reopening.

GENDER, SPACE AND TERRITORIES IN CONTEXT

The problem with relating this material to existing literature on gender, nationality, space, locality and post-communism is that there is both too much and too little of it. There is too little in that no discrete literature deals directly with the question of places which border post-communist states, or with communities which straddle those borders in terms of changing gender identities; and there is too much in that each of the issues has its own specialist literature.

Most ethnographic studies of gender in Greece have focused on the household, marriage, the village, the coffee shop and/or some general notion of Greek or even Mediterranean cultural constructions, with a frequent focus on either the 'honour/shame' complex, Greek 'machismo' or religion, or all of these.[2] Some studies have also focused on the relationship between constructions of identity and gender (Herzfeld 1985) or more recently, on the practice and performance of gender within different contexts (Cowan 1990; Loizos and Papataxiarchis 1991).[3] Neither masculine nor feminine gender is here taken as a universal, generalisable category or status: rather, there is an interweaving of what are *taken* to be 'timeless universals' of gender (usually expressed as rhetoric rather than practices) and changing conditions in context which result in the ways particular peoples experience gender. All of these studies, either directly or indirectly, consider the way gender operates within physical space, particularly in terms of issues such as 'public and private' spaces and the ways men and women use, or are related to, different kinds of space. This is hardly surprising, as one of the immediately noticeable characteristics in Greece is that many spaces are gender-divided. Even those who do focus specifically on territoriality centre mostly on people's ideas of their own space, rather than on how they define themselves with reference to other people's spaces next door (Hirschon and Gold 1982). My concern is first how gender constructions relate to a spatial level above the village and below the state, but which is nevertheless related to both. To put it crudely, the household or village, or city coffee shop, does not, or not always, have a direct and unmediated link to large-scale structures, institutions or even dominant discursive rhetoric. There is, or there was in the recent past, something in between. In the Pogoni area, it is in this somewhat fuzzy, slightly bigger than local level, where issues involving gender often come into contact with other issues such as state politics, ethnicity and nationalism. And second, my concern is to consider the impact of recent changes on a community which straddles the border between a post-communist and a non-communist state.

Studies of the social construction of the spaces within which people live – whether defined as landscapes, environments, ecologies, places with borders or whatever – have gathered apace within anthropology in recent years.[4] The general trend in this work has been towards a rejection of seeing the physical environment as some kind of static backdrop against which people do the things which they do. 'There is not one absolute landscape . . . but a series of related, if contradictory, moments – perspectives – which cohere in what can be recognised as a singular form: landscape as a cultural process' (Hirsch and O'Hanlon 1995: 23).

Within this perspective, the spaces within which people live are constructed by and interwoven with their social, political, economic and cultural existence: changes in any of these will inevitably have an effect on the others. This is perhaps nowhere so obviously the case as on international borders (Donnan and Wilson 1994: 1–14).[5]

POGONI COUNTY AND THE ETHNOGRAPHIC AREA: BACKGROUND TO THE CURRENT CONDITIONS

Two groups of villages on either side of the Kasidiares Mountain (Map 6.1) were the focus of the study. Here I consider only the villagers on the west side of the mountain; when I refer to Pogoni, I mean these villages and a few on the Albanian side of the border (Map 6.2).[6]

Before the Albanian border was closed in 1945 under Enver Hoxja's socialist regime, the villages on both sides formed part of the same communities (Map 6.2).[7] Three of the groups illustrated on Map 6.2 clearly straddled the border.[8] The group in the southeast contains a total of twenty-three villages, only seven of which are on the Greek side of the border. This community was generally referred to as the Dropoulis people (after the valley in which it is located), and the villages are located along the banks of the Drinos River, which runs between Albania and Greece. Note also the small gap in the middle of the groups of villages: this is the village of Chrisodouli, and nobody claimed it as being part of their past community groupings. This was because, I was told, it had been entirely populated by Albanian Muslims until the end of Ottoman rule in 1913. It is now populated by Greek-speaking households.

In addition to the villagers, there were Sarakatsani, Vlach and various Gypsy groups living in or frequently moving through the area, and on the Albanian side of the border, besides a large number of Muslims, there was a significant Catholic or Orthodox minority (Jacques 1995). During my year of fieldwork (1993–94), villagers on the Greek side invariably stated to which group they belonged, unless they were illegal Albanian immigrants. Villagers who were Greek-speaking but did not belong to any of the culturally distinct Greek-speaking groups such as the Sarakatsani sometimes called themselves 'Grekis'. The usual Greek term for Greek – 'Ellinas' or 'Hellene' – was used by all Greek-speaking groups and therefore did not distinguish between them. Obviously, Hellene is the unifying national term, which deliberately ignores any differences. But as those differences were significant locally, the word 'Greki', which is usually considered a non-Greek word for Greeks, was often used so as to have a name for those not covered by any other name.

In the border area of Pogoni, villagers on both sides were also sometimes considered, in historical terms, as 'Northern Epirots'. It was said that Northern Epirots shared certain distinctive traditions – a local argot and very distinctive musical tradition quite unlike that in the rest of Epirus, similar clothing styles and generally the same kind of economic and social life. Importantly, Northern Epirots considered their distinctive cultural character to be rooted in the north, towards Argyrokastro (Gjirokastra in Albanian),

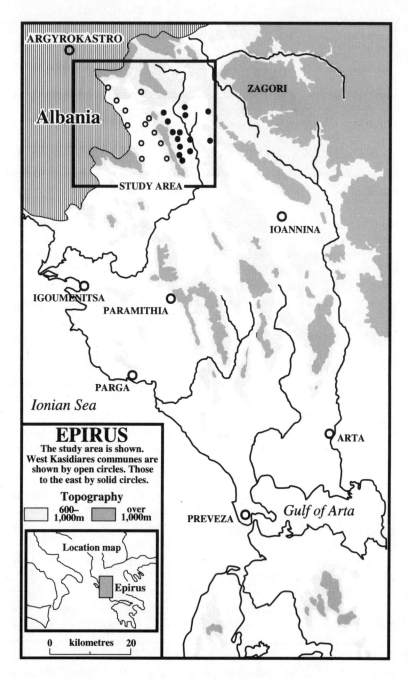

Map 6.1 Epirus: topography, main towns and case study areas

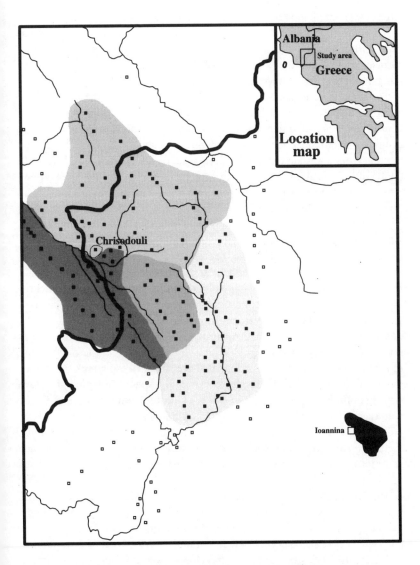

Map 6.2 Epirus: case study area in detail, showing distribution of villages

the main town in southern Albania, rather than southwards towards Ioannina and southern Greece.

After the border opened,[9] the vast majority of the border villagers on the Greek side were happy to refer to themselves as Northern Epirots – that is, the same as the Greek-speaking people on the Albanian side of the border. This willingness on the part of Greek borderland villagers to associate themselves with Northern Epirus changed as the phrase began to take on much more negative connotations.

The issue of southern Albania, or Northern Epirus, was the source of an ongoing dispute between the Greek government, the Greek Orthodox Church and the Albanian government during the fieldwork period.[10] A central aspect of that dispute involved the Greek state's and Church's claims that the Albanian state had been denying the Greek minority their rights to their cultural, religious and ethnic heritage – that is to say, their Greek national heritage.[11] The distinction between ethnicity and nationality is rarely made clear in these disputes.[12] For its part, the Albanian government complained of the deliberate promotion of Greek nationalism in southern Albania and felt that Greece, or at the very least the Greek Orthodox Church, has and always had designs upon that territory.[13]

In the process of this dispute, a great deal has been said in Greece about what being Greek is about, which includes strong gender imagery concerning the Greek 'mother' and the Greek woman in general as the symbol, guardian and reproducer of 'Hellenism'. This symbolism has been present in Greek nationalism since the earliest period of the Greek state, and it is no less powerfully used today.[14] Within that stereotypical rhetoric (taking the 'Madonna' side of the 'madonna/whore' model), the Greek woman as mother is the centre of the family household, a sphere in which she stays with her children, whom she protects and nurtures with traditional Greek culture, and she is therefore not sullied by the changes and disruptions of political or economic life. Her role in creating and controlling the family, the cornerstone of Greek society, is held up as crucial in the maintenance and reproduction of the Greek heritage, most especially during periods of threat to the Greek nation.

This imagery has highlighted certain divergences between national rhetoric about the ideal Greek woman and the history of the Northern Epirot peoples precisely because of the long closure of the border. Since, in effect, the joint lives of these borderland communities took two divergent paths in 1945, the memories of life before the closure were metaphorically kept in a cupboard and saved until the current conditions allowed the cupboard to be opened again. For the admittedly few villagers who remained permanently on the Greek side, that history was not forgotten, although the social memory has been somewhat mixed in with today's renditions of the past.

Anna Collard's (1989) findings from her study in central Greece show that certain moments in Greek history were focused upon as constituting part of the people's social and spatial history, whereas others were ignored. Collard's suggestion that there was a particular focus on the Ottoman period (as a very long period of hardship and oppression, but stability), the Second World War (as the beginning of the break with the past) and the Greek civil war which followed it (as a revolutionary time that changed everything), precisely matched my findings in Pogoni county, in today's typically Balkan situation.

POGONI HISTORICAL GENDER AND TERRITORIAL CONSTRUCTIONS

Pogoni was regarded as a kind of a poor cousin to most of its neighbours during Ottoman rule (1453–1913; Clogg 1992) and in fact this impression continues to the present day. Largely due to economic factors, the Pogoni people, unlike their neighbours, had no cushioning from Ottoman rule. On the Greek side, and parts of the Albanian side, the area was unsuitable both for the high summer grazing required by the transhumant pastoralists and for cultivation. Villagers concentrated on small-scale mixed cultivation and animal husbandry, taking the animals up to summer pastures and down on to the post-harvest fields in winter. Moreover, each village was directly ruled by one or more *aghas*, or Ottoman-appointed landlords – mostly Albanians – who took a large portion of what little was produced. Not that these landlords were terribly fortunate: they could have been far wealthier had they had control of the large plains further east or south on the Greek side, or the richly fertile plains further northwest on the Albanian side. Just as the Pogoni villagers were regarded as poor, so too were their masters.

By the eighteenth century a system of long-term labour migration became widespread. In the majority of border villages, almost all, if not all adult men travelled to other areas of Greece, to Constantinople and to other areas in the Balkans (particularly Romania) to work in cities. They would be absent for three to five years at a time, return for three months or so to hand over any saved earnings and to develop a family, and then leave again, until they were too old to continue.

In effect, this meant that historically, the village was organised, on a day to day basis, by women. These women cultivated the fields, ran flocks of sheep and goats, took odd jobs such as collecting wood for the making of plaster or charcoal, went to market to sell any surplus goods, as well as raising their children and running their households. In the Ottoman period they were effectively under the control of a male *agha*, but the male migration pattern continued until the mid-1940s, according to local reports.

On the Greek side of the border, the majority of the actively working Pogoni population emigrated after the civil war to Athens, Germany, the USA or Australia, leaving a few villagers carrying on small-scale agricultural activities.

Therefore, between the end of Ottoman rule and the closure of the Greek–Albanian border, the women of these villages could be said to be, on the face of it, fairly autonomous and self-sufficient in every area of their lives. And, in fact, they developed a reputation, still in existence today, of being 'tough' women, hardworking peasant women who could carry twice their own weight on their backs even in old age, and who could hold their own in any argument with anyone, man or woman. Indeed, numerous politicians and newspaper feature writers in recent years have been tempted to suggest that these women, alone and without their men – who were most often in some foreign country – were the conduits through which Greek culture and heritage was continued and reproduced. However, that is not the way the women (as opposed to the men) I spoke to described that period. First, the division between Albania and Greece was historically almost entirely irrelevant to them in their daily lives. They located themselves in terms of their communities, and not in terms of nations or states. 'Look,' one 87-year-old woman called Kariklea said, speaking in early 1993, 'Thesprotia is in Greece, right? In the old days, Thesprotia was full of those goat thieves. Northern Epirus is in Albania, but that contained all our relatives and friends. What difference does it make to me where they drew their lines?'

The second aspect which did not quite accord with the national rhetoric was the past pattern of marriage in the area. In the early period of research, I frequently found people who said that their mothers were Albanian, often speaking no Greek at all when they first married. They were always Christians rather than Muslims, but in no way could they be described as ethnically Greek.[15] I also came across examples of men marrying Sarakatsani and Vlach women. While the groom had to be a born member of the community, the background of the bride was not quite as important.

This clearly did not accord with the ideal of the mother as symbol, protector and reproducer of Hellenism, but it did with the local tradition of virilocal marriage and the belief that the father was responsible for passing on community membership. The mother was the carrier and the carer. As far as I understand it, national identity was not a clearly held concept in the past; community membership was the crucial point.[16] Children automatically became members through their father, who was not only born of a local patrilocal family (whatever *its* cultural history), but crucially was born there, in that landscape, defined by its location and orientation *vis-à-vis* neighbouring and different landscapes.

There is, however, an additional point here: Pogoni were among the poorest people in the region, and often literally the day after the marriage the new husband would leave for some distant shore and would be away for most of his wife's life, leaving her to do all the work necessary to survive. These men were therefore not only relatively powerless because of their economic position, they were also relatively powerless to the point of being actually absent. The main source of their influence and authority in their villages seems to have been their ability to find male relatives jobs in the distant cities where they worked. Upon their return in old age, they could make both symbolic and material capital out of this by requiring the respect and assistance of families made beholden to them.

If the image of the traditional Pogoni woman is stronger in people's minds than that of the traditional Pogoni man, this has more to do, to my mind, with his physical absence than her identification with the image of the Greek mother as guardian of the Hellenic household.[17] Looked at from this perspective, the prospect of marrying a Pogoni man was not a pleasant one even for Pogoni-born women. To marry in Pogoni meant to have 'black knees' from working in the fields, a 'bent back' from continuously having to carry heavy weights, and an absent man. His absence was his location in the local gender order, in a sense, and as such it was at the bottom of the complexly subdivided regional hierarchy of masculinities. Marrying a Pogoni man was very different from the fate of some Zagori women, who, in marrying a wealthy merchant or professional, could live a life of relative leisure with fine clothes, no black knees and a man who was often around. One old woman, who thought my interest in the whole business hilariously funny, explained:

> Don't get the idea that marriage in those days was about love. That's what you girls do these days, but in my day, your family arranged it and you just had to make do. We always hoped that a family in the Zagori would take us. They were wealthy, and professionals, and cultured. We were peasants, and poor, and the women worked very hard. The men were always away.

For these women, the characteristics of stereotypical Zagori marriage, household and gender relations gave the very different Pogoni arrangements a particular, and rather low, value. Pogoni womanhood was most certainly not to be admired for the autonomy and self-reliance it afforded, and the fact that Pogoni women had a reputation for hard work and speaking back to their men – or even worse, ignoring them – was not regarded as a plus-point in expressions of gendered practice, even by women. Old women would frequently say disparagingly that their men were 'daft' (*hazoi*), and did not have a proper education and, in short, did not deserve respect. The fact that the majority of Zagori residents were also poor, and many women had husbands who did the same migrant work as Pogoni men, did not affect the Zagori stereotype.

There is a slightly complicated issue of agency here. As I understand, it was not that women felt they had no personal agency – in fact, far from it. But the man was the head of the family, and therefore he represented the family. His absence reflected badly on his own expression of masculinity and on Pogoni women as well – on the kind of gender status they had within the gender order of the slightly larger than local scale in the area. So, while women in Pogoni did in practice control their daily lives, and recognise themselves as making the choices and doing the work, they perceived this as an unfortunate state of affairs, hopefully temporary, which was the result of economic necessity. Most would have preferred to be much less autonomous and living in a wealthy household in the Zagori.

This brings me to a third aspect of Pogoni women's lives in recent times which diverged from the nationalist rhetoric of the Greek woman. They not only worked in the fields and with their flocks, but for wages when they could, they sold their goods in markets and they dealt with local administrative problems in government and financial offices. Moreover, in times of war, Pogoni women were among those from Epirus who went out to fight, in addition to providing support and care for the men.

A good example of the contrast between these conditions and the national rhetoric about the Greek woman current at the moment occurred in November 1994 while I was revisiting the area for some follow-up research. A statue has been erected in the Zagori region to honour the actions of Epirot women during the Second World War. The statue is bronze and some fifteen feet tall, and shows a strong, muscular woman with flowing robes reminiscent of classical Greek attire, marching forward carrying an Olympic-style burning torch. The symbolism involved is obvious.

Most local women I spoke to felt this represented the full extent of what Epirot women did for the war effort: their traditional toughness meant that they put their all into it and even fought when necessary. However, the Greek VIP who gave the speech at the opening ceremony – the then Minister for Foreign Affairs, Karolos Papoulias – emphasised instead the crucial role of the Epirot woman in the home, the woman who raised her children in those trying times and who kept the household going despite it all. Many Pogoni women might have liked to have been this ideal-typical type, but in practice they were not. Some local women expressed a degree of confusion about the speech, others simply dismissed it as another politician 'puffing out hot air'.

I do not wish to create the impression that the people of Pogoni do not or did not consider themselves thoroughly Greek, for they do, and that has been the cause of more recent problems. The point is that there are considerable differences across Epirus in the ways in which both being Greek and being a woman were practised, and the ways in which those practices were perceived were closely interrelated with location. Furthermore, I am arguing that such perceptions were informed by brief encounters with, and patchy knowledge of, other areas. Inevitably, the unifying intentions of nationalist rhetoric clashes somewhat with local knowledge practices; where the two became mixed and confused was on that slightly bigger than local level.

HISTORICAL CONDITIONS AND CHANGES ON THE ALBANIAN SIDE OF THE BORDER, 1939–92

While general conditions in Albania during the socialist period are relatively well known,[18] there is currently sparse ethnographic data on the experience of the northern Epirot peoples during this period. As it was the policy of the Albanian government to treat all its citizens as 'equal' (meaning that any asserted differences between groups was discouraged), few official sources specifically identify the Greek-speaking populations in southern Albania. Furthermore, since Greece and Albania remained officially in a state of war until 1984, partly because of Greece's past claims to southern Albania, the Albanian government was extremely reticent to recognise the Greek-speaking minorities (Gage 1993).

Most information consists of accounts about the Albanian state's handling of its Greek-speaking minority under Enver Hoxja (1944–85).[19] Veremis *et al.* (1995), focusing on the changing conditions of the Greek-speaking minority, and the occasional personal account, such as Papaconstandinou's (1991),[20] provide a little further information. With these sources and some informants' accounts, it is possible to outline what was happening on the other side of the border just before, during and after Hoxja's socialism.

Before the Second World War, the Northern Epirot/southern Albanian region was ruled by feudal lords who carved up the plains, and ran each large estate almost as an independent unit. In Greece, the slow process of placing lands in private hands and governing from the centre began with the fall of the Ottoman empire (1913), while at the same time Albania's first ruler, the infamous King Zog (1912–39), established its feudal system.

For the Albanian Pogoni communities, this feudal period more or less maintained the system of Ottoman control over agricultural lands and the members of this community continued to cross the border fairly freely and the men continued as before to travel abroad to work. Similarly, Sarakatsani and Vlach shepherds would pass through the area on their way to and from the winter pastures on the southern coastlands of Albania. Thus, the experience of those on the Albanian side of the border was more or less the same as those on the Greek side during this period, and they were in constant communication. Some village territories even straddled the border.

However, the Second World War, which brought the end of King Zog's reign and the beginning of Hojxa's command socialism, marked the onset of an entirely different experience. First, the villagers on the Albanian side were strongly restricted in their movements. Permission was necessary both to move out from and into an area. The southern Albanian region was an important source of agricultural production and this, combined with the problems of language and social relations Greek-speaking people experienced in the more northern regions, made it difficult to leave. Furthermore, the tight closure of Albania's international borders meant that villagers could no longer carry out periodic migrant travels as they had done, and the setting up of agricultural co-operatives in the area meant people were more or less forced to stay where they were and work for the state. Those few who did leave often did so in order to pursue higher education, which always required them to be fluent in Albanian and often also to change their names to something less 'Greek-sounding'. In essence, leaving Northern Epirus was seen by many as akin to losing Greek identity.

Thus, while the families on the Greek side of the border were joining in with the processes of emigration and urban industrialisation, those on the Albanian moved into sedentary agricultural work. Both men and women equally participated in this work, and the villages were continually being given (as was everyone else in Albania) Hoxja's brand of communist ideology concerning all the people of Albania being equal, particularly men and women (Emadi 1993). In the Northern Epirot area, it was made abundantly clear that there would be no tolerance of asserted ethnic Greek rights if those rights appeared in any way to threaten the security of the Albanian state, which in the eyes of the Albanian police and secret service they almost always did.

These villagers therefore began to feel strongly constrained by a government they perceived to be hostile to their cultural background. The most common comments I received from Northern Epirots were that they felt imprisoned and constantly watched by undercover agents. This is understandable given the level of suspicion Hoxja's regime had about possible enemies, but it was also particularly acute for these people, who had maintained a pattern of labour migration for many decades, and were now cut off from the other half of their communities, within sight of the border they could no longer cross. Reports suggest that any attempts to cross that border (which was at the time demarcated by barbed wire and full of land mines) were dealt with extremely harshly.[21]

Most informants said they hoped that it was a temporary state of affairs, and they looked forward to the day, one day maybe, when they might be reunited with their Greek neighbours. Until 1967, when Hoxja abolished religious worship, they could still attend Orthodox churches, and during that period the Church provided a focus for Greek identity.[22] Thus the closure of the border, which made national differences starkly obvious at the local level, was combined with the Albanian state's concerted attempts to 'flatten' any differences among its people. This shifted the previously regional sources of identity towards a more national, and more abstract, form of identity. To be sure, Greek identity had been problematic for the Albanian state since its formation due to the fact that Greece had attempted to carve a piece of Albania for itself (Kostelancik 1996; Clogg 1992; Jacques 1995). But this stance was not personally felt in daily life by the Northern Epirot communities until the communist period. From that point on, nationality clearly made a very big difference to people's lives, enforced on them, in a sense, by the new conditions.

Verdery's work on the relationship between command socialism and (ethno)nationalism (Verdery 1993), as well as on socialist attempts to re-work gender relations in Romania (Verdery 1996: ch. 3) is relevant here. Although there were significant differences in the way Romania and Albania practised command socialism, there were also considerable overlaps, particularly in these areas. As in Ceaucescu's Romania, Hoxja's Albanian state took a stance of 'socialist paternalism', in which people became the dependent recipients of the state's redistributed social product and the state was represented as a kind of family which 'took care' of its people. As in Romania, this was almost indistinguishable from 'ethnonationalism' (Verdery 1996: 63), in which Albanian ethnic identity, and the history of the Albanian struggle to become a state, alone and unaided according to Hoxja's rhetoric, became the model for 'the people'. In this, of course, the Greek-speaking peoples found themselves somewhat out in the cold, unless they agreed fully to take on Albanian identity as defined by Hoxja.

Equally, the 'gender regimes' described by Verdery for Romania and the ways they intersected with Albanian ethnonationalism hold many echoes, with local variations, for informants' descriptions of their experiences on the Albanian side of the border. First, as has already been described, there was a tradition in the area that women's local identity was set by male kin and by virilocality after marriage. Second, there was the Greek gendered nationalist rhetoric concerning the 'mother nation', and Pogoni peoples on the Albanian side of the border were well aware of this rhetoric. And third, there was the Albanian state's asserted intention of eradicating male–female differences in the socialist project. As Emadi (1993) outlines, Hoxja made a point of continually emphasising that women should be treated equally with men, and a variety of changes was made (in the state's terms and interests) to help ensure this was the case, setting up a women's movement, education for women, day-care centres, kindergartens, health institutions and so on, to allow women to work.

However, despite these changes, women still remained in charge of most of the household work, and in Northern Epirus, which was almost entirely an agricultural area, they carried out most of the childcare as well, generating the by now extremely familiar model of the 'double' or 'triple burden' in much of the former USSR and eastern Europe.[23] The point of interest here, however, is that women remained in charge of the one area where 'Greekness' was seen to be maintained despite opposition – in the village, in people's houses and neighbourhoods – which dovetailed very easily with Greek nationalist rhetoric concerning the 'mother nation', and which directly contradicted Hoxja's promotion of women having children for the Albanian nation. By maintaining 'Greek traditions' within the household, women could thus see themselves as directly resisting the state's wishes. Thus, while the changes occurring in Greece and Albania were extremely different, the progressive uncoupling of women's identity from local regional interrelations, and their relocation in a more unlocated and abstract home and household, which was, in Greek nationalist rhetoric, described as the bedrock of Greek national identity, was occurring on both sides of the border.

For the Greek-speaking men on the other hand, the process of 'dislocation' had begun. Their labour migrations had been curtailed and so they were increasingly sedentary, but at home their work lives were controlled by co-operatives, and their identity as ethnically Greek was treated with hostility. While their previous status might have been relatively low, their status under the Hoxja regime was even lower. The overtly 'masculinist' model (military imagery mixed with paternalism) used by the Albanian state was not easily accessible to the Pogoni men, for this imagery was mixed in with Albanian ethnonationalism. There was an increasing sense for many Northern Epirot Greek-speaking men that their 'location' had been removed, and the only way to retrieve it would be to reunite themselves with the Greek communities on the other side of the border. In this, it was Greek national identity, and not the previous regional identity, which became the focus of attention. It was their 'Greekness' which was the source of their dislocation in Albania; it would be their 'Greekness' which therefore might be the source of their relocation, and that was currently only maintained within families and households, which was not their sphere, but that of the women.

PRESENT-DAY CONDITIONS ON THE BORDER

Now let me return to the present day and developments on the border since 1992. The rural exodus which occurred in Greece following the civil war and in the 1960s affected most of rural Epirus, but it was particularly acute in Pogoni. In conjunction with the economic and political changes, local identities became increasingly disconnected from their local regional interrelations. While the location of the village in which people were born remained important in terms of personal identities, the structure of the interrelations between clusters of villages, which I have argued was the historical source of people's gendered identities, began to dissipate. Anna Collard also noted this change in her research in central Greece, and comments:

> In general, the historical past of the village is conceptualised through a dichotomy within space ... After the Civil War, however, the fact of this spatial opposition could no longer be maintained because the village and the State became in one sense a single unit, and because the spatial boundaries of the village had been challenged, first by evacuation and then by wide-scale 'emigration'. Spatially 'them' now included all those who had left the village but who were still looked to as part of the community.
>
> (Collard 1989: 99–100)

On the Greek side, therefore, younger Pogoni people's knowledge and understanding of their area comes from the vantage point of an urban centre and involves a mixture of what they read in the papers and what their aged relatives tell them. Many of these younger people have built new houses in the villages where they spend their holidays and local festival days. They explained that they returned every summer to be reminded of their 'roots' and their 'heritage', to get out of the city and to grow their own vegetables. But these 'roots' are no longer embedded in the past interrelations described above.

During this period, most older men ceased their practice of long-term migrant labour, and moved permanently with their families to large cities, often, at first, near relatives and former neighbours in Pogoni. This provided many men with a fairly positive source of identity in the cities, in that they became 'present' as opposed to 'absent' heads of households, and they tended to maintain their former 'location' as people who helped younger (male) relatives achieve their careers through the use of their personal networks. Their links with their previous Pogoni villages were maintained when they visited at Easter and/or during the summer, and through ex-residents' village associations (*adelfotites*, or 'brotherhoods'). In recent years, some older men have begun to move back from distant cities, either to Ioannina to work while maintaining weekend and vacation links with the village (and some of these men have been elected presidents of their village), or to the village itself to retire.

The pattern of emigration meant that women increasingly became, at least in conservative rhetoric, 'relocated' within a more or less abstract notion of the household, rather then being specifically related to their regional location, relative to neighbours. They were the 'mothers' of the Greek family, wherever that family may be located. This is not to say that changes in women's status inspired by various hues of feminism have not had a considerable impact in recent years, amongst the younger women at least. However, these kinds of changes are very much associated with the city and with 'modernisation', and the Pogoni area has been glossed as one of these places that retains 'tradition'. In that sense, location is still important in terms of the different contexts in which different notions of 'womanhood' are expressed. The rhetorical view of the women of Pogoni, *as* women of Pogoni, is that while there, they represent the retention of traditional Greek 'womanhood' which is associated with the 'mother nation' idea discussed above. Those women who have either never left or who have moved back to retire to the villages are therefore regarded as retaining that 'tradition', though this is a current-day rendition of what that 'tradition' represents, rather than reflecting the way Pogoni women were historically located within the local gender order. With this new situation and until the border opened, therefore, Pogoni had become a sleepy backwater, and it rarely caught the spotlight of either the newspapers or the tourist industry.

When the border fully opened in 1992 things changed dramatically. At first there was delight and excitement among Pogoni villagers at the prospect of seeing their long-lost relatives again. Local villagers happily proclaimed that they were one with the Northern Epirot people, that they too were Northern Epirot and would do anything they could to help their old kin and friends. However, the scale of the flood of both Greek-speaking and Albanian-speaking immigrants which resulted was not predicted by anyone.[24] The border villages were rapidly overwhelmed, and while they gave all assistance they could at first, the immigrants simply did not stop coming, and they ran out of resources to give. At the same time, the immigrants would do almost any job for any price, and so as they worked their way further south, the first reaction was that everyone had to have a Northern Epirot or Albanian working for them in some capacity, with the almost inevitable result that complaints began about these mostly illegal immigrants undercutting Greeks' wages.

Also inevitably, reports of trouble between the immigrants and local villagers in Pogoni began after a short time. Incidents of violence and of theft from houses became more frequent – all those brand-new and usually vacant vacation homes full of mod-cons belonging to the absent villagers were rather easy targets for organised burglary gangs. The permanent residents began to be fearful and to lose their patience, and the absent villagers whose houses were being burgled began to be outraged. In Greek cities, the red-light districts started to fill up with illegal immigrants offering their services. As far as I am aware, these were both men and women. However, the most common story I heard told about this in the Pogoni region was that Albanian men were forcing their women into prostitution. One man said, 'Their wives, their sisters, even their daughters.' And he continued, 'See, that's the kind of people they are over here. They're animals.' As further 'proof' of his claim, the man drew my attention to a rape which had occurred a few days earlier near his village. The raped women was Albanian and in her teens. She had been so badly hurt in the attack that she was now fighting for her life in Ioannina hospital. He said he knew it had been a gang of Albanians that had done it to her, that was the kind of people they were. There had been no witnesses and the young woman had made no statement as yet, but this seemed to him the obvious conclusion to draw.

This kind of 'demonising' of illegal immigrants was more or less complete by late 1993, though a clear distinction was made initially between Albanians and Northern Epirots. It was the Albanians who were the thugs, criminals and animals, not the Northern Epirots, who were Greek and therefore would not behave in that way. It was at this stage in my fieldwork that Pogoni locals were still happily telling me they were Northern Epirots and discussing their Albanian mothers with me. Over time, however, the distinction between the two groups of immigrants in this local area blurred, and the phrase 'Northern Epirot' came to mean quasi-Albanian. I increasingly heard people outside the border area express the opinion that they did not know what Hoxja had done to them, but these people had fundamentally changed and had become bad people. And more significantly still, some suggested that the reason for their bad behaviour was that they had contracted mixed marriages in Albania while the border was closed, marrying Albanians, and were therefore no longer properly Greek.

It was at this point that the distinction between national identity and community identity became clear to local villagers in Pogoni. It was no longer such a good idea to claim to be a Northern Epirot or to speak of the complex backgrounds of one's parents. During this year, people began to say that they were Epirots and Greeks, rather than Northern Epirots, and they became strangely reticent about discussing their family trees. The memories in the cupboard had caught up with today's rhetoric.

At the same time, however, the Greek government and the national media continued its crusade against the Albanian government concerning the Greek-speaking people in southern Albania, who were increasingly being called the Greek ethnic minority in Albania rather than Northern Epirots (Pettifer 1994; Angjeli 1995). For the absent Pogoni villagers who visited in the summer, the issue became more and more distant and abstract. They generally supported the efforts of the Greek government and Church to help the Greek-speaking people living in southern Albania, but somehow these people had ceased to be anything to do with them personally.

In effect then, Northern Epirots, and particularly Northern Epirot men, now have a rather ambiguous identity in terms of their location, being dislocated from Albania but not relocated in Greece. Rather, they have been identified, in Greek politics, as a besieged Greek minority in Albania. Their 'location' once in Greece is not covered by the rhetoric of the Greek national campaign on their behalf, and so somehow they have come to be seen as an abstract idea rather than as the people they feel themselves to be.

It is interesting to note in this context that a number of Northern Epirots from Albania who have moved to Greece have entered a trade that used to be the exclusive activity of Gypsies – another kind of outsider – that of musicians at Greek festivals, weddings and dances. The dance is a crucial part of the expression of gender in many parts of Greece. As Cowan describes for the Macedonian village of Sohos, the musicians, who are always male and non-local, possess a kind of neutral gender identity, or at least an external and therefore locally unrecognised gender identity, in order to provide the backdrop for the performance of gender of the dancer or dancers (Cowan 1990: 126–30). Northern Epirots from Albania living in Greece have begun to feel very much a part of that 'no-man's land', and the role of musician is somehow quite resonant of their current location within the gender order.[25]

I spoke to a number of young Northern Epirots who were studying in a technical college set up specially for them by a Greek shipping magnate whose grandfather was Northern Epirot. One young boy expressed the group's general opinion quite succinctly:

> While we were inside, we were told about Greece, and how Greece was our motherland. We dreamed of the day that we could come here and leave Albania, because the Albanians, they didn't like us much, you know. But when we came here, we found that people here don't think we're Greek, they think we're different. Not Albanian of course, but not like them either. So what are we? Where do we belong? Do you know?

Thus one half of that community divided by the closure of the Albanian border is now having to relocate itself with little assistance, and a certain amount of hindrance, from both official discourses and the other half of their old community located in Greece. At the moment, Northern Epirot men do not appear to have a location, and the women have been incorporated into a debate about how Albanian versus Greek men 'treat' their women – a very familiar theme in nationalist debates (Verdery 1996: ch. 3). Again, a contributory factor is that slightly bigger than local level: Northern Epirots used to be located within smaller and larger scales through being Northern Epirots and all that that meant in relation to neighbouring regions. Now, with the geographical area fragmented by national boundaries, historical changes have relocated Greek men, reshaped Northern Epirot women's location in terms of the 'Greek household' and dislocated Northern Epirot men. National rhetorics of both countries have negated their regional location and the Greek side has increasingly rejected the Albanians when they arrive in Greece; as a result, Northern Epirot men have, for the time being, lost their location. And that appears to have had considerable impact on their gender identities. It is not, I think, as many people have argued about conflict situations which dislocate people, a matter of the men being 'feminised' and the women being either literally or metaphorically raped and destroyed as a part of that process. Northern Epirot men from the Albanian side of the border have perhaps lost their prior masculinity, but that has not 'feminised' them so much as it has left them with little in the way of an unambiguous gender identity at all.

Pogoni men from the Greek side of the border are a somewhat different matter. As it became increasingly important to distance oneself either from anything smacking of mixed ethnic origins, or from anything smacking of Albanian, there was a rejection of Northern Epirot status, and a replacement of that with Greek status. Increasingly, the older men in Pogoni are, in conjunction with the economic and demographic changes already discussed, actively erasing the significance of the slightly bigger than local scale, and aligning themselves instead with Greek nationalist rhetoric, which casts the region of Northern Epirus in terms of nationalist, and not locally con-structed, identities. And as I have also mentioned, the image of woman (in the singular) as mother of the nation, as located in the domestic sphere and protecting the Greek family and heritage, is extremely strong in that nationalist rhetoric. Whereas Pogoni women were often cynical about this idea, many Pogoni older men seemed all too keen to endorse it. This usually went along with complaints that the Greek traditions were under threat in modern times, and that this must be reversed if Greek culture was to be preserved.

This might seem like the typical male complaint against the few gains women have made in recent decades, but I want to argue something different. The Greek older men who have either stayed in or returned to the Pogoni area have over recent years altered their location. For a start, they are 'present', rather than 'absent'. But more importantly, their gender location, while still related to the Pogoni area, is not based on the past interrelations between area, but on more wide-ranging social and political networks, and on the idea of Pogoni as constructed within present-day nationalist and 'modern versus traditional' rhetoric. The appeal of the nationalist campaign on behalf of Northern Epirots for these men is bound up with the attempt to relocate themselves in local spatial structures. The place is now 'tradition', but one which has been in a sense reinvented to meet today's conditions. Those conditions are of Pogoni being a post-communist neighbour, and of these older men being relocated in Greece's economic, social and political fabric essentially through their location in cities. In short, the location of Pogoni has become relevant to ideas of nation and tradition, rather than to local spatial interrelations.

The attraction for many of these men of nationalist rhetoric, which strongly asserts a return to 'traditional' Greek values and in particular Greek family and gender relations, becomes somewhat more comprehensible in this context. And that has led to some odd situations on the Greek–Albanian border. While Pogoni men now underemphasise any personal links with Northern Epirots, many are at the same time strongly voicing their support for the Greek national campaign on behalf of Northern Epirots' rights. So long as the Northern Epirots remain in Albania and represent, in an abstract way, Albania's infringement against the Greek nation, many local Pogoni men vociferously advance Northern Epirots' rights. At the same time, when Northern Epirots move to Greece, the same men accuse them of being uncivilised and quasi-Albanians.

This strength of feeling about nationalist rhetoric in the local area amongst some older men seems to be closely linked not so much to overt statements about the Greek minority's rights in Albania, but to changes which have been under way in Greece for these Pogoni men. Nationalist statements about Northern Epirus seem to be motivated by the wish to recreate a new location in the area, based on community interrelations which have now more or less disappeared, creating a space which is not this time defined by their absence, but by their active agency. While their old wealthy neighbours in the Zagori are once again attracting all the tourists, money and attention, the Pogoni remains poor, little visited (except by border police, the army and illegal immigrants), and little known. Some men in the Pogoni want to change both their old location in the local gender order and their new one, and the nationalist rhetoric appears to be a good vehicle for this. A campaign which from Athens looks like it is about Greek national unity and protecting Greek interests wherever they are, from the Pogoni looks more like an issue of relocating gender.

The experience of the younger people suggests that this situation is likely to change in the future. Very briefly, both young men and women have begun to view their relation to Pogoni and the kind of identities it represents from distant and urban locations. The distance is perceived very much as one of time as well as space, so that even when they are there, they feel somewhat apart from it, as if they are visiting another time as well as another place. The young women often express the opinion that they are 'well out of it', and would never return to live in those 'traditional' conditions, even if they had the opportunity. The men look at it from a rather more romantic perspective, and many express the wish that one day, they might return to their 'topos', their landscape, but that at present there are no economic opportunities. In Athens, or New York, or wherever they live now, they still say they are Pogoni people, but that is used to locate themselves there, not in the Pogoni.

CONCLUSION

I have argued in this chapter that, in the more distant past, particularly before nationality was of great significance to these borderland communities, gender was constructed spatially (in combination with cultural, political and economic conditions), in terms of interrelations between clusters of village communities and neighbouring regions. These spatial relations formed the basis of people's sense of identity generally, including their gender identities. Further, I have suggested that it is in this slightly bigger than local level, which is neither the village nor the state, that issues involving gender often come into contact with other issues such as state politics, ethnicity and nationalism. Gender is here regarded as being constructed through practices and performances, and is more of a process than it is a status or a category. Once nationalism started to have greater significance, particularly after the closure of the Greek–Albanian border, a new layer of gender constructions was added on both sides of the border (which did not entirely replace earlier constructions and often contrasted with them), but these were different in each, though both were related to state-led assertions of national identity. At the same time, considerable economic, social and demographic changes were taking place, which in Greece involved heavy depopulation of the Pogoni area, a growth of urban industrialism and abandonment of men's periodic seasonal labour migration patterns, and in Albania involved a transition to collective farming and the development of ethnonationalism. Following the reopening of the Greek–Albanian border, renewed rhetorics concerning national and ethnic identities affected gender constructions for the people of this community.

In conclusion, I would suggest that by focusing on the ways in which people had historically constructed their identities and 'locations' in the world, a greater understanding of the kinds of change occurring with the advent of post-communism can be achieved. It is an old chestnut to say that the ways history, nationality and gender are represented in the dominant debates are constructed for current purposes, but the analysis often fails to look very closely at how this operates in practice in the local level. I have suggested that one of the most important changes which has occurred over the same period as the advent and fall of communism in this area is the uncoupling of gender identities from their construction within local inter-relations, both in Albania and Greece, and their reincorporation into more abstract notions of locality related strongly to nationalist, rather than local, ideas of identity. Ethnographic and historical research allows us to unravel these kinds of change at the slightly bigger than village level, where the interactions between gender identities, national and ethnic identities are most strongly felt and fought out.

NOTES

1 This research was part of an EU-funded Archaeomedes Project, Contract Number EV5V-0021, and Environmental Perception Programme (EV5-CT94–0486). I am grateful to the European Union for financial support for the research. Different versions of this chapter were presented as papers at the departmental seminars of the London School of Economics and Keele University departments of Social Anthropology.

2 See, for just a few examples, Friedl (1962), Dubisch (1986), Seremetakis (1991), Loizos and Papataxiarchis (1991), Papataxiarchis and Paradelis (1992), du Boulay (1974), Greger (1988), Herzfeld (1985), Hirschon (1989).

3 See also Lindisfarne (1994), Herzfeld (1985) and Pina-Cabral (1989) for a critique of the 'honour/shame' complex as characteristic of Mediterranean constructions of masculinity.

4 See, for example, Malkki (1992), Croll.and Parkin (1992), Hirsch and O'Hanlon (1995), Donnan and Wilson (1994) and Bender (1995).

5 However, their argument that 'an anthropology of frontiers must incorporate the analysis of inheritance, negotiation, and invention of cultural boundaries between and among groups of *people who identify themselves as members of one nation*' (Donnan and Wilson 1994: 11–12, my emphasis) does not quite accord with my own. While I agree that the analysis must focus on process and negotiation, I am also concerned with the way in which the idea of 'nation' and 'nationality' becomes incorporated into a cross-border community's conceptions of themselves, rather than take it for granted that such a notion exists.

6 To the east of Pogoni is the ruggedly mountainous area of the Zagori, which is where John Campbell studied the Sarakatsani (Campbell 1964). To the north and northeast, above the Zagori (not shown on the map), is the region of Konitsa, also very mountainous and the summer home of the other major transhumant pastoralist group in Epirus, the Vlachs. Many villagers of that area had a long tradition of stonemasonry. Directly to the south is the region of Thesprotia, which historically, but no longer, contained a high proportion of an ethnic group called Tsamithes, most of whom spoke an Albanian dialect. To the southeast are the major plains of Epirus and the capital city, Ioannina, which was and is the business and administrative centre of the region. And to the west is southern Albania. This region of Albania, called Northern Epirus (Vorios Ipiros) in Greece, contains a high proportion of Greek-speaking peoples.

7 I am extremely grateful for the help of Geoffrey King in the production of these maps.

8 Through reports from local informants, I constructed Map 6.2, groups of villages which considered themselves to have been part of 'the same community', related to neighbouring communities, in pre-war years.

9 Relations between Greece and Albania began to improve and border restrictions relaxed in 1985, following the death of Enver Hoxja and the introduction of the much more liberal government under Ramiz Alia, but the communist period did not end until 1992, when Sali Berisha was elected president under a new democratic system. It was really only after 1992 that the border was fully opened. See Jacques (1995)

10 See Branson (1994), Veremis (1994) and Angjeli (1995).

11 See also Gage (1993), who strongly supports the Greek claims.

12 See Jacques (1995) for an historical explanation for the lack of distinction between religion, ethnicity and nationality in this region, and Verdery (1996) for an exploration of the relationship between socialism and nationalism in Eastern Europe.

13 See Jacques (1995, esp. pp. 342*ff*) for support of this claim. It is interesting to note that complete disagreement about the historical relations between the two nations is reflected not only in political rhetoric, but in the work of foreign scholars (compare, for example, the arguments of Gage (1993) with those of Jacques). This paper is therefore in no position to make any definitive statements on the matter.

14 See, for example, Herzfeld (1987).

15 It would have been perfectly possible for Greek-speaking Northern Epirots to marry some Albanian-speaking locals in religious terms, as many Albanian-speaking locals were Orthodox Christians. See Jacques (1995).

16 This was not only because the relevant local sources of identity were the community and its relations with neighbouring communities and regions, but also because the Ottoman state had grouped peoples into *milets* according to their religious affiliation (see Clogg 1992), and in Northern Epirus, there were both Greek-speaking and Albanian-speaking Orthodox peoples (Jacques 1995), who were thus grouped together.

17 It might be worth noting here that the majority of traditional Pogoni songs are a kind of local equivalent of the blues, in which a woman singer laments the absence of her husband. Nowhere else in Epirus is this type of song so prevalent.

18 See, for example, Jacques (1995) and Biberaj (1990) on detailed histories of the country; Stavrou (1996) on the advent of Albanian communism and relations with the Orthodox Church, Sjöberg (1994) on restricting population movements during the communist period; Kostelancik (1996) on Albanian minorities and education; Emadi (1993) on the changes for women in general during that period.

19 See, for example, Gage (1993), Veremis *et al.* (1995), Sevastianos (1984), Kostelancik (1996) and Papadopoulos (1992).

20 Papaconstandinou lived in Ktismata, just on the Greek side of the border, but he crossed it frequently as a child before its closure.

21 Those caught were either shot in the act or publicly punished in village squares later.

22 The strength of the Orthodox Church's feelings on the matter of preserving Greek identity in Northern Epirus can be seen in Sevastianos (1984), who was, until his death in 1995, the bishop of Orthodox peoples on both sides of the border.

23 See, for example, Funk and Mueller (1993) and DeSilva (1993).

24 See Peckham (1992), Pettifer (1994) and Branson (1994) for descriptions of the increasingly tense relations between Albania and Greece as a result of this rapid immigration.
25 The phrase 'gender order' is taken from Connell (1987), and refers to the hierarchical structured relations in which different constructions of gender are embedded.

REFERENCES

Angjeli, Anastas (1995) 'Problems of Albanian Democracy'. *Mediterranean Quarterly*, 6, 4: 35–47.
Bender, B. (ed.) (1995) '*Lanscape: Politics and Perspectives*'. Oxford: Berg.
Biberaj, Elez (1990) *Albania: A Socialist Maverick*. Oxford: Westview Press.
Branson, Louise (1994) 'Fear grips refugees in holiday resorts as Greece cracks down'. *Sunday Times*, 28 August, pp. 1 and 13.
Campbell, John (1964) *Honour, Family and Patronage*. Oxford: Oxford University Press.
Clogg, Richard (1992) *A Concise History of Greece*. Cambridge: Cambridge University Press.
Collard, Anna (1989) 'Investigating "Social Memory" in a Greek Context'. In E. Tonkin, M. McDonald and M. Chapman (eds) *History and Ethnicity*. London: Routledge.
Connell, R.W. (1987) *Gender and Power*. Cambridge: Polity Press.
Cowan, Jane K. (1990) *Dance and the Body Politic in Northern Greece*. Princeton: Princeton University Press.
Croll, Elisabeth and David Parkin (eds) (1992) *Bush Base: Forest Farm. Culture Environment and Development*. London: Routledge.
DeSilva, Lalith (1993) 'Women's Emancipation Under Communism: A Re-evaluation'. *East European Quarterly*, 27, 3: 301–15.
Donnan, Hastings and T.M. Wilson (eds) (1994) *Border Approaches: Anthropological Perspectives on Frontiers*. London: University Press of America.
Dubisch, Jill (ed.) (1986) *Gender and Power in Rural Greece*. Princeton: Princeton University Press.
du Boulay, J. (1974) *Portrait of a Greek Mountain Village*. Oxford: Clarendon Press.
Emadi, Hafizullah (1993) 'Development Strategies and Women in Albania'. *East European Quarterly*, 27, 1: 79–95.
Friedl, Ernestine (1962) *Vasilika*. New York: Holt, Rinehart and Winston.
Funk, Nannette and Magda Mueller (eds) (1993) *Gender Politics and Post-communism. Reflections from Eastern Europe and the Former Soviet Union*. London: Routledge.
Gage, Nicholas (1993) 'The Forgotten Minority in the Balkans: The Greeks of Northern Epirus'. *Mediterranean Quarterly*, 4, 3: 10–29.
Greger, S. (1988) *Village on the Plateau: A Mountain Village in Crete*. Studley: KAF Brewin Books.
Herzfeld, Michael (1985) *The Poetics of Manhood: Contest and Identity in a Cretan Mountain Village*. Princeton: Princeton University Press.
—— (1987) *Anthropology through the Looking Glass: Critical Ethnography in the Margins of Europe*. Cambridge: Cambridge University Press.
Hirsch, Eric and M. O'Hanlon (eds) (1995) *The Anthropology of Landscape: Perspectives on Place and Space*. Oxford: Oxford University Press.

Hirschon, Renée (1989) *Heirs of the Greek Catastrophe: The Social Life of Asia Minor Refugees in Piraeus*. Oxford: Clarendon Press.

Hirschon, R. and J.R. Gold (1982) 'Territoriality and the Home Environment in a Greek Urban Community'. *Anthropological Quarterly*, 55, 1: 63–73.

Jacques, Edwin E. (1995) *The Albanians: An Ethnic History from Prehistoric Times to the Present*. Jefferson, NC, and London: McFarland & Co.

Kostelancik, David J. (1996) 'Minorities and Minority Language Education in Inter-war Albania'. *East European Quarterly*, 30, 1: 75–9.

Lindisfarne, Nancy (1994) 'Variant Masculinities, Variant Virginities: Rethinking Honour and Shame'. In A. Cornwall and N. Lindisfarne (eds) *Dislocating Masculinity: Comparative Ethnographies*. London: Routledge.

Loizos, Peter and Evthymios Papataxiarchis (eds) (1991) *Contested Identities: Gender and Kinship in Modern Greece*. Princeton: Princeton University Press.

Malkki, Liisa (1992) 'National Geographic: The Rooting of People and the Territorialization of National Identity among Scholars and Refugees'. *Cultural Anthropology*, 7, 1: 24–44.

Papadopoulos, Alexandros K. (1992) *O Alvanikos Ethnikismos kai o Oikoumenikos Ellinismos: 'Apeiros' Chora*. [Albanian Nationalism and Universal Hellenism: The Area of 'Aperios'] Athens: A.A. Livan.

Papaconstandinou, F. (1991) *Anthropino Hreos*. [A Human Debt]. Ioannina: Dodoni.

Papataxiarchis, E. and T. Paradelis (eds) (1992) *Taftotites kai Filo Sti Synchroni Ellada*. [Identity and Gender in Modern Greece]. Athens: University of the Aegean.

Peckham, J.R.S. (1992) 'Albanians in Greek clothing'. *World Today*, 48: 58–9.

Pettifer, J. (1994) 'Albania, Greece and the Vorio Epirus question'. *World Today*, 50: 147–9.

Pina-Cabral, J. de (1989) 'The Mediterranean as a Category of Regional Comparison: A Critical View'. *Current Anthropology*, 30, 3: 399–406.

Seremetakis, C. Nadia (1991) *The Last Word: Women, Death and Divination in Inner Mani*. Chicago and London: University of Chicago Press.

Sevastianos, Bishop of Drinoupolis (1984) *Northern Epirus Crucified* (2nd rev. ed.). Athens: Kaphouros.

Stavrou, Nikolaos (1996) 'Albanian Communism and the "Red Bishop"'. *Mediterranean Quarterly*, 7, 2: 32–59.

Verdery, Katherine (1993) 'Ethnic Relations, Economies of Shortage, and the Transitions in Eastern Europe'. In C.M. Hann (ed.) *Socialism: Ideals, Ideologies, and Local Practice* (ASA Monograph 13). London: Routledge.

—— (1996) *What Was Socialism, and What Comes Next?*. Princeton: Princeton University Press.

Veremis, Thanos (1994) 'Falling out with the neighbours'. *The Times*, 24 June, p. 20.

Veremis, T., T. Kouloumbis and I. Nikolakopoulos (eds) (1995) *O Ellinismos tis Alvanias*. [Hellenism in Albania]. Athens: I. Sideris (University of Athens, Department of Political Science and Civil Government).

Wolchik, Sharon L. (1981) 'Ideology and Equality: The Status of Women in Eastern and Western Europe'. *Comparative Political Studies*, 13, 4: 445–76.

7 Dealing with fragmentation

The consequences of privatisation for rural women in central and southern Poland

Frances Pine

'You remember what it was like before. Everything was so cheap we could afford it, but there was nothing in the shops, so we couldn't buy anything. Well, now there is everything in the shops but it is all so expensive, we still can't buy anything. What's the difference?'

(Polish village woman, 1993)

'TRANSITIONS': TO CAPITALISM, WITHIN CAPITALISM

Post-socialist Poland is an extraordinarily diverse place. Very shortly after the 1989 elections which ended the era of one-party rule and command economy, Warsaw and Cracow became full of elegant restaurants, exclusive shops with beautifully displayed merchandise, Ford, BMW and Mercedes showrooms, chic and sophisticated art galleries – in short, the overt public face of twentieth-century western consumer culture. The busy affluence of the urban centres has continued throughout the initial post-socialist period, and there is little to distinguish these cities, or Wroclaw and Poznan, from other European metropolises. In other cities and towns, particularly those whose economies revolved around one particular industry, the public display is much shabbier, and the years of hardship under socialism, quickly followed by new kinds of impoverishment and privation under the new system, are visibly engraved on to the surfaces of the buildings and etched on to the faces of the people. In the countryside too, some areas, particularly those near historic sites or western borders, are becoming visibly more affluent by the moment; much of this new affluence is based less on traditional agricultural pursuits than on new forms of entrepreneurism, both agricultural and non-agricultural, and on temporary migration (see Buchowski 1996). In more remote areas, those furthest from western borders, or those with little to offer any outsider in the way of attraction or distraction, levels of rural poverty are increasing and standards of living visibly falling. This occupational and regional diversity makes any coherent analysis of the national economy very complicated; it also, it seems to me, reflects vividly the processes of fragmentation, entitlement and exclusion which are characteristic of Poland in the 1990s, and indeed of post-socialist states generally.

David Harvey prefaces his discussion of the political-economic trans-formation of late twentieth-century capitalism, in *The Condition of Post-modernity*, with a quotation from John Calhoun: 'The interval between the decay of the old and the formation and establishment of the new, constitutes a period of transition, which must always necessarily be one of uncertainty, confusion, error, and wild and fierce fanaticism' (Harvey 1990: 119). Harvey is using Calhoun's words as a lens through which to examine the transition from Fordism to 'flexible accumulation' in late twentieth-century capitalism; his own description of this phenomenon stresses fragmentation, and the replacement of the apparently holistic or unitary organisation of the Fordist industrial system, which attempted to permeate all areas of social and economic life with a correct, even moral, productive order, by a dispersed collage of economic activities and social interactions. Harvey writes:

> The revival of interest in the role of small businesses (a highly dynamic sector since 1970), the rediscovery of sweatshops and of informal activities of all kinds, and the recognition that these are playing an important role in contemporary economic developments even in the most advanced industrial countries, and the attempt to track the rapid geo-graphical shifts in employment and economic fortunes, has produced a mass of information which seems to support [the] vision of a major transformation in the way late twentieth-century capitalism is working. A vast literature has emerged ... that tends to depict the world as if it is in full flood of such a radical break in all of these dimensions of socio-economic and political life that none of the old ways of thinking and doing apply any more.
>
> *(Ibid: 190)*

These ideas seem to me to be equally applicable to what is often referred to as the 'transition' from communism to capitalism, or from centrally planned one-party states to free-market democracies, in eastern Europe and the former Soviet Union.

Recently, as the economic uncertainty which is pervasive in all but the most developed urban centres has become difficult to ignore, it has been generally acknowledged that 'there is still a long way to go in the transition' (EBRD 1996: 5). The point of departure of the transition is clearly state socialism and all that this implied, although the recent appointment to government of former communists and their affiliates suggests that the past and present are not as distinct as initially might have appeared. The *to* part of the transition equation, however, seems to me to be far less clear, even in the countries taken by the OECD as the indices of successful transition, that is to say Poland, Hungary, the Czech Republic and Slovenia (OECD 1996; Howell 1994). In the more successful countries, both random and organised crime and violence appear to be more widespread than in the socialist period, as do prostitution and pornography; inflation and unemployment continue to give cause for concern; and many of the new private enterprises which might be taken as signs of growth are in fact shortlived, collapsing due to shortfalls in profit or market after only a few months.

To the economists, politicians and management consultants orchestrating the restructuring process, these are the small details. They are more impressed by what they see as the total picture: the number of joint ventures, the investment in local industry by such international giants as Pepsi Cola, Fiat and Pierre Cardin, and the gradual recovery of productivity levels and of import/export balances. From the point of view of the anthropologist, however, the details of local strategies and forms of adaptation are most interesting, and it is on these that I shall concentrate in this chapter.

Some commentators on the new order in the former socialist countries have pointed to similarities between emerging patterns of inequality and dependency in the East–West 'partnership' and those already entrenched in the Third World (see, for example, Moghadam 1992). They suggest that the path along which the former socialist countries appear to be being propelled is not one which leads to western capitalism but to dependency and underdevelopment. Hobsbawm, for instance, in *The Short Twentieth Century*, claims that:

> The capitalist economy clearly decided to write off a large part of the Third World. In many countries, net foreign investment fell to zero. A large part of the world was dropping out of the world economy. After the collapse of the Soviet bloc, this also looked like being the case with the area between Trieste and Vladivostock. In 1990 the only socialist states which attracted net foreign investment were Poland and Czechoslovakia. One way or another, most of the former Second World was being assimilated to Third World status.
>
> (1994: 7; see also Rai, Pilkington and Phizacklea 1992)

I must confess to having a great deal of sympathy with this view. I think, however, that another way of examining the process of change is to shift the focus slightly on to the disjuncture in western capitalism itself. In a sense, one could say that the transition to capitalism is in fact taking place as anticipated in 1989, but that the *form of* western capitalism which the former socialist countries are approximating is not that of Fordism, or of the post-war boom period, but of the disintegration, polarisation and fragmentation of the late twentieth century.

Let me push this a little further. It seems to me that in the many models of late twentieth-century capitalism which exist, two mega schemes are particularly pervasive and quite opposed. One, promoted in government analyses and the reports of international business and banking, stresses productivity, GNP, balance exports and imports, and public-sector expenditure, and sees the recession as a finite episode, from which most economies, certainly in the West, will emerge. Here the emphasis is on growth and recovery, and the model is basically a 1950s development one, based on the premise of 'modern' progress underpinned by the inherent rationality of the market. The other, and the one more frequently promoted by social scientists who work at the micro rather than macro level, stresses irreversible fragmentation, disarticulation, and the growth of a new and geographically ubiquitous underclass; this view is more reminiscent of 1970s theories of core and periphery, world economy and underdevelopment. The interesting thing about these two quite different explanatory models is that both are being utilised in the context of the former socialist countries, not only by academics, analysts and policy makers, but also by local people struggling to make sense of their daily lives. However, while the analysts and academics tend to belong either to one school of thought or the other (and I am aware that this is a vastly simplistic and inadequate dichotomy), local actors appear to combine the two. They tend to fluctuate in their own interpretations and ways of understanding between a search for the solution that will transform their economy into one of ideal capitalism or their own lives into stories of success and security on the one hand, and a belief, either resigned or backed by a bitter and frustrated anger, that their situation will continue to be constrained by unemployment, economic uncertainty and exclusion from the fruits of development, on the other.

LOCAL MODELS AND UNDERSTANDINGS – DARK SATANIC MILLS AND *DYNASTY*

Here is an anecdotal example of what I mean. One day three summers ago I was talking to a woman in a village in rural Poland, and I asked her what she thought could be done to alleviate the problems of unemployment, deindustrialisation and general hardship. This woman is a former local councillor, well respected locally for her shrewd grasp of politics and economics as well as for her firm and continuing commitment to the ideals of socialism. She answered without hesitation, enthusiastically: 'What we need here is a Blake.' Slightly bemused, with visions of heaven and hell, innocence and experience, and the dark satanic mills of the British poet

William Blake conjured up by my mind's eye, I responded, rather weakly, 'Blake?' 'Yes,' she insisted, 'you know, *Blake*. He is exactly what we need. He is very, very rich but he is also good. He is firm, and he understands business. He puts his family first. We need Blake.' Light dawned. The American soap serial *Dynasty* was being shown on local television and *her* Blake was not the visionary poet of the dark satanic mills but the icon of popular culture, the paternalistic, rich and rather ruthless businessman Blake Carrington. And, of course, completely fictitious.

In many other conversations I had with villagers in this area over the next two years, Blake's name was also mentioned, much in the way that Margaret Thatcher's had been in the 1980s, as a perfect example of strength of character and business acumen which could set things right. What interests me about what I came to think of as the Blake syndrome is that on one level the people I was speaking to did not fully recognise or acknowledge that this was a Hollywood image, and that the life represented on such serials is a fantasy life. Rather, Blake Carrington was taken as the epitome of a kind of firm but benign style of economic leadership which could produce the transformation into the world of ideal capitalism. This vision of capitalism appeared to be based far more on received (distorted) images centred on consumption and style than on actual practices of economic structure, employment or work. On the other hand, both the ex-councillor and many other villagers I spoke to also expressed their great *fear* that Poland was becoming like the West, with rising prices and high rates of unemployment, an increasing sense of the pervasive nature of crime and resultant personal danger, and a growing polarisation between the haves and the have-nots. Further, a third level of local interpretation portrayed eastern Europe as the victim of the West; here western businesses were seen as stripping eastern Europe of its assets for their own gain, western consumer goods as dominating eastern European markets, and the West generally as excluding eastern Europeans from any role in economic partnership other than the provision of cheap commodities and above all labour. It appeared therefore that at least two distinct images of western capitalism were being held simultaneously. One looked back to the (idealised) era of Fordism, in which steady employment, good wages, affluence and access to the world of consumption were represented (whether accurately is another matter) as the entitlement of all solid working people. The other was a fragmentary, frightening image of a western world out of control, a runaway world in which neither personal safety nor individual or regional entitlement was in any way protected. A variation of this second theme portrayed an East–West dichotomy, in which western governments and businesses ruthlessly pursued their own interest, and effectively excluded the East from any possibility of equal participation.

I would argue that for the people to whom I was speaking, each of these images arose from and reflected certain realities, and that the one which was stressed varied according to context. Bad capitalism represented everyday life as they were experiencing and witnessing it around them, or anticipating it with fear and anxiety: for instance, local unemployment, corruption and breakdown of social services, exploitation at a local and national level by western economic interest and even a more elusive sense of contagion from moral decay in the West. Good capitalism represented above all a quality of life which they had glimpsed, believed in and aspired towards both during the socialist period and since. While growing poverty and discontent are increasingly visible throughout Poland, so too are a small but striking number of success stories, people who have 'made it' in some sort of business and who display to the world continual proofs of affluence and conspicuous consumption: BMWs and Mercedes, mobile phones, large and ornate houses guarded by dogs and minders, and elegant clothes to be paraded at lunches in expensive restaurants. That many of these public displays of consumption and affluence are made possible not by steady work in new, well-organised business empires but by highly idiosyncratic and individualistic entrepreneurial activities is a fact by no means lost on the less advantaged audiences. In the current climate, it seems to me, moral judgements are continually being made, based both on a strong positive and highly selective social memory of what socialism *was*, and on the alternative models of capitalism I have discussed above. Not only the past but the present appears to be being continually reinvented.

To a great extent, these moral judgements serve as ways in which people can interpret the world of the 1990s. The complexity of this world is at times overwhelming, and understandings of it are largely dependent upon the social, economic and regional position within which one is located. Furthermore, even within one region different groups and categories of people experience the new system in diverse ways. In any area where light industry and the service sector have been subjected to 'structural adjustment', for example, and/or where the social services, health care and childcare facilities have been severely cut back, women are likely to be the first to feel the impact of the changes. In this chapter, I consider some of the different ways in which the new system is affecting people, particularly women, at the local level.

The research on which this chapter is based was conducted in two quite different areas of Poland: the area around Łódź which is highly industrialised but also retains a strong agricultural base, and the historically more marginal, and highly diversified, region of the southwestern Carpathians. In these two regions, very different ideas about both the nature and role of the state, and about work, employment and the gendered nature of various types of labour were held prior to and during the socialist period. I would argue that it is only through considering such historical and regional differences that we can begin to interpret the types of strategy that are being developed in response to the current situation (see also Ciechocinska 1993). In the remaining sections, I focus on ways in which local representations of gendered work effects responses to the process of privatisation and economic restructuring.

REGIONAL DIFFERENCES: CENTRAL WORKER–PEASANTS AND MARGINAL ENTREPRENEURS

During the period between 1990 and 1995 the Łódź and Sieradz *wojewódswa* (provinces) in central Poland, and the Nowy Sącz *wojewódswo* (province) in the Podhale, the two areas where the research was conducted, appeared to be quite similar in statistical terms. Both experienced a high proportion of factory closures and liquidations, and both had in 1994 a registered unemployed population of about 15 per cent of the local workforce, with figures as high as 25 per cent in certain sectors. In both regions, women account for higher percentages of unemployed in light industry and the service sector. There are, however, substantive differences in the ways in which unemployment and restructuring affect the lives of rural women in these two regions, which can only be understood in relation to local ideologies of gender, kinship and work.

The Łódź region

The textile industry grew up in and around Łódź in the mid-nineteenth century, when the area was part of the Russian Partition. Local practice of favouring one single heir meant that in this region a large number of both sons and daughters from peasant households were excluded from farming as a primary occupation, and had to look elsewhere for their livelihood. The existence of work in local textile factories provided opportunities for these rural residual siblings; here, as elsewhere, the textile trade employed large numbers of women. As a result, there was a continual flow of peasants from outlying villages into the local towns, but the existence of an extensive local industry provided an alternative to the high levels of regional or national emigration commonly found in rural areas where practices of impartible inheritance dominates. During the socialist period, the experience of this local rural–urban migration changed. Infrastructure development, particularly in terms of railway services, allowed villagers to live in their natal villages and commute to work. For female workers particularly, work conditions improved radically during the socialist period. The possibility of commuting meant that instead of leaving their children in the care of rural kin while they themselves boarded in worker accommodation in town, they could continue to live with their families in the countryside. Although travel to and from work was time consuming, and often had to be conducted late at night or in the early hours before dawn, for most women the fact that they could see their children every day, rather than only briefly on Sunday, made the physical hardship worthwhile.

> After the war, the socialist government built a railway station in the village. The wagons in which we could travel to work were called cattle cars, because they were open and very crowded, like cars for animals. But we didn't mind that. On the day the train station opened the entire village formed a procession from the church to the station. The priest and the organist led the procession and all the villagers carried flowers and ribbons. When the train came the priest said a blessing, and sprinkled the locomotive with holy water. Then everyone went back to the church, and the priest said a mass for the train. It was so important, you see, because it meant that we women could stay with our children.

I was told this story by a 70-year-old grandmother in 1993, some forty years after the station had been opened. Her voice resounded with a vivid enthusiasm and vigour that made it seem as if the railway station had been opened the week before, rather than decades ago. The story reflects, among other things, how even at the height of Stalinism, the state's actions could attain moral legitimacy, reflected in beautiful paradox by the blessings of the Church, through acting in a way which was seen as being 'for the people' – and here, as so often in rural Poland, the good of the people was equivalent to the good of the mothers and children.

Other factors under socialism also had profound influences on women's lives. Better working conditions developed in the factories, and regular health checks, dental care, and sickness and maternity leave were made available to all working women. Many factories also had attached childcare facilities, and subsidised shops for workers and their families; some had attached housing. While the factory workers recognised that their working conditions continued to be extremely hard, they also saw the positive changes which were implemented by the new system.

In agriculture, on the other hand, things continued much as before in terms of local work practice. In this region, as elsewhere in Poland, the division of labour in the farming household was and continues to be based on age and gender. Women, including those who work for wages outside farming, are responsible for most domestic labour, and participate in most farming activities. However, farming is represented on the whole as a male activity; the work which women do is viewed as part of their kinship role as wife, sister or daughter of the main farmer, and hence in some senses masked, or undervalued. While women who had worked only briefly in the public sector, or not at all, often describe themselves as 'on the farm' when asked about work, they are equally likely to represent themselves as farmer's wives, or as at home, not working. Women who work or worked in the public sector describe themselves as seamstresses or weavers; when they lose their work, they see themselves as 'without work' despite the fact that they are often working equally long hours on the farm.

Loss of work for these women means substantial loss of income to the farming household, as well as increased expenditure in terms of healthcare, purchase of previously subsidised goods and so on. Although they have more time to work on the farm, and most do so, agriculture is also experiencing difficulties, in some cases extreme, as local markets are flooded with imported produce, government subsidies are being cut and prices deregulated, resulting often in reduced outlets for and less income from local produce. A further complication is caused by the return of women who have lost their jobs to their natal villages and the farms of parents or siblings. Such women provide labour for the household and farm, but also add to the burden of subsistence.

> Things are difficult at the moment. I've lost my job because the collective farm has closed down. We are working our small holding. But now my wife's sister and her kids have come to live with us too. She was a seamstress but the factory has closed and now she's on the '*Kuronówka*' [unemployment benefit, nicknamed after Jacek Kuroń, the first post-socialist minister of employment who orchestrated the benefit scheme]. We don't have enough to support us all.
>
> (middle-aged male employee of a PGR (collective farm), made redundant when the collective was liquidated in 1992)

Various factors make the situation of unemployed women more difficult than that of men, and that of rural women different from, and in some ways harder, than that of urban women. Men are often able to find work as builders, drivers, or manual labourers. Women may take in sewing, or provide domestic services, but, as several women to whom I spoke pointed out, in this region all women can sew and they are unlikely, particularly in times of economic hardship, to pay others to provide services they can do themselves. While there are many retraining schemes in the region, the experience of most women I spoke to suggested that even after retraining very few were likely to find regular work. As one woman put it quite graphically, 'They only want to employ young attractive women, women without children, women who are willing to do a strip-tease. There will be no work again for older women like us.' Statistics back her up:

unemployment is extremely high among women over 40 and, equally tragically, young school leavers.

When factories are closed down, their assets are sold off, often in public auction. As a result, small *chałupnicwa*, or cottage industries are springing up in private houses all over the countryside. These are usually run by local men, who have been able to raise the collateral to borrow funds to buy some machinery, for example two or three machines to make stockings, or sewing machines. Women often find it difficult to get loans, as they do not have access to collateral. Rather, they become the new casual workers; they are often employed, for very low wages, for just less than three months and then let go, so that the owner will not have to pay state-regulated benefits and insurance on their behalf. Often these enterprises are themselves fly-by-night, folding after several months when the owners are unable to make ends meet.

Work in this new private sector is usually obtained through ties of kinship or *znajomosci*, the ubiquitous Polish word meaning acquaintance but also having the connotation of people who can arrange favours. While kin may be treated more equitably than non-kin in the sense that they are less likely to lose their employment as the three-month period draws to a close, their work, like farm work, may be disguised as 'helping' kin rather than as formal employment; this is true particularly for women of the same household as the owner, whose individual interests are subsumed under those of the farm or establishment. Equally, women often work for male kin who have set up small businesses, fast food outlets and the like; here again, they are often seen as 'helping' rather than employed, and paid irregularly, almost as favour, or in kind, rather than with cash.

The majority of unemployed women I spoke to in and around Łódź between 1991 and 1995 were adamant about their feelings with respect to work. They identified themselves as textile workers, and did not want to do anything else. They were proud of their skills, and their strength, and often identified strongly with social life in the workplace where, although conditions had been very hard, they often worked alongside close female kin and neighbours. As one women in her late forties put it, 'I am a weaver. That is my work. I don't want to do anything else.' When I asked them about looking for permanent work in other trades, or about leaving the region to search for work elsewhere, even migrating to the West temporarily, most were definite in their rejection of these possibilities. Again, their kinship networks and obligations were a crucial factor here. They said that they could not leave their children, or their elderly parents. They spoke of relying on their mothers and sisters for all sorts of assistance, from childcare to economic help, and could not imagine surviving without this support (see CBOS 1994). Finally, they stressed the impossibility of going somewhere

where they had no kin and no friends: where would they live, how would they find housing, how would they survive? Here the networks of kinship and neighbourhood provided the security that the state had ceased to give; this was not a new pattern, as these networks had been essential under socialism as well, in terms of dealing with shortages and other difficulties of daily life. What was new was the removal of the balancing framework of state support, particularly in terms of employment. Suddenly these 'safety nets' of kin were responsible for bearing what seemed like the full load.

In 1994, however, I became aware of a change in responses, particularly in those of young unmarried women. These women, without husbands and children, increasingly expressed their willingness and indeed eagerness to move in search of work, and even to go abroad. Nearly all of the older women I spoke to then still identified themselves as textile workers, but they too showed signs of shifting their identity somewhat, many saying that they would do any other work if they could. What is significant here is the timing of the shifts in attitude. After almost fifty years of guaranteed employment, many workers could not really envisage the possibility of long-term unemployment. Although they were shocked and depressed by the changes, and many said that they were sure they would never work again, at some level they also felt that the consequences of privatisation were only temporary. Waged employment had, after all, been a consistent reality for most of them all of their working lives. However, with the passing of time, it seems that these women are adjusting their views about the nature of the work, and beginning to imagine alternatives to what they have 'always' done. The tragedy, I suspect, lies in the probability that in some ways their earlier, pessimistic assessments were accurate. The likelihood of most of these women, particularly those who are middle aged and have children, ever regaining regular work such as they had before seems slim. Rather, they are likely to continue to be involved in their invisible, highly labour-intensive farm work, which is masked by an ideology of reproduction, and to be denied access on any regular basis to the productive sphere of waged labour. Many will also find temporary work, in the service sector, as piece workers in the new cottage industries, and possibly as homeworkers for foreign-owned factories and businesses. Thus, their work identity will become increasingly fragmented in the productive, or public, sphere and remain solid, but masked, in the private sphere of reproduction (see Pine 1996a).

However, another dimension to the economic changes is found in the nature of farm work, food production and distribution itself. As food prices and other costs rise, town dwellers are increasingly relying on their rural kin for access to food. Women, traditionally associated with domestic care, nurturing and feeding the family, are particularly likely to spend a great deal of their time 'helping' in the fields of their village kin, and are rewarded for their help with sacks of potatoes, eggs and fruit, which they use either for their own consumption or sell in the market. Again, this labour is represented as kinship reciprocity and as being about reproduction and consumption rather than production. It is an increasingly important survival strategy for the unemployed or low-paid urban dweller; whether it is more of a help or a drain to the resources of the rural households is not always clear.

The Podhale

The experience of unemployed women in the mountain villages of the Podhale is very different from the picture I have drawn for the Łódź region. Although, as I have already pointed out, the statistical patterns in the two areas are similar, Górale (the inhabitants of the Podhale) experiences of unemployment, privatisation and restructuring are of quite another order from those of many of the people living in the rural areas around Łódź. This I would argue is at least partly because of their particular history of marginality. The Górale were originally pastoralists; the village in which I have done research was first settled in the early seventeenth century. During the partition period, the area fell under Austro-Hungarian rule, and the practice of partible inheritance allocated equal shares of parental property to all sons and daughters. This meant that women as well as men owned land and other productive resources. It also meant that by the mid-nineteenth century, when Łódź was developing as a centre for light industry, the farms of the Podhale were becoming increasingly fragmented and dwarfed. The Podhale was on a major trade route across the mountains, and villagers were able to supplement subsistence farming by marketing of produce, crafts and commodities. Young girls also went to work as domestic servants, and both women and men worked as day labourers. However, there was at this point no equivalent to the factories of Łódź, and many Górale, both men and women, became temporary wage migrants, travelling as far afield as Budapest or even, quite frequently, Chicago (Pine 1987).

For both men and women, social and work identity were and continue to be based on belonging to a named farming household, owning and working land, and cooperating with kin and other villagers in reciprocal farm labour (Pine 1996b). A wide range of other activities have long been pursued in order to subsidise and maintain the farm. Regular local waged work, however, only became available during the socialist period when, in keeping with their programme of rapid industrialisation, the government built small factories throughout the Podhale. Simultaneously, the development of roads and train services through the mountains opened the villages up to tourism, and a growing service sector in local towns also offered employment to villagers. While the villagers around Łódź recall the opening of the railway in terms of benefits to mothers and children, the Górale villagers with whom I work speak of the event in their village as 'the opening of a window to the world'. In the Łódź area, where waged work was an integral part of social identity, the opening of a local train station increased villagers', and particularly women's, integration into the central economy; in the Podhale, where identity is located in place and kinship but supported through sporadic interaction with the outside world (both national and international), the train station allowed villagers to widen their informal networks rather than integrate into the centre.

In household and farming activities, the division of labour is here, as in the Łódź area, based on gender and generation. However, it is in practice more flexible than in the Łódź region – it is common, for instance, to see men cooking or caring for small children, or women driving horses or tractors – and perhaps even more significantly, women's work is rarely if ever invisible. It may be less valued than that of men, but it is acknowledged and valued in its own right, and firmly embedded in a set of reciprocal rights and obligations of kinship and community. During the 1960s–80s, a girl would normally begin waged work in the state sector immediately after leaving school, work until marriage and the birth of her first or second child, and then spend more and more time in farm labour, craft production at home, local marketing, and so on, until she finally left the public waged sector altogether. Most women organised their labour around the demands of childcare; long-distance traders, for instance, only began serious travelling when a daughter or daughter-in-law was able to take over care of the house and younger children.

In terms of socialist ideology, social worth and entitlement was inextricably linked to productive labour. Both men and women in the Podhale, as in the Łódź area, define themselves, and are defined by others, largely on the basis of their work. In this sense, it might be assumed that, as with many of the women in the Łódź area who linked a work ethic to general social entitlement, they were in sympathy with the dominant ideology of socialism. However, this was not the case, the Górale tend to view work differently. There is no one area of work with which most Górale women are associated. Factory work, or other waged labour in the public (state) sphere, was not perceived by these women as the crucial part of their personal identity – that is to say, they did not speak of being a leather worker in the same way that a woman in central Poland would speak of being a seamstress or a weaver. Rather waged labour was seen more as a necessary evil which had the advantage of bringing them some small amounts of money and, more importantly, connections which were essential during the economy of shortage, benefits such as healthcare, pensions and so forth (see Pine 1996a).

Because there was no established tradition of industry with which to make comparisons, the socialist state was not viewed as having improved working conditions; village life and farming remained the source of identity for both men and women, and the state was viewed with hostility both because villagers always suspected that collectivisation was its intent, and because of its attempts to regulate other kinds of (informal) economic activity.

Hence, with the closure of the factories, women's lives were not radically altered as they were in the Łódź region. Factory work was just one small bit of all kinds of work that women do, do visibly, and are valued for doing. When border restrictions were lifted, more women went abroad, to work as au pairs in Italy and Greece, to work as housekeepers and farmworkers in Germany, to trade their wares as far afield as Turkey. Many Górale villagers, male and female, continue to go to America. Young women as well as older women are among the growing numbers of wage migrants; they leave their children with their mothers, an act acceptable because the financial gains are high enough to outweigh the demands of motherhood.

FRAGMENTATION OR DEVELOPMENT?

The comparison between this region and the Łódź area is complex; I have been very brief in my discussion of each, but I hope the main points I wish to make are clear. The division between private and public was perceived differently during the socialist period in the two regions. Górale women's work identity did not come only from participation in the public sphere, but from a range of activities basically centred on, or radiating from, the farm and the village. Loss of factory work or work in the formal public sphere did not result in exclusion from, or masking of, women's productive activities, because in Gorale culture production and reproduction are not radically separated. On the one hand, patterns of fragmented labour, migration and entrepreneurial activity are long established in this region; on the other, identity and personhood are associated with the house, the farm and the village community, to which people can always return. Equally importantly, neither work for the state, nor the state itself, was viewed positively as something within which local people were incorporated and in which they had a vested interest. Rather, the state was part of the 'outside', which was at best morally neutral, and at worst seen as a potential source of oppression and exclusion. Hence, unlike in the Łódź region, very few women I spoke to in the Podhale experienced unemployment in terms of betrayal by the state, or mourned the loss of the socialist system. In the Łódź area women feel they are being forced by unemployment back into agriculture, into piecework and into kin-based enterprises; Górale women even under socialism gave moral and practical precedence to these areas, and now when faced with unemployment channel even more energy into them.

The comparison between these regions, and between local histories and ideologies of work and identity, production and reproduction, and public and private, must I think raise more general questions about the kind of working lives rural people, and particularly women, can expect in the future. I suggested at the beginning of this chapter that in Poland at the moment people interpret the emerging world of capitalism in several different ways, and that the same people can hold different explanatory or interpretative models simultaneously. The Górale and the villagers of central Poland on the whole use the same models of bad capitalism, good capitalism, bad west and good west, and bad socialism and good socialism to talk about their lives and their worlds. The Górale however have consistently viewed entrepreneurialism and economic fragmentation with approval; these formed a large part of their own economic world long before either socialism or post-socialism. In their representation, bad capitalism tends to be that from which they are excluded. Thus, they complain about the expensive foreign goods which are flooding the shops, but they themselves see no moral dilemma in selling consumer goods which they bring back from America or western Europe.

The villagers of central Poland, when I first began to do this research in 1991, regularly raised objections to capitalism, foreign goods and foreign ownership, and voiced a deep distrust and disapproval of entrepreneurial activity generally. This reflects both a highly developed work ethic in which there is a strong moral association between the obligation of the individual to be involved in productive work and the obligation of the state to provide and protect that work. The end of socialism itself, as well as the loss of work, created in many people a deep sense of loss and disruption. Over the following three years, however, the language used by many villagers has changed. In 1992 unemployment was a major issue but still a relatively new phenomenon. The people I spoke to then always defined lack of work as the main problem in their own lives and for the nation, and defined work in a specific and highly personal way. As unemployment continued, however, I saw evidence of this bounded identity beginning to shift and fragment. Industrial unemployment continues, but other alternatives are starting to seem possible. Last summer, the problem most commonly identified by the same people was not lack of work but lack of money; as I mentioned already, many women talked about retraining or getting on a course. As more than one woman explicitly stated: 'I am willing to do anything, as long as I can get money.' The poignant aspect of such statements is that for many people in this region, particularly older women, it seems unlikely that developing a wider understanding of what work means, or going on a course, will help them to obtain it. For some younger women and for many men, however, the picture may be less bleak. A few young villagers have gone to the Wroclaw region to find work, and have returned with enough money to build big new houses. Several men have bought up combines and other agricultural machinery from liquidation sales at agricultural cooperatives or PGRs, and are earning very large sums of money renting out their labour and machines. While no Blake Carrington has yet emerged, it seems to me that local meanings of work are changing as these formerly incorporated workers begin to develop survival strategies for coping with the new system.

I have argued that the Górale developed such complex survival strategies in the nineteenth century, in response to poverty and marginality, and have maintained them since. They have, however, also remained on the whole peripheral to the central economy. The Łódź area was highly integrated into the central economy, in terms of both industry and farming, from the nineteenth century onwards. What the villagers I have been discussing appear to be doing now is learning the survival skills associated with marginality. While such flexibility is undoubtedly beneficial and probably essential in coping with the immediate problems of unemployment and rural poverty, as a long-term or permanent pattern it would lead to an extremely fragmented economy. Part of the reason that marginal peoples like the Górale are able to survive indefinitely on the basis of such strategy is that they have a very strong kinship system and local community which is a source of opposition, or resistance, to the state. Trust and morality are implicit at the local level, but do not extend to the wider society. Rather, the 'centre' is viewed almost as a field of opportunity, in which gaps can be located to pursue entrepreneurial dealings; these dealings are imbued with little or no sense of moral obligation, and there is little sense of shared identity with the centre. The new mafias which are developing in the former socialist countries seem to me to share this attitude to the centre, or the wider society, but to lack the morality of local kinship and community ties which characterise closely knit peripheral social groups like the Górale. If large sectors of the population which were formerly incorporated into the centre become increasingly marginalised and turn to the types of strategy such as migration, petty marketing, and various semi-legal alternatives which are pervasive among small local populations like the Górale, it is difficult to see how the wider society will accommodate them all. Some will obviously be very successful, and extend their successes through their own kin networks. The potential for an increase in mafia-type patronage, divorced from the trust and morality of local community obligation, also seems to me to increase as the part played by the state in providing social and welfare services and above all opportunity for regular work retracts. What seems most probable, however, is that until such time as a new industrial base develops, and agriculture is built up to the point that farmers can easily produce for the market as well as for subsistence, such areas as central Poland with long-established mixed economies will continue to stagnate, and large sectors of their population will occupy a rather ambiguous position, balancing irregular waged work with subsistence farming, neither totally integrated through work and market into the main economy nor totally peripheral to it. While I would certainly not deny that there are specific problems associated with post-socialist restructuring, this particular picture is not very different from that seen throughout the capitalist world in the late twentieth century. Fragmentation and flexibility may be useful as survival skills in times of crisis, but I suspect that the important question for women in the Łódź area is whether one kind of work, based on training, expertise and years of experience, will ever again be a possibility. The Górale developed their particular skills as marginal peasants living in a backward area; the idea that such skills may be becoming almost a prototype for work in developing economies must give pause for thought.

ACKNOWLEDGMENTS

This chapter is based on research funded by the ESRC between 1992 and 1995, on Grant No. R000233019. It also draws on earlier research in the Polish highlands in 1977–79 which was funded by the SSRC and between 1988–90, which was funded by the ESRC, Grant No. R0002314. Some of the material is also drawn from a national survey of Polish women's attitudes, conducted by CBOS in 1993 and funded by the ESRC.

REFERENCES

Buchowski, M. (1996) *Klasa i Kultura w Okresie Transformacji: antropologiczne studium przypadku spolecznosci lokalnej w Wielkopolsce*, Berlin: Centre Marc Bloc.
CBOS (Centrum Badania Opinii Spolecznej) (1994) *Kobiety 93*, Warsaw: CBOS.
Ciechocinska, M. (1993) 'Gender Aspects of Dismantling the Command Economy in Eastern Europe: the case of Poland', in V. Moghadam (ed.) *Democratic Reform and the Position of Women in Transitional Economies*, Oxford: Clarendon Press, 303–26.
EBRD (European Bank for Reconstruction and Development) (1996) *Transition Report Update*, April 1996, London: EBRD.
Harvey, D. (1990) *The Condition of Postmodernity: An Enquiry into the Origins of Cultural Change*, Oxford: Blackwell.
Hobsbawm, E. (1994) *Age of Extremes: The Short Twentieth Century, 1914–91*, London: Michael Joseph.
Howell, J. (1994) *Understanding Eastern Europe: The Context of Change*, London: Ernst and Young.

Moghadam, V.M. (1992) 'Gender and Restructuring: a global perspective', in V.M. Moghadam (ed.) *Privatization and Democratization in Central and Eastern Europe and the Soviet Union: The Gender Dimension*, Helsinki: World Institute for Development Economics Research of the United Nations University, 9–23.

OECD (1996) *Agricultural Policies, Markets and Trade in Transition Economies: Monitoring and Evaluation 1996*, Paris: OECD.

Pine, F. (1987) *Kinship, Marriage and Social Change in a Polish Highland Village*, PhD thesis, University of London.

—— (1996a) 'Redefining Women's Work in Rural Poland', in R. Abrahams (ed.) *After Socialism: Land Reform and Social Change in Eastern Europe*, Oxford: Berghahn, 133–56.

—— (1996b) 'Naming the House and Naming the Land: kinship and social groups in the Polish highlands', *Journal of the Royal Anthropological Institute*, 2: 2.

Rai,S., Pilkington, H. and Phizacklea, A. (1992) *Women in the Face of Change: The Soviet Union, Eastern Europe and China*, London: Routledge.

8 Gypsy self-governments in post-socialist Hungary

Martin Kovats

> The majority always determines the fate of the minority.
> (Florian Farkas, president of the National Roma Self-Government)[1]

Times have often been hard for the vast majority of Hungary's Roma (Gypsy) population. Buffeted by social, political and economic changes that have swept across the country over the centuries, the Roma have usually been left to their own devices to make a living however they might. Occasionally state or local indifference has been replaced by periods of sustained and vicious persecution which, in turn, have contributed to the Roma occupying a position on the periphery of society. From the start of the 1960s the cycle seemed to be broken, with the state investing significant amounts of financial resources and political determination to reduce the disadvantageous position of most Roma and allow them to enjoy the benefits of modernisation (clean water, sanitary housing, healthcare, education, rising incomes, etc.). The economic crisis beginning in the 1980s brought these policies to an end and has created a new set of difficulties as well as opportunities by which Roma interests can be advanced. Emphasis has been placed on constructing a 'dialogue' between Roma (representatives) and administrative organs. Roma are expected to enter the 'democratic' game and lobby for increased resources and opportunities through the articulation of their interests and negotiation. This chapter examines the primary institutions of this new environment, the system of minority self-governments, and considers the extent to which Roma representatives have been able to exploit new opportunities to enhance the survival of their communities as well as their opinions as to the appropriateness of the current legal and institutional environment for addressing their most fundamental needs.

On 7 July 1993 Law LXXVII on the Rights of National and Ethnic Minorities received almost unanimous approval from the Hungarian Parliament. The law acknowledges the existence of thirteen national and ethnic minority groups in Hungary and provides a number of individual and collective rights which members of these communities may exercise. The most significant element of the Minorities Law is the creation of a system of representative institutions for minorities at both the local and national level: minority self-governments. Local minority self-governments can be formed in a number of ways; however, the overwhelming majority to date have been established through direct elections. Each minority is entitled to form a national minority self-government, which is elected by an electoral college made up of local representatives. The term 'self-government' is somewhat misleading as these institutions do not have the authority to govern in the conventional sense of the word. The activities of self-governments are regulated by the Minorities Law, the primary aim of which is to allow minorities to take control over cultural affairs and, to a lesser degree, the education of members of the minority.

The Roma are the largest minority group in Hungary, indeed throughout all Europe (7–8.5 million people).[2] Roma have been living on the territory which is now Hungary since at least the fourteenth century. The population has continually altered with the movement of Roma groups in and out of the area over the centuries. The current Hungarian Roma population is therefore culturally and linguistically diverse. In the late nineteenth and early twentieth centuries the Romany language went into rapid decline and the largest group in today's Roma population are the Romungro (literally, Hungarian-speaking Rom). Some 20 per cent of Hungarian Roma speak Romany, while a further 7 per cent speak an archaic form of Romanian. Historically, Hungary has had a relatively ambiguous relationship with the Roma, encouraging Roma skills, particularly music making, and being the birthplace of Romani studies,[3] but also treating Roma with harassment and oppression. Today, the half-million Roma population accounts for around 5 per cent of the total population of Hungary and 50 per cent of the country's non-Magyar citizens.[4]

The self-government system is designed to 'ameliorate the disadvantages of being a member of a minority',[5] that is, systemic political weakness. The need to find a political mechanism by which their interests can be effectively represented is even more acute for the Roma than for the other minorities, given the devastating impact the transition to a market economy has had on Roma employment. Almost three-quarters of the Hungarian Roma now live in poverty compared to 15 per cent of the non-Roma population.[6] The relaxation of controls against discrimination and prejudice, and the general rise in social tension, consequent of a decline in living standards throughout the country, has further reduced opportunities for Roma and made mainstream politicians wary of addressing these problems.

The influence of Roma within mainstream politics is negligible. Most Roma are under eighteen and therefore have no vote. The distribution of Roma throughout the country means that in only a handful of villages do they form a majority of electors. The obstacles to explicit Roma representation were shown at the 1994 elections when the most successful Roma candidate not aligned with a mainstream party polled only 5.4 per cent of the vote in his single constituency. Establishing a mechanism by which Roma could win elected office was first advocated in 1989 by the last communist and subsequently first post-communist HDF-led governments' principal advisor on Gypsy affairs, János Báthory.[7] The first election to local self-governments, held in December 1994, saw the formation of 422 local Roma self-governments out of a total of 641. The self-government system is the backbone of post-communist Hungary's minorities policy. As the most numerous minority, and having formed the most self-governments, any analysis of the efficacy of this policy must examine the Roma and their experience of the system and the extent to which it caters to the needs of Roma communities.

THE RESEARCH

The research on which this chapter is based examined the experiences of local Roma self-governments after the first year. In addition to considering the consistency of experiences in different localities, the research focused on concerns raised by individual Roma and Roma organisations, as well as other minority representatives regarding the authority and financing of self-governments. The self-government system plays a definitive role in the way Roma politics develops in Hungary and so the research sought the opinions of Roma representatives as to how the system has affected inter-Roma relations and the position of Roma politics within the national political environment. The research also examined what the Roma Parliament has called the 'legitimacy' of self-governments, that is, the degree to which Roma communities themselves support the establishment of Roma self-governments. The final aim of the research was to ascertain what programmes and activities Roma self-governments have been able to initiate and to what extent Roma politicians believe the system addresses the needs of their Roma communities.

To provide a full account of the experiences of Roma self-governments would require a much more substantial project involving interviews with dozens of self-governments. Given the novelty of the system, as well as the wide variation in circumstances of Roma self-governments, the findings contained in this chapter do not claim to give a definitive picture of the self-government system. Nevertheless, in many respects the system is a 'leap in the dark' and if problems are identified at an early stage it may reduce difficulties in the future. The modest aim of the research was to examine a number of specific issues employing two variable factors: the known political alignment of the self-government, and the location of the self-government by settlement type. Interviews were carried out in December 1995 with representatives of eight local Roma self-governments, on all but one occasion (Csepel) with the president of these five-member institutions. The self-governments were selected on the basis of the known political alignment (membership, association) of the interviewees on information provided by the two leading Roma organisations Lungo Drom and Phralipe and the former Free Democrat MP Aladár Horváth. The self-governments were selected to reflect the different types of settlement in which Roma live. Of the eight self-governments studied, three are in villages (Kakucs, Emőd, Vestő), two in small towns (Heves, Kisújszállás) and one in a large provincial town (Nyíregyháza), one in a suburb of Budapest (Csepel), and one in an inner-city district of the capital (VII).

The two aims of the research were reflected in the way the interviews were structured. The first was to find out details about the size and situation of the local Roma population, the election of the self-government and what activities it had engaged in during the year and what financial or other support it had received from a variety of sources. The second aim was to discover how the self-government representatives felt about their position, their relationship with other Roma, the local government and other institutions. The research also sought the representatives' views of the Minorities Law and how they felt it would contribute to the position of the Roma. Therefore, interviews involved a number of detailed questions but also allowed interviewees to discuss more general matters. Allowing interviewees to talk at length about their perceptions established greater confidence with the interviewer, as many had never been asked (by an outsider) about how they viewed the situation of the Roma.

THE LOCATION OF THE SELF-GOVERNMENTS

Since the 1960s the locations of Roma settlements and the conditions in which the people live have changed significantly. Before the communists' slum-clearance programme the vast majority of Roma lived in isolated settlements in derelict buildings or structures they had made for themselves out of whatever materials were available.[8] Industrialisation saw a drift into towns, though the majority of Roma (60.1 per cent) still live in the countryside. János Ladányi's research in 1993 found a strong pattern of residential segregation among Roma in Budapest, though this was closely related to class, with Roma being disproportionately represented among unskilled and semi-skilled workers.[9] In villages and towns Roma were often rehoused in low-value 'Government Regulation' accommodation or in vacated peasant dwellings, often on the periphery of the settlement. The 1993 National Roma Survey found that 'powerful residential segregation defines the spatial distribution of around 60 per cent of Roma'.[10] In all eight of the areas surveyed in this research, Roma housing had been affected by the slum-clearance programme. The physical segregation of Roma housing is particularly strong in the villages of Emőd and Kakucs and the town of Heves.

In all eight areas Roma form a minority of the total population ranging from 4 to 5 per cent (Kisúljszállás) to 22 per cent (Vesztő). All were populated by Hungarian-speaking Roma, though in some places there were also families of native Romani speakers; however, this fact did not seem to affect the outlook or composition of the self-governments. In all five of the urban areas studied, the composition of the Roma population had been affected by the immigration of Roma workers from the 1970s, most notably in Csepel, an industrial suburb of the capital. The full employment policies of the previous regime had conditioned the lives of Roma in all the areas studied. Many Roma, particularly from the villages, had commuted to urban areas to find work. Roma had been employed in construction (mentioned by all interviewees), factory work (Heves. Nyíregyháza, Csepel) and agriculture (Kakucs, Emőd, Kisújszállás). The transition to a market economy led to a rapid rise in Roma unemployment (see later section for details) and the re-emergence of poverty as a serious problem for both Roma individuals and communities.

THE SELF-GOVERNMENT ELECTIONS

All eight of the local Roma self-governments examined in the course of the research were formed by direct elections on 11 December 1994, on the same day that local authority elections were held throughout Hungary. The research focused on two issues; the effect of the elections on the internal politics of the Roma and the relationship between the Roma self-government and the wider political community. Each interviewee was questioned about the number and political allegiance of candidates who stood for places on the five-member Roma self-governments. In addition, information was sought as to how many people voted for the self-governments and to what extent local Roma voted for these institutions. A breakdown of election results by constituencies has not been published, but each self-government possessed information for their area. Unfortunately, in most cases these data were not to hand, so the figures provided by interviewees were mainly their own estimates. The Minorities Law prohibits the creation of a separate electoral register for members of minorities and voting took place by secret ballot so it is not possible to identify exactly how many Roma voted for Roma self-governments. However, all those interviewed offered an opinion of the degree to which local Roma voted in these elections based on their own observations and anecdotal evidence.

In the eight areas studied the number of candidates standing for Roma self-governments ranged from six (Emőd and Budapest VII district) to seventeen (Vesztő and Nyíregyháza). In line with the national trend,[11] around half of those who stood did so as independents. In some areas where Lungo Drom (Kisújszállás and Heves) and Phralipe (Emőd and Kakucs) have well-established organisations, the candidates supported by these organisations all won. However, this was not the case in Csepel where a Phralipe branch had been established in 1992 and five independents won the election, or in Nyíregyháza where, despite the presence of a Lungo Drom branch, the elections saw only two Lungo Drom returned and three independents. Detailed research is required to assess the motivation of Roma activists in joining organisations or presenting themselves as independents, as well as the significance of these choices in determining electoral outcomes. While Lungo Drom and Phralipe have clearly emerged as the two dominant organisations, Roma politics has not yet developed into providing clear-cut political and institutional choices with a degree of conformity across the country; however, these do exist at the national level (in competition for places in the National Roma Self-Government), and in some local areas.

The question of who voted for Roma self-governments raises one of the anomalies of the system. While self-governments are conceived of as allowing minorities a degree of cultural autonomy, the fact that all registered voters are entitled to vote in these elections, of whom those who are the subject of the legislation are (by definition) a minority, means that non-members of the particular ethnic or national group potentially have a determining role in the selection of minority representatives. This paradox became a reality in December 1994, with almost 900,000[12] people voting for Roma self-governments across the country, whereas the number of registered Roma electors (some of whom could not vote if there was no self-government election where they lived) is convincingly estimated as probably not greatly exceeding 200,000.[13] Concern over the participation of non-Roma in Roma elections was raised by the Roma Parliament who said it would undermine the legitimacy of these institutions.[14] In one of the eight areas studied, Csepel, the five independents originally elected immediately resigned, claiming they had no mandate as most of those who had voted had not been Roma.

In examining whether interviewees believed they had received mandates from Roma electors an even more diverse picture was presented. In Kakucs,

Nyíregyháza, Csepel and Heves, the interviewees believe that not only did Roma constitute a minority of those voting, but that participation among Roma was significantly lower than among the non-Roma population. In the first two areas this was specifically interpreted as illustrating the scepticism of local Roma as to the utility of a separate institution. In Vesztő, Emőd and the Budapest VII district it was felt that Roma had voted in relatively high numbers, even forming a majority of those who cast ballots for the self-government. In Kisújszállás, Mrs Kovács believed Roma voters to have been in the minority (the Roma population is relatively small in the town), but that Roma had enthusiastically supported the self-government. Interestingly the size of the turnout and the perception of the extent to which Roma voted cuts across both the type of settlement where the elections took place and the political allegiance of the successful candidates. This indicates that the degree of enthusiasm of Roma for separate institutions might vary according to the degree to which the system is understood and the perception of the position of the Roma in relation to their non-Roma neighbours and the local authority in particular.

THE EXPERIENCES OF THE SELF-GOVERNMENTS

The self-government system is an innovative form of minority representation. The activities of self-governments are regulated by the Minorities Law and fall into two categories: cultural affairs and interest representation. On the one hand, local self-governments are entitled to take charge of certain cultural activities, such as the erection of monuments, and to organise festivals/ celebrations. They also have the right to set up and run educational institutions and economic enterprises.[15] Self-governments are entitled to request information from official bodies, offer opinions, initiate proceedings and have the right to veto certain decisions of the local authority.[16] From the time that it became clear what form the legislation was going to take, the most consistent criticism of the system, not only by Roma organisations but also bodies such as the Minorities Roundtable and independent legal experts,[17] has been the lack of guarantees, most notably financial, that self-governments will be able to carry out some or any of these activities. The vagueness of the legislative background allows for the possibility that the interpretation and practice of the rules may vary enormously across the country, a danger made even more likely in this early period as those involved get used to the system.

Material support for self-governments

Apart from the state budget, the Minorities Law entitles local self-governments to seek financial support from a variety of sources such as charities and individuals, and to use the profits of whatever enterprises they set up. The government has also set up the Foundation for National and Ethnic Minorities and the Foundation for Gypsies, with 400 million and 150 million forints respectively at their disposal. Delays in establishing these bodies meant this money was not available in 1995. The main source of material support for self-governments is conceived both politically and by the Minorities Law to be the respective local authority. Paragraph 59 of the Minorities Law states that 'of the total assets possessed by the local authority in its competence, those necessary to the local minority self-government to perform its duties within its sphere of tasks and authority shall be made available'. However, this does not constitute a guarantee that self-governments will receive anything, as the paragraph goes on to state that, 'This transfer . . . must not prevent the local authority from carrying out its normal duties.'[18]

Most interviewees expressed concern about the level of resources made available both to their own self-government and to the system in general. This view was most clearly articulated by Menyhért Lakatos (Vesztő), a leading figure in Hungarian Roma politics since the early 1970s, who believes that the chronic underfunding of self-governments (consequent of austerity throughout the public sector) will prevent the self-government system from developing into a mechanism for the protection and development of Roma interests. The Roma are in a much weaker financial position than the other minorities in Hungary due to the high rate of Roma unemployment and the lack of a mother country from which support might be expected. In addition to financial support, self-governments require help in providing the infrastructure for the institution (office space and equipment). In three areas (Kakucs, Vesztő and Kisújszállás) the local authority provides Roma with public agricultural land rent free, but this had been done prior to the formation of the self-governments.

In 1995 every local minority self-government, regardless of which nationality had established the institution, where it was based (small village, large town, district of Budapest) and the size and needs of the local minority community, received 220,000 forints (£1,100) from central government. This money was disbursed in two stages and ensured that each self-government had some money to play with. The amount was far too small to allow self-governments to exercise their rights and failed even to cover the annual administration costs of these bodies and honoraria for representatives. Therefore, most self-governments sought financial support from their corresponding local authority. Two of the eight self-governments covered by the research (Heves and Vesztő) did not do so. Of the remaining six, two village self-governments (Kakucs and Emőd) had their applications turned down and received nothing in 1995 from the local authority. The self-government in the provincial town of Kisújszállás received 760,000 forints. Self-governments in the larger urban areas faired better: Nyíregyháza received 3 million forints, the Budapest VII district 2 million and Csepel 5 million.

To prevent local authorities considering self-governments a burden, the government developed a scheme whereby local authorities were compensated for whatever property they made available to self-governments. Most of the self-governments were provided with office space. Usually this comprised two rooms, and all had a telephone line. The main exception was the VII district where the self-government was allocated a whole building (300 square metres). Three self-governments (Kakucs, Kisújszállás and VII district) were given buildings in such a dilapidated state that they required substantial renovation before they could be used. In Csepel the Roma self-government is located in a council property which, prior to the formation of the self-government, had been the Roma community centre. The self-government protested against the decision of the local authority to make this the headquarters of the self-government as it effectively meant the end of the community centre. Ferenc Kovács believes the council infringed the right of the self-government whose agreement is required (according to the Minorities Law) for decisions affecting the local institutions of the minority. However, he does consider there to be an accessible legal remedy or body which could review the decision and ensure that the Roma are able to exercise their rights. One of the self-governments studied (Emőd) had received no office space or other property.

Local authorities are also entitled to provide minority self-governments with other property or land. The Vesztő self-government received two large school buildings in which it planned to provide the local Roma with education and work-related skills (see below). Prior to the establishment of self-governments, Roma organisations in Kakucs and Vesztő had been provided with agricultural land by the local authority, 3 hectares amd 46 hectares respectively. While the self-governments now contributed to deciding how the land is used, in Kakucs the establishment of the self-government coincided with the local authority taking away the land originally allocated to the Roma and replacing it with a plot of similar size but of much lower quality and less productivity.

It is clear that for the self-government system's first year of existence, the amount of money guaranteed to these institutions by the state was pitifully low. Such small sums indicate not only a squeeze on the resources that government can make available, but questions the commitment of the state to enabling self-governments to fulfil a useful and practical role in their communities. Many self-governments were therefore thrown back on to their local authorities for support. The research revealed a wide variation in the degree to which self-governments have been supported by the local authority, with those in larger urban areas receiving the most generous allocations. If not exactly a lottery, clearly the degree to which self-governments could obtain financial assistance in 1995 was haphazard and reflected neither the wishes nor needs of the minority communities involved.

The relationship with local government

Financial support and the allocation of property or land to self-governments is only one aspect of the relationship between these institutions and their corresponding local authorities. Others include the degree to which the local authority respects the rights of the self-government and the extent to which the self-government can participate in the work of the authority. One of the most common criticisms of the self-government system has been that, despite being recognised legal entities, self-governments lack authority and have been 'subordinated' to local government. The absence of a mechanism for resolving conflicts between these two bodies, and of guarantees that the rights of self-governments will be respected creates the possibility that there might be wide variation in practice across the country. This is an issue of particular concern in relation to the Roma, as their low social status has meant that on both the local and national level the needs of Roma people are not considered a priority by politicians.

All the interviewees considered a good relationship with the local authority to be crucial for the effective running of the self-government. In every area bar one (Nyíregyháza), the representatives viewed their relationship as good. In Csepel and Kisújszállás, the members of the self-government had received advice from the local authority and in Kakucs they had attended training courses run by the county council and the National Roma Self-Government. In Heves and Nyíregyháza there were complaints about delays or difficulties in obtaining information about the decisions of the local authority, and in Csepel and Kakucs the self-governments have found it a problem to get agreements with the local government set down in writing. The only complaint about misinformation came from Emőd, where Gusztav Kökény felt that they had been misled by the clerk into believing they could allocate 29,000 forints for an interest-free loan fund to provide temporary assistance to Roma in financial difficulty. On presenting this plan to the council they were told this was illegal and felt themselves publicly humiliated.

Most of the self-governments studied participated to some extent in the work of local government committees. This form of cooperation works best in Kisújszállás and Vesztő. In the former the Roma have signed an agreement whereby the council agrees not to harm Roma interests and the self-government has been declared an official advisor to the local authority. As president of the self-government, Mrs Kovács had a seat on the social services committee. One of the benefits of this arrangement is that the local authority provides unemployed Roma with public employment when requested to do so by the self-government. In Vesztő there are Roma on the council and the self-government participates in the work of the social services, education and land committees. In the Budapest VII district Dr Reményi attends most council meetings and regularly spoke with councillors. He also had a seat and voting rights on the social services committee, which he believed demonstrated the goodwill of the authorities and their appreciation of Roma needs. He hoped that, on the basis of the good relations already developed, the local authority would approve the self-government's application for 17 million forints to finance projects in 1996. In other places these links are less comprehensive. In Heves, Mihály Lólé received occasional invitations to attend the social services committee. He would prefer to have the right to do so and did not feel it worthwhile to attend other council fora. Nevertheless, he was successful in persuading the local authority to provide ninety days' employment to all Roma who, because of changes to benefit regulations, otherwise would have lost their entitlement to income support. In Kakucs, Jenő Redics claimed a good personal relationship with the chair of the education committee and hoped this would lead to council support for the self-government's plan to establish education classes for both adults and children.

In Emőd and Csepel there was no formal or informal cooperation between the local authority and the self-governments. Furthermore, Ferenc Kovács (Csepel) complained that the rights of the self-government had been ignored by the local authority, particularly in regard to cuts in support for a local nursery which is attended by a large number of Roma children. The failure of the former president of the self-government to veto this decision led to his dismissal and caused conflict with the local authority. By far the worst relationship between a local authority and the self-government was in Nyíregyháza. It is the view of Artúr Balogh (president) that the self-government was incapacitated because of an unhealthy relationship between a minority of its members and the local authority. At the time of the interview, the local authority had not allowed the self-government to establish its own bank account and held all its income (220,000 forints from the state, 3 million from the local authority and 60,000 forints won from the Ministry of Education and Culture) in a council bank account. The self-government was only allowed access to its own money after submitting a formal request to the clerk, who then decided whether to release funds. The self-government had not been invited on to any committees and its suggestion that minority committees be set up in the areas of education, health and employment was rejected by the local authority. The self-government had not been able to influence the decisions of the local authority or enjoy its right to be informed of decisions affecting the Roma community, such as the 100 million-forint redevelopment plan for the largely Roma Husszár neighbourhood.

The research revealed a mixed picture of the relationships between local authorities and the self-governments. While the variation in circumstances throughout the towns and villages of Hungary means that differences will emerge from place to place, the fact that some self-governments have not been able to exercise some of the most basic rights granted them by the Minorities Law is a matter for concern. Participation in local authority committees carries a minimal cost and the fact that some councils have been accommodating indicates that those that have not are guilty of making a political decision to exclude Roma representatives. The opportunity to articulate community needs in the decision-making processes of the local authority is one of the more meaningful provisions of the Minorities Law, one made even more important in areas where lack of resources means that self-governments have little chance of initiating change by themselves.

THE PROGRAMMES AND PLANS OF THE SELF-GOVERNMENTS

As 1995 was the first year of operation of the self-government system, all involved had to spend time learning the rights and obligations of self-governments, developing procedures and coming to terms with the local political environment. The representatives from Kakucs, Csepel and Kisúj-szállás specifically mentioned that the first six months had been a learning period during which few concrete decisions were taken. Nevertheless, in addition to providing advice to Roma (and non-Roma) and seeking to influence decisions of the local authority, many had managed to initiate a number of different projects during 1995 and all had developed plans for what they would like to achieve in the future. This process had taken up much of the time of the self-governments. While priorities varied between self-governments, the types of programme fell roughly into four categories: employment, education, health and welfare, and culture.

Employment

The move towards a market economy has had a devastating effect on the employment of Roma throughout Hungary. Most unemployed Roma no longer receive unemployment benefit and few sign up for training programmes, meaning that the number of Roma officially classified as unemployed is a dramatic underestimation of the true figure. The Roma self-government has carried out a survey of the size and situation of the local Roma population in only one area (Emőd), although a number of others were planning to do so in the following year. Therefore, the figures provided by the interviewees were estimates based upon their personal knowledge of the local Roma community. The lowest estimate of Roma unemployment, 30–60 per cent, came from Dr Géza Reményi of the VII district. In contrast, Mihály Lólé estimated that of the adult Roma in Heves (around 750), the number with regular work could be counted on the fingers of one hand. All the other interviewees estimated local Roma unemployment to be around 75–80 per cent. The survey carried out by the Emőd self-government found of the 171 adults of working age in the village only 13 had regular work, 77 received some form of welfare benefit, 5 were in prison and 75 of all adults (42 per cent) have no visible form of income at all. Discrimination certainly reduces opportunities for Roma workers and the representatives from Kakucs, Emőd, Nyíregyháza, Csepel and Heves all described instances of local Roma being refused interviews due to their ethnicity. More fundamentally, there simply are not enough jobs available. In many cases the relatively high rate of unemployment in the locality was felt to affect the chances of Roma obtaining places on public work schemes run by local authorities. Only in Kisújszállás did the local authority provide public work to Roma unemployed when asked to do so by the self-government.

Despite the lack of emphasis in the Minorities Law on job-creation programmes, given the extremely high rate of Roma unemployment it is not surprising that many Roma self-governments wish to explore opportunities of providing local Roma with work. Many of the representatives interviewed believed the greatest danger facing the Roma is not cultural assimilation, but long-term poverty and social marginalisation. Given the early stage of the process, it was not surprising that most employment programmes were still at the planning stage, though the Kakucs self-government had set up a small enterprise where Roma were engaged in broom making, carpentry and weaving. The Vesztő self-government planned to establish a small manufacturing enterprise in a building provided by the local authority. Men would be employed to make metal bars, security grills and so on, and women in dressmaking. The Roma self-government in the VII district of Budapest proposed the establishment of a 4 million-forint enterprise fund. The money would be used to provide business advice to Roma entrepreneurs, as well as to provide a modest source of start-up capital.

Few self-governments have the resources to become directly involved in job creation. In greater conformity to the spirit and provisions of the Minorities Law, as well as the budgets of these institutions, many self-governments planned to develop programmes to provide local Roma with employment skills. In the eight areas studied, the most sophisticated scheme was in Vesztő where an adult education centre had been established. Twenty-two women were enrolled and were learning dressmaking, and twenty-two men were studying carpentry and plumbing. The course lasts for one year and students receive a grant of 9,000 forints a month (funded by the Ministry of Labour). On completion, students receive a diploma recognised by the Ministry of Education and Culture. However, Menyhért Lakatos is pessimistic about the trainees' employment prospects due to the lack of jobs in the area and the discrimination of employers. In Emőd, Nyíregyháza and Kisújszállás the self-governments wished to capitalise on the experience of Roma in the construction industry and initiate training schemes in construction skills and/or in the production of materials for the construction industry. In Kakucs the self-government hoped to reach an agreement with the local labour centre to provide Roma with computing and secretarial skills.

Self-governments have also been brought into a scheme launched by the government in 1992 and known as the 'Social Land Fund'. The scheme allows Roma communities to cultivate unused agricultural land at a low rent or free of charge. The food produced provides a valuable supplement to the diet of many poor people and the scheme provides opportunities for some Roma to learn or develop agricultural skills. Of the eight areas surveyed, the most extensive scheme was, once again, in Vesztő, where work (and food) was provided for over 100 people. In the areas where self-governments have received land from the local authority, and in Emőd where the self-government purchased a strip of land, the Roma wished to increase the area under cultivation. The self-governments in Kakucs and Nyíregyháza wished to persuade their respective councils to provide them with agricultural land.

Education

The mass of Roma were only brought into the public education system during the second half of the communist period. Despite improved access to education, developments throughout society meant that the gap between Roma and non-Roma did not diminish. An increasing number of Roma children completed eighth grade, but few made it into secondary education. The National Roma Survey (1993–4) shows that since the change of system Roma educational attainment has fallen significantly.[19] Poverty is widely seen as being an important factor in this decline.[20] In 1995, the self-governments in Kakucs, Emőd, Csepel and Nyíregyháza allocated money to support local Roma children through the purchase of books and clothes, and provision of travel costs and scholarships. All intend to continue to do so and similar programmes are planned in Heves, Kisújszállás and the

Budapest VII district. Nursery education is of particular importance to the Roma given the relative high proportion of young Roma. In Vesztő, Csepel and Heves the self-governments extended financial assistance to nurseries to offset local authority budget cuts.

The self-government in Kisújszállás had a well-developed scheme for providing additional educational support to Roma children. Inheriting the goodwill and opportunities created since the establishment of Lungo Drom in the area in 1992, the self-government runs the Barna Gyöngyök club which meets once a week and provides Roma and non-Roma schoolchildren with after-school activities supervised by professional teachers. In Kakucs and Heves the self-government hoped to receive property from the local government in which a community centre could be established, providing facilities (library, supervision) for after-school study and recreation for Roma children.

Some of the self-governments had plans to establish adult education classes to take advantage of a scheme supported by the Ministry of Education and Culture, whereby those who have not completed eighth grade may study and pass two grades in a year. Such a programme was most developed in Kakucs where the self-government hoped to start classes in January 1996. In Vesztő, the self-government was waiting for school buildings to be renovated. In Heves and Nyíregyháza the realisation of such plans depended on the appropriate resources being made available. In Csepel the self-government planned to run an adult education camp in the summer of 1996.

Health and Welfare

The deepening poverty of most Roma has made many dependent on welfare benefits and services for survival. The general state of physical health of Roma has always been below the Hungarian average and this situation is being aggravated by poverty in the form of poorer housing, stress and a decline in ability to purchase food and clothing. The self-governments in Heves, Emőd, Nyíregyháza and the Budapest VII district had all drawn up plans for the provision of regular advice about health. In Nyíregyháza Artur Balogh was less optimistic as the council had rejected the self-government's plan for the establishment of a network of health advice centres for the minorities. The self-governments in Kisújszállás and Csepel included presentations on healthcare and crime prevention at cultural events organised in 1995. Crime-prevention information is considered important by many self-governments, not only as a means for educating Roma but also for improving relations between Roma and the police. Education about drugs was mentioned by a number of representatives, though none considered this to be a significant problem for the Roma yet.

There was particular concern expressed in a number of areas about issues of women's health and fertility. As families become impoverished there is a chance that women may be driven into prostitution, increasing their risk of contracting HIV or other STDs. This fear was felt most acutely in Heves, which is near an international transport route. The issue of Roma fertility is one of the jokers in the pack of contemporary Hungarian politics. In the past it was generally accepted (and demonstrably proven) that the high Roma birth rate was a product of poverty and that it fell significantly with urbanisation and increased incomes.[21] More recently the fashion for seeking genetic explanations for behaviour has started to give so-called 'scientific' grounds to irrational prejudices about Roma 'inferiority' as illustrated by a high birth rate. This approach is best exemplified by the work of Tamás Bereczki, a biologist at the University of Pécs, who has argued that Roma fertility is characteristic of the reproductive strategies of 'lower' animals and concludes that '"humanist" oriented politicians may increase problems in the coexistence of the two ethnic groups (Magyar and Roma) because they are convinced that political and legal equality is based on biological identity.'[22] Events in the former Yugoslavia demonstrate that it is a matter of concern when the fertility of an ethnic minonty becomes perceived as a threat to a society.

For a number of reasons, such as limited access to contraception and economic insecurity, the conscious reduction in family size witnessed during the period when Roma enjoyed practically full employment is no longer occurring.[23] In Emőd the Roma population has increased 40 per cent since 1990. Due to traditional stereotypes and profound fears for Magyar national identity the issue is developing into a powerful element of anti-Roma prejudice. However, the main reason why many self-governments place particular emphasis on family planning is that it is not in anybody's interest, especially not in the Roma's, that a large number of Roma children are growing up in deep poverty. Artúr Balogh (Nyíregyháza) argued that only schemes organised by Roma themselves can have credibility and influence, particularly in relation to sex education. The development of health programmes are all at the planning stage. Whether these projects can be realised depends on physical and financial resources as well as the cooperation of local health specialists.

Culture

One of the main aims of the self-government system is to allow minorities to take charge of the cultural development of their communities. In Kakucs the self-government allocated some of its budget for the purchase of musical instruments and sponsoring public performances of a local Roma band.

However, budgetary constraints have meant that this had to be discontinued. A similar situation occurred in Nyíregyháza where a twenty-piece Roma band was only able to do two public performances before running out of money despite the self-government winning a 60,000-forint grant for the purpose, but to which access had been restricted. In Csepel the self-government organised a cultural festival (Cigánybál) which was generally considered a great success and received the blessing of the local authority with the attendance of the mayor. A Friendship Day (Barátság Nap) was held in Kisújszállás by the Roma self-government with Roma music and dance combined with information on healthcare and crime prevention. In Kakucs the self-government was encouraging the development of sport among the Roma through sponsorship of a football team and the organisation of a soccer tournament which they hoped to make an annual event.

The scope of the programmes aspired to by those interviewed indicates that, given the opportunity, many Roma self-governments would like to engage in a number of important and diverse activities. Some of these, such as the promotion of culture and health awareness, seem ideal activities for self-governments and rely less on expensive materials than on cooperation with outside agencies. Though the Minorities Law allows self-governments to undertake some educational activities, it is less clear how effective these may be without qualified educationalists and appropriate materials. The fact that some self-governments felt compelled to direct some of their resources to cover the withdrawal of local authority funds for nursery provision is a matter for serious concern as the existence of a self-government might become an excuse for local authorities to cut services. Significantly, all the representatives interviewed considered employment to be a crucial area; however, self-governments and the Minorities Law are not well suited to have much influence in this area. It is true, though, that the self-government system provides a network through which centrally funded employment and training programmes could be developed throughout the country if there was the political will to do so.

THE VIEWS OF ROMA REPRESENTATIVES WITH RESPECT TO THE SELF-GOVERNMENT SYSTEM

The authority of self-governments

Each of the interviewees believed the Minorities Law needed to be amended in order to give self-governments greater authority in determining policies of local government, particularly in the areas of social services, health, education and employment. The Minorities Law does grant rights to self-governments to intervene in the decision-making process and even veto some decisions. However, the major problem is that self-governments lack the power to compel local authorities to take account of their views, even if they are obliged to do so by the law. The representatives from Kakucs, Csepel, Emőd and Nyíregyháza each felt that their rights had been ignored by the local authority and that they could do nothing about this. Going to court is viewed as too time consuming and expensive. None of the interviewees mentioned using the recently appointed Parliamentary Commissioner for Minority Affairs (Ombudsman) as a means for resolving conflicts with a local authority.

Political relationships

One consequence of the lack of legal teeth of self-government is that considerable importance was attached to developing good relations with the respective local government and other institutions (ministries, foundations, etc.). In only one of the areas studied (Emőd) had the self-government planned a demonstration against the council, but this had not taken place after the president, Gusztav Kökény was warned off by the local chief of police. The establishment of goodwill is a two-way process and this was felt to be lacking in a number of areas (see above). In the view of Jenő Redics (Kakucs) in order to function a self- government requires 'support, empathy and tolerance' on the part of the local authority. Of the three areas where this relationship seems to be best (Heves, Vesztő and Kisújszállás), Roma had been represented on the local authority prior to the creation of the self-government in the capacity of spokespersons.

Finance

Closely related to the issue of the authority of self-governments is that of the lack of financial guarantees. The only money which self-governments could be sure of was the 220,000 forints allocated by the state budget, a sum considered insufficient to cover even the most basic programme. The creation of the two state foundations opens up a new source of finance to which self-governments can apply. However, none but those in Heves and Kisújszállás saw this as a credible option, fearing that only those with political ties to the trustees will receive funds. Interestingly, the most trenchant criticism of the lack of resources made available to self-governments came from Menyhért Lakatos (Vesztő) whose self-government had been the most successful of the eight in winning financial and other support from a variety of sources. He believed the system to be fatally undermined by lack of funds with little prospect that this situation will change for the better given the state of the economy and the low priority of the Roma. The fact that Roma self-governments must seek the approval of other agencies in order to receive funds with which they can finance programmes can be seen as a serious limitation on the authority of self-governments. Jenő Redics (Kakucs) was particularly critical of the inconsistency of funding arrangements across the country. He felt that self-governments 'nearer to the fire' either politically or geographically (in Budapest) are more generously supported even if this is not necessarily merited by the quality of their work and the needs of local Roma communities.

The Minorities Law

The greatest difference of opinion between the interviewees lay in their interpretations of the utility and purpose of the Minorities Law. The most positive views were expressed by Mrs Kovács (Kisújszállás) and Mihály Lólé (Heves), both Lungo Drom members, who saw the law as a major step forward for the Roma, both in the opportunities it provides for developing programmes catering to Roma needs and because of the improvement in status it gives the Roma both at the local and national level. The view was strongly voiced in Kakucs, Nyíregyháza and Csepel that the emphasis of the law (and the self-government system) on the cultural development of minorities does not address the fundamental problems facing the majority of Roma: poverty, unemployment and exclusion. In the words of Jenő Redics, 'You can't go on stage if you have no clothes to wear.' Furthermore, the emphasis on the 'difference' of Roma obfuscates the need for Roma to be allowed to live lives similar to those of non-Roma, enjoying equal status and opportunity. They felt the law, in its current state, does not really empower the Roma to exercise their rights and implement programmes which may make a genuine contribution to improving their lives; self-governments are dependent on the approval of others and have no powers to counter discrimination. Concern that the government is not interested in developing policies which can lift the Roma out of poverty had been heightened with the abolition, in December 1995, of the Office of Gypsy Crisis Management Programmes, set up in 1994 by the incoming socialist/liberal coalition.

Profound anxiety for the fate of the Roma was expressed by Artur Balogh (Nyíregyháza) and Menyhért Lakatos (Vesztő). Both believed that the current situation cannot last for long as Hungarians will not tolerate 'keeping' substantial numbers of Roma who are unable to find work. Neither believed that the Roma are capable, either politically or economically, of resolving these problems by themselves and therefore Hungarian society must become aware that policies need to be implemented to facilitate the social and economic integration of the Roma. However, neither expected that the Minorities Law and the self-government system would do this as there is neither the political will nor the resources available to make the system work. Ferenc Kovács considered the Minorities Law says to the Roma, 'You can sing and dance, and then go to hell.'

The representatives from Csepel, Nyíregyháza and Vesztő saw the flaws in the system as resulting from the purpose for which the Minorities Law was drawn up. They considered the law not to be aimed at Hungary's domestic minorities, but to be part of the country's foreign policy seeking to facilitate Hungary's entry into European supra-national institutions such as the European Union and providing some protection for the substantial Magyar minorities living in neighbouring countries. The law, therefore, is essentially symbolic, not designed to address the needs of minorities in Hungary. In the words of Menyhért Lakatos it is a 'window-dressing policy', a phrase commonly heard in Roma political circles. Ferenc Kovács was even more sceptical, believing that after Hungary has achieved its foreign policy goals, the self-government system will be reviewed, considered to have failed and allowed to die.

Political development

Opinions were mixed among those who expressed a view about the possible effect of the self-government system on the future political development of the Roma. The representatives from Kakucs and Emőd maintained that, if the system is allowed to evolve, then it can make an important contribution in drawing Roma into public life. However, those from Vesztő and Nyíregyháza believed that the system is so flawed that it will not stimulate interest in politics among Roma. Ferenc Kovács (Csepel) considered that the system had already caused a great deal of harm to Roma politics by stifling possible cooperation between Roma organisations, undermining self-organisation as support is switched towards self-governments, and further dividing the Roma by doubling the number of Roma organisations (previously there were around 270 self-organised Roma groups in Hungary and now there are almost 500 self-governments). Interestingly, both Menyhért Lakatos (Vesztő) and Jenő Relics (Kakucs) expressed the view that this generation of Roma activists, while being able to achieve little themselves, is laying a foundation for the next generation who will be much better prepared to fight for the interests of Roma people.

CONCLUSION

The research was predicated on the view that, as a unique system of minority representation, the self-government system needs to be carefully monitored to assess the degree to which it contributes to improving the lives of Hungary's domestic national and ethnic minorities. As they comprise the largest minority group and have formed the most local self-governments, the views of Roma representatives are of particular significance in such an assessment. The research also sought to investigate the extent to which concerns raised prior to the introduction of the system have been shown to be justified in practice. Though the self-government system is still in its infancy, some significant issues emerged during the course of the interviews which should be further examined.

Perhaps the most striking feature to emerge from the research was the wide variation in experience and perceptions of the system on the part of the eight representatives interviewed. One of the variable factors in the research was the known political allegiance of those interviewed. This factor was only of significance in perceptions of the relationship with local authorities. The two Lungo Drom members (from Heves and Kisújszállás) and Menyhért Lakatos (Vesztő), whose name was provided by Lungo Drom, all positively evaluated their relationship with their local councils. Rather than being a direct consequence of political allegience, good relations with local authorities may well be due to the previous existence of formal links between Roma and the local authority. The three Phralipe members (from Kakucs, Csepel and Emőd) were less positive, but in each case this was seen as a result of local factors rather than related to the political allegiance of the Roma. Local conditions also seem to play a determining role in influencing the local authority–self-government relationship in the areas where the Roma presidents were not members of the two main Roma groups. However, in Nyíregyháza the paralysis of the self-government seems to be caused by the local authority's exploitation of splits among the Roma. Perceptions of the relationship with the local authority seems not to be related to the type of settlement.

The location of a self-government seems to play a role in determining the scale of material support from the local authority. All three large urban settlements had received significant grants, while none of the village self-governments had received any money, though land and buildings had been provided. In the two smaller towns both had received office accommodation but only one had any financial support. Personal and/or political links were considered important when applying for external funding, including from the two new government-backed foundations. There were significant differences in the kinds of project the self-governments had either initiated or are planning to. Some placed great emphasis on the need to establish jobs and provide skills training, whilst others sought to promote education and cultural events. These positions seem to be independent of political allegiance or the location of the self-government, but related to perceptions of what can be achieved within the local political environment. A matter of concern for those responsible for the system must be that some representatives interpreted the lack of authority and the absence of financial guarantees fundamentally undermined the credibility of the system. There were also differences of opinion about the whole emphasis of the law, some believing the emphasis on culture and education to be appropriate while others saw this as a deliberate attempt to prevent the real problems of the Roma being addressed.

A welcome finding of the research was the enthusiasm and commitment from the research of those involved to make the system serve their communities. However, the extent to which they may achieve their plans lies beyond their control, in the hands of others. The significant differences in the financial support provided to self-governments, the extent to which they participate in the work of the local authority and the strongly felt perception that good personal links are required to make the system work clearly indicate that the system is not underpinned by a central authority (the Minorities Law and the Office for National and Ethnic Minorities which is responsible for minority affairs) capable of ensuring consistency of approach and equality of opportunity across the country. As such the system does not succeed as the comprehensive mechanism of minority protection which it seeks to be. Nevertheless, the first years of the system were always going to be a period of learning for all involved. The strength and value of the system will depend on the extent to which the flaws identified at this early stage can be corrected, and its positive elements identified and built upon.

NOTES

Interviews were carried out in December 1995 with:

Jenő Redics – Kakucs	Gusztav Kökény – Emőd
Menyhért Lakatos – Vesztő	Mrs J. Kovács – Kisújszállás
Mihály Lólé – Heves	Artúr Balogh – Nyíregyháza
Ferenc Kovács – Csepel	Dr Géza Reményi – Budapest VII district

1 Interview with Florian Farkas, 3 May 1995.
2 J.-P. Liegois and N. Gheorghe (1995: 7).
3 The link between India and the Romani language was first made by István Lali in the 1750s and the first series of articles analysing Roma life were written by the Hungarian Lutheran pastor Samuel Augustini ab Hortis and was published in 1775–6 (Fraser 1995: 190–3).
4 G. Havas, G. Kertesi and I. Kemény (1995) 'The Statistics of Deprivation', *Hungarian Quarterly*, vol. 36, Summer: 67–80.
5 Preamble to the Minorities Law: 'Évi törvény a nemzet és etnikai kisebbségek jogairól', *Magyar Közlöny*, 22 July 1993.
6 *Népszbadság*, 13 May 1995
7 Báthory's advice was predicated on the view that mass impoverishment combined with the emergence of a 'Gypsy movement' could become a source of political instability. He admired the way 'democratic systems successfully

channelled "pacified" aggressive ethnic movements . . . by building them into a system of democratic institutions'. Taken from a confidential document entitled, 'The Aspiration for National Unity and the Gypsy Ethnic Movement', prepared by Báthory for the Hungarian Socialist Workers Party and reproduced (in Hungarian) in 'Verőviszonyok' [Losing Positions], *Phralipe*, VI, 7–9: 105.

8　A. Faludi (1964: 12).
9　J Ladányi, 'Patterns of Residential Segregation and the Gypsy Minority in Budapest', *International Journal of Urban and Regional Research*, 17, 1: 30–34.
10　*Beszámoló a magyarországi roma (cigány) népesség helyzetével foglalkozó 1993 októbere és 1994 februárja között végzett kutatásról* [Report on the research carried out between October 1993 and February 1994 into the circumstances of the Hungarian Roma (Gypsy) population], Hungarian Academy of Science – Institute of Sociology, unpublished report, p. 33.
11　'Nyerőviszonyok', [Winning Positions] *Beszélő*, IV, 19: 19.
12　*Beszámoló az Országgyűlésnek a helyi önkormányzati képviselők és polgármesterek 1994 évi választásáról* [Report to Parliament on the 1994 election of local government councillors and mayors], Országos Választási Bizottság, Budapest 1995.
13　I Vajda (1995) 'Minket ne Válasszanak Külön' [Don't Set Us Apart], *Amaro Drom*, March, p. 4.
14　*Népszabadság*, 6 December 1994.
15　Minorities Law, *op cit*, paragraph 27.
16　*Ibid.*, paragraphs 26 and 29.
17　For example: *Népszabadság*, 2 and 17 February 1995: G. Noszkai (1994) 'Örvénybe Iktatva' [Into the Whirlpool], *Respublika*, no. 6: 42.
18　Translation taken from Guglielmo and Waters (1996: 147) which includes English translations of a number of passages of the Minorities Law.
19　G. Havas *et al.*, *op cit.*
20　Z. Szilágy and A. Heizer (1996: 14).
21　P. Bánlaky (1993) *Cigánycsaládok vizsgálata* [Study of Gypsy Families], Budapest: Népjóléti Minisztérium, p. 23.
22　T Bereczkei (1993) 'Selected Reproductive Strategies among Hungarian Gipsies: A Preliminary Analysis', *Ethnology and Sociobiology*, no. 14: 86.
23　B. Mezey (1986: 276).

REFERENCES

Báthory, J. (1995) *Kisebbségi kodex* [Laws affecting Minorities], Budapest: Auktor.
Boda, P., Cseresnyés, J. and Vánko, T. (1994) *A Kisebbségek Jogai Magyarországon* [The Rights of Minorities in Hungary], Budapest: Közgazdasági és Jogi Könyvkiadó.
Faludi, A. (1964) *Ciganyok* [Gypsies], Budapest: Kossúth.
Fraser, A. (1995) *The Gypsies*, Oxford: Blackwell.
Fehér, G. (1993) *Struggling for Ethnic Identity: The Gypsies of Hungary*, New York: Human Rights Watch.
Guglielmo, R. and Waters, T. (1996) *Rights Denied: The Roma in Hungary*, New York: Human Rights Watch.
Liegois, J.-P. and Gheorghe, N. (1995) *Roma/Gypsies: A European Minority*, London: Minority Rights Group.

Mezey, B. (1986) *A Magyarországi Cigánykérdés Dokumentumokban 1422–1985* [The Gypsy Question in Hungary in Documents 1422–1985], Budapest: Kossuth Könyvkiadó.

Szilágy, Z. and Heizer A. (eds) (1996) *Report on the Situation of the Gypsy Community in Hungary*, Budapest: Office for National and Ethnic Minorities.

9 Divergent responses to land reform and agricultural restructuring in the Russian Federation

Louise Perrotta

'What do I think about restructuring? We've been restructured about once every five years for as long as I can remember. And every time things get worse instead of better. I don't see why it should be any different this time. Restructuring usually means that things get worse.'

(72-year-old woman farmworker, Voronezh Oblast, May 1995)

'I was to learn later on in life that we tend to meet any new situation by reorganising, and a wonderful method it can be for creating the illusion of progress, while producing confusion, inefficiency and demoralisation.'

(Gaius Petronius, AD 66)

One of the central features of 'transition' in the former Soviet Union has been reform of the agricultural sector. The structural aspects of these reforms emanate largely from the centre in the shape of laws, presidential decrees and government resolutions. These have created the legal framework for the private ownership of agricultural land and non-land assets, and for the restructuring of former state farms (sovkhozy) and collective farms (kolkhozy) into independent, private-sector businesses. However, the practical implementation of these reforms varies widely, not just between oblasts and rations (administrative districts), but between neighbouring farms; similarly, understandings of and attitudes to reform vary between members of the farms' populations. In this chapter I attempt to give some sense of the varying interpretations, understandings and practices that have developed in the wake of legal innovations. I suggest that 'transition' is characterised by contradiction between the 'opportunities' presented by privatisation and practical and structural constraints. Some of these constraints are inherited from the Soviet period, while others are the often unforeseen consequences of the reform process itself. The fieldwork on which this chapter is based was conducted between 1993 and 1995 in nine oblasts of European Russia,[1] while working as an advisor and/or researcher on internationally funded land-reform and agricultural-reorganisation projects.[2]

Problems in the agricultural sector have dogged the Soviet economy ever since the collectivisation of agriculture in the 1930s. At the end of the 1980s, it was estimated that crop yields were up to 30 per cent lower and livestock yields 40–50 per cent lower than in comparable climatic zones in the West. It has also long been acknowledged that yields from the small 'private plots' of state and collective farmworkers are consistently higher than on the broad acres of the farms themselves. Similarly, yields of privately owned livestock inevitably compare favourably with yields from sovkhoz or kolkhoz livestock. Although figures vary with political interests, it is commonly stated that private plots accounted for less than 3 per cent of all agricultural land in the Soviet Union, while their produce accounted for some 30 per cent of household foodstuffs.

The relative success of the contract-leasing brigades,[3] comparisons with yields on privately owned and managed agricultural enterprises in the West and acknowledgement of superior performance on the small privately worked plots of state and collective farmworkers combined to create a consensus that the key to agricultural reform lay in the direction of 'privatisation'. A large number of laws, government resolutions and presidential decrees relating to the agricultural reform have been issued since 1990. The most significant of these relate to land reform, the establishment of private (peasant) farms, and the allocation of land and property rights to current and former state and collective farmworkers.

LAND REFORM

The private ownership of land became legal in the Russian Federation with the passing of the law 'On Land Reform' in October 1990. Subsequent laws, decrees and resolutions have dealt with the criteria for the allocation of land ownership to agricultural workers and others, mechanisms for the transfer of ownership of land through sale or inheritance, land registries, taxation, care and maintenance of land, land use and land pricing. There are a number of forms of 'land title' under Russian law, including outright ownership, 'possession for life', leasehold, indefinite or permanent use and temporary use. Title to land may be held by various legal entities including Russian citizens, citizens of the 'near abroad' (the former Union Republics of the USSR), any physical person (including foreigners), or any juridical entity (organisation). Land title may be issued to individuals, or to collectives in either joint collective ownership or joint share ownership. There is con-siderable confusion at the local level about these different forms of land title; many of the former state and collective farmworkers interviewed were unable to specify the form of title they had acquired, or to define the different forms of land entitlement. Less frequently, local bureaucrats of the oblast or raion administration or from the Department of Agriculture were equally unable to explain adequately the difference between different forms of land title. Although indigenous definitions are vague, it seems that where a 'collective' enjoys *joint collective ownership*, individual shares are not necessarily clearly defined, making withdrawal of land shares less likely. The 'owner' is conceptualised as the collective, regardless of its individual membership. Where a collective enjoys *joint share ownership*, individual shares are clearly defined (but not necessarily demarcated into physical land parcels on the ground), which facilitates withdrawal should an individual share owner so desire. The land is owned by (named) individuals, who have opted for joint occupation and use of the land.

In general, the rights and obligations that attend land ownership are poorly defined in law and even more vaguely understood by the new legal owners. For example, when the initial moratorium on land sales was eventually lifted, many locals asserted that the sale of land was still not legal because the state had not specified the procedures for land sales, or the 'price' of land.

Private peasant farming

The law 'On Peasant Farms', which established the right to private peasant farming in November 1990, has been followed by decrees and resolutions regarding criteria for the allocation of land and property to private peasant farmers, taxation and interest rates for private peasant farmers, different forms of legal entitlement to land, land use, sale and inheritance. By July 1994, the 'Union of Private Peasant Farmers' (AKKOR), reported that almost 280,000 private peasant farms had been established in the Russian Federation. Many of these are former state or collective farmworkers who withdrew from the state or collective farms, taking with them land and property entitlements and acquiring extra land as necessary from local (raion) land-redistribution funds. Others have emigrated from the urban centres, and a significant minority are refugees from the 'near abroad'. Private peasant farms vary in size from a few hectares to several thousand with an average of 43 hectares per private peasant farm.

In order to encourage the establishment of private peasant farms, the Russian government initially offered a number of sweeteners to prospective peasant farmers. These included cash incentives for people moving from one oblast to another (reportedly subject to much abuse), freedom from some taxes for the first five years and preferential interest rates.[4] If the proliferation of private peasant farms was seen by many both inside and outside the former Soviet Union as an ideal solution to the problems of Russian agriculture, it has become increasingly clear that at best it is only ever going to be a partial solution. Many of those who have embarked on private peasant farming are now facing extreme financial difficulties. The exceptions are serious entrepreneurs who set up in 1991–92, and who benefited from low interest rates and subsequent inflation. Some of those who are now equipped and debt free are enjoying considerable success. Later entrants are doing less well as the withdrawal of credit at preferential interest rates has combined with increasing price disparities to cause insuperable financial difficulties for even the most entrepreneurial private farmer. Attitudes to private farmers vary, but rural populations prefer to point out local failures, emphasising corrupt practices by local private farmers, the agricultural incompetence of urban migrants, or the general impossibility of surviving outside the fold of the former state or collective farms. The establishment of new private peasant farms has now stalled as it becomes increasingly difficult to acquire affordable credit to finance necessary machinery and equipment. Low prices for agricultural produce combine with rapid inflation for agricultural inputs to discourage even the most rash entrepreneur.

THE 1992 FARM REORGANISATIONS

The third thrust to the government's agricultural reform programme has been directed at the restructuring of the state and collective farms. Government Resolution No. 86 entitled 'On Procedures for the Reorganisation of Collective and State Farms' was issued on 29 December 1991. State farm directors and collective farm chairpersons who failed to comply with this resolution were threatened with fines or imprisonment. Reorganisation was to have been completed by 31 December 1992.[5]

Where an individual or group of individual entitlement holders wants to set up a private peasant farm or other juridical form of independent enterprise, they have the right to be given physical land parcels and assets in accordance with their legal entitlements. The Intra-farm Privatisation Commission is responsible for deciding which land parcels and which assets (in cash or in kind) to allocate to aspiring independent farmers. Not surprisingly, many of the private peasant farmers who had withdrawn their land entitlement from the collective claimed to have been allocated the worst land, located far from their houses, the worst machinery and equipment, and/or an inadequate cash compensation.

The process of reorganisation required that farm members be given the opportunity to vote both on the form of land title and on the legal–organisational form of association they wished to adopt in accordance with their new status as 'owners' of land and assets. This decision was taken at a general meeting of the collective, that is, of all those entitlement holders who had not chosen to withdraw their land and property entitlements for the purpose of independent enterprise. Some of the former state and collective farms were legally exempt from the reorganisation process as a result of their status as 'special breeding stations, experimental farms, vineyards, tea-growing enterprises or peri-urban horticultural specialists'. Of the farms not exempt from reorganisation, almost 97 per cent of former state and collective farms had completed the obligatory reorganisation process by January 1993.

However, it is widely acknowledged that compliance with these top-down directives has had minimal impact on the management or production practices of the former state and collective farms. The vast majority have become joint stock companies or limited or so-called 'mixed' partnerships. Whatever the new legal–organisational format adopted by the collective, land and assets are still very often held in collective ownership. The management of the new enterprises has remained largely unchanged in terms of both personnel and structures of participation (or non-participation) in decision making. Responsibility for the 'social sphere' (social services, etc.) very often still rests with the old state or collective farm management. Yet it is from this point on that we begin to see the emergence of different perceptions of the nature of the problems, their causes and possible solutions. If observers and participants are fairly unanimous in assessing the extent of change after the 1992 reorganisation, evaluation of the causes and consequences of minimal improvement varies.

INTERNATIONAL AID AGENCIES[6]

Representatives from the Know How Fund, USAID and the World Bank all agree that the results of the 1992 farm reorganisation have been disappointing. They have noted that the changes have been 'superficial', 'purely formal', 'changes in name only', and have had little if any effect on improving the efficiency of agricultural enterprises. The reasons for the failure of the 1992 reforms include inadequate changes to the structure of ownership and continued poor management.

According to assessments by the international aid agencies, the reform of land and property ownership is an absolute prerequisite for efficient agricultural production. This view is based on experiences of the higher efficiency of agriculture where land and assets are privately owned. Private ownership is thought to guarantee better husbanding of resources, and more rational decision making motivated by the pursuit of profit. Private ownership and management of productive assets is thought to increase personal responsibility, reward risk-taking and increase labour discipline as the returns on investments (capital or labour) accrue to the original investors instead of being siphoned off by the state. According to this view, farm reorganisation in Russia has failed to produce the hoped for results because the structure of ownership has remained largely unchanged in practice. The technical transfer of legal property rights has not created the anticipated 'feeling of ownership' (*chuvstvo khoziaina*). This is linked to the fact that land and assets are still very often held in 'collective' ownership, to the absence of legally certified title to land, and to the fact that land is rarely demarcated into individual land holdings. As no one knows where their land lies or which plough is theirs, traditional neglect of resources combines with continued poor labour discipline to create gross inefficiencies.

According to many foreign commentators, Russian farm management is inefficient. Efficient financial management, it is stated, is hampered by accounting systems designed for use in a centrally planned economy; management accounts which allow for relative assessments of profitability between sectors are unheard of. The financial discipline imposed by western-style banking procedures is not in evidence as losses are accumulated in the certainty that the state will rescue defaulters. Resources are not efficiently husbanded as the old system encouraged wastefulness. Production structures do not reflect market forces and no attempts are made to adapt production to changing demands. Farms are grossly overstaffed; labour discipline is poor. Finally, responsibility for maintaining a variety of assets and services (the 'social sphere'[7]) creates a constant drain on the farms' resources, as they struggle to fulfil both productive and non-productive functions.

The aid agencies are almost unanimous in their preference for 're-visiting the reorganisation process'. In support of this, in 1993 USAID provided funding to the International Finance Corporation (IFC) for the development of a model farm-reorganisation programme in Nizhnii Novgorod. The technical aspects of the programme were developed in association with the Agrarian Institute in Moscow. As most land reform and agricultural restructuring projects are heavily influenced by the experiences of the Nizhnii Novgorod programme, a brief description is in order here.

The Nizhnii Novgorod model was designed to encourage real re-structuring of former state and collective farms, in a manner that is '*fair, open and transparent*'. Although the model bears formal resemblance to the legal requirements of reorganisation, it goes beyond these by encouraging higher rates of participation and by introducing an element of market competition. Better-informed participation is accomplished both by a high-profile publicity campaign, mostly in the mass media, and by providing accessible expertise and advice at the farm level.

This increased emphasis on communication and participation was accompanied by the development of market-oriented mechanisms, aimed at forcing people to make decisions about the use of their land and property entitlements. Once lists of entitlement holders have been posted and approved, and land and assets inventoried and evaluated, formal certificates are issued. These can then be combined by groups of individuals to bid for land and assets at auction. The auction introduces an element of market competition into the redistribution process, as newly established private farmers, partnerships and joint stock companies compete both for entitlement certificates and for physical land parcels and assets. Assistance and advice is freely available to emergent entrepreneurs. As a result of this input, farm reorganisation in Nizhnii Novgorod has resulted in a number of new enterprises of varying shapes and sizes. If land and assets are still very often held in joint share or joint collective ownership, this is the result of reasonably well-informed choices rather than inertia, poor understanding or outright misinformation. The Nizhnii Novgorod model effectively achieves the objective of restructuring the former state and collective farms. It is (or at least was) assumed by the original designers of the programme that restructured ownership would automatically lead to improved efficiency. In the course of this process, responsibility for the 'social sphere' is transferred to the local (raion or village) administration, while funding is provided by the oblast administration.

Opinions vary as to whether the Nizhnii Novgorod model contributes to improved efficiency. Post-reorganisation farm business management advice is available to the managers of new enterprises, and is partly paid for by the aid agencies. Although the situation throughout the agricultural sector has deteriorated rapidly over the last two years, some observers argue that the Nizhnii managers are coping better than most due to their increased autonomy and/or their improved access to western-style advice and expertise. Some critics argue that the Nizhnii farms are doing neither better nor worse than comparable farms elsewhere. Others suggest that they are performing better but that the cost of this improved performance is extremely high, and that it will not be possible to replicate the Nizhnii model elsewhere in terms of inputs from abroad. All agree that the political situation in Nizhnii Novgorod makes a major contribution to its success; the presence of a young, dynamic, high-profile governor ensures that local-level political support for reform is unusually reliable.

THE RUSSIAN BUREAUCRATS

If bureaucrats at all levels agree that the 1992 reorganisation has resulted in little real change, they differ markedly in their understandings of the causes of continued adherence to Soviet-era practices and, consequently, potential solutions.[8] Federal-level representatives are invariably overtly pro-reform and keen to establish good working relationships with representatives of the aid agencies. Some are undoubtedly sincere, while it is clear that others have a more complex private agenda. At the federal level, the reasons given for the failure of the 1992 reforms include opposition from conservative oblast-level officials, farm directors and/or workers, overly hasty implementation/poor planning, and lack of cooperation from other ministries or departments. The Ministry of Agriculture, for example, blames the State Land Committee for not fostering the development of a market for the efficient redistribution of agricultural land.

However, the opinions of federal-level officials and bureaucrats are less significant than those of oblast- or raion-level representatives, as the former are far removed from the day to day management of agricultural and economic policies. The continued weakening of the centre in Russian politics is well documented, as is the attendant rise in autonomous behaviour by oblast-level officials. One of the most important factors is the degree of commitment of members of the State Land Committee (*Goskomzem*), whose efficiency in registering and transferring land titles is the single most important influence on the development of a land market. If the federal State Land Committee is guilty of incompetence in the issue of consistent legal documentation, how this is dealt with at the local level varies. The more 'conservative' the local land committee, the more likely its members are to throw up their hands in despair. In other areas, the local land committee has issued temporary documentation and assured title holders that this is legal. The enthusiasm of the chairperson of the Blagodarnenskii Raion Land Committee in Stavropol Krai, for example, was instrumental in developing innovative reforms on a former state farm.

Whether the local land committee can map and survey individually demarcated plots of land is a basic issue in the development of private peasant farming. If it cannot, this is often an absolute bar to real reform. Thus the local land committee can 'make or break' land reform. Perceptions of corrupt practice in the allocation of land from the raion redistribution funds do little to increase confidence in the reform process. Rumours of bribes paid to members of local land committees are supported by the widespread appearance of new housing on supposedly agricultural land. While some members of the land committee remark on their willingness to repossess land that is not being farmed 'properly', others appear to ignore all regulations in pursuit of gifts and sweeteners.

It is important to remember that the privatisation of land ownership entails a significant loss of power for State Land Committee officials. The suggestion by western experts that infractions of the land-use code should be met with fines instead of repossession, in order to protect the principle of land ownership, is often met with strong disapproval. Retaining control of land, its use and disposition, creates real divisions within land commit-tees. Some struggle to retain Soviet-era-style controls while others are keen to establish new positions of power and influence over an emerging land market.

Other important influences on the progress of agricultural reform emanate from oblast- and raion-level officials, both in the administration and in the Department of Agriculture. Here we need to distinguish between the overtly expressed attitudes and opinions of officials and the actual outcomes of their activities. In discussions with foreign advisors, local officials almost always express a favourable attitude to agricultural reform in general. This is usually qualified by one or more negative opinions. For example, the reforms have been 'too hastily implemented' or were generated from above/from Moscow, and therefore reflect ignorance of local/agricultural realities, or would have worked but for unfair competition from imports/ humanitarian aid. Alternatively, local people are not ready for private land ownership or for individual entrepreneurial activity. This is why they have largely chosen to 'stay the same'. Reforms were necessary but restructuring ownership of land and assets was not the main priority. The more important issues are improving the technical capacity of the farms and reducing the disparity between costs for agricultural inputs and the price of agricultural outputs. Interestingly, it is common for these reservations to be expressed 'in private', while overt approval is reserved for more formal meetings.

A comparison of the outcomes of the reorganisation process across oblasts or between raions indicates the extent to which overt consensus masks divergent local interests and practices (Table 9.1). The results of agricultural reorganisation vary widely, both in the proportion of farms choosing a particular status ('open' or 'closed' joint stock company or limited partnership) and in the ways in which change is defined and recorded. There are also critical differences in the extent to which oblast administrations are willing to take over responsibility for the 'social sphere'. In Nizhnii Novgorod Oblast, responsibility for the social sphere has been transferred to raion administrations and is funded by the oblast adminis- tration; in Voronezh, however, the oblast administration has refused to take over this financial responsibility and new agricultural enterprises are forced to continue to support social sphere provisions. Some argue that this responsibility is the main cause of their financial difficulties.

The responses of those such as farm managers who are most closely affected by the actions of local officials reflect a range of practices. At one end of the spectrum, we find highly motivated officials visiting farms, answering questions and encouraging the exploration of different options. At the other end, support for reorganisation has been minimal, with brief visits from officials ensuring that the Intra-farm Privatisation Commissions have fulfilled the basic legal obligations.

Other responses reveal widespread use of threats and bribes to control the

Table 9.1 Agricultural reorganisation across oblasts and between raions

Stavropol Krai: original large agricultural enterprises

Type	1991
Sovkhoz (state farm)	257
Kolkhoz (collective farm)	159
Mixed enterprises	21

Agricultural enterprises after transformation

Type	May 1994
Kolkhoz (unchanged)	48
Sovkhoz (unchanged)	36
Closed joint stock companies[1]	291
Collective agricultural enterprises	45
Associations of peasant farms	16
Agricultural cooperatives	8
Mixed enterprises	5
Agro-firms with joint collective ownership	3
Private peasant farms	11,949

Rostov Oblast: agricultural holdings, pre-reform

Kolkhoz	414
Sovkhoz	395

Agricultural enterprises after transformation

Type	1993	1994
Total 're-registered' sovkhoz and kolkhoz	584	775
Retained previous status	163	200
Open joint stock company[2]	15	10
Limited partnership	234	328
Peasant associations	21	27
Agricultural cooperatives	6	11
Subsidiary farm enterprises	2	25
Other	143	174
Specialist state farms	N/A	384
Individual farms	7,817	12,431

Tver Oblast: transformation of original 700 kolkhoz and sovkhoz

Type	July 1994
Retained status as kolkhoz or sovkhoz	350
Joint stock company or limited partnership	219
Agricultural cooperative	115
Association of peasant farms	9
Small enterprises	8
Other	45
Individual (peasant) farms	3,720

Saratov Oblast: results of transformation

Type	July 1994
Total large farming units	755
Joint stock companies	491
'Unrestricted'	189
State specialist farms	75
Individual farms	13,457

Pskov Oblast: transformation of original 350 kolkhoz and sovkhoz

Type	March 1994
Kolkhoz (unchanged)	54
Sovkhoz (unchanged)	12
Limited partnerships	162
Joint stock companies	85
Production cooperatives	32
Miscellaneous enterprises	16
Associations of (peasant) farms	3
Other entities	3
Non-registered farms	2
Individual (private) farms	3,110

Rostov Oblast, Zernogradsky Raion: transformation

Type	pre-reform	post-reform
Kolkhoz and sovkhoz	20	
Specialist state farms		12
Joint stock companies		8
'Fully restructured' joint stock companies		1
Private farmers		700
Proportion of arable land farmed by private farmers		5%

Rostov Oblast, Pyshchanavsky Raion: transformation

Type	pre-reform	post-reform
Sovkhoz	11	
Kolkhoz	12	
Joint stock companies or limited partnerships		23
'Fully restructured' joint stock companies or limited partnerships	1	
Private farmers		500
Proportion of arable land farmed by private farmers		10%

Rostov Oblast, Martinovsky Raion: after transformation

Proportion of arable land farmed by private farmers	28.6%

Krasnodar Krai, Temriuk Raion: transformation

Type	pre-reform	post-reform
Sovkhoz	27	
Sovkhoz		2
Specialist state farms		3
Closed joint stock companies		22
Private farms		1,176

Krasnodar Krai, Sochi Raion: transformation

Type	pre-reform	post-reform
Sovkhoz and kolkhoz	32	
Join stock companies with land owned by state		6
Specialist state farms		5
Cooperatives		1
Experimental state farms		1
Closed joint stock companies or limited partnerships (with land owned by collective)		7
Private farms		219

Krasnodar Krai, Ust Labinsk Raion: transformation

Type	pre-reform	post-reform
Kolkhoz	11	
'Privatised Collective Partnerships' with collective land ownership		11
Total private farms		2,496
'Independent' private farms		600
'Substructures of kolkhoz' private farms		1,896

Notes:
[1]Ownership of shares in 'closed' joint stock companies is restricted to farm members.
[2]Ownership of shares in 'open' joint stock companies is not restricted to farm members.

Source: 'Report on Farm Reorganization and Privatization in Russia', prepared by Arthur Andersen & Co. for USAID, August 1994.

extent and direction of the reorganisation process. Some farm managers said that representatives of the Department of Agriculture made it clear that any innovation would result in strained relations. In one case, the farm director was told that if he 'gave the cattle to the workers', he would find it 'very difficult to get the fuel rations he needed for the harvest'. In another case, a farm manager who wanted to slaughter some of the cattle because livestock production had become unprofitable was told that he would be personally prosecuted for tax evasion. When asked why the local Department of Agriculture did not want him to slaughter cattle, he replied, 'if we make losses, we remain dependent on them for access to state credits, fuel rations, seeds, etc.'

Policy makers at the oblast level exert considerable influence on the extent and direction of reform through the regulation of production, trade, pricing, taxation and policies concerned with social sphere provisions. In some cases seemingly arbitrary restrictions on agricultural imports into or exports out of the oblast reflect the administration's desire to retain control over agricultural production. In one oblast, the prices of agricultural foodstuffs were still being controlled in spite of directives from Moscow that prices were to be freed. Whilst oblast administrators claimed that the controls were aimed at keeping consumer prices low, agricultural producers claimed that it was to keep them impoverished and dependent. Officials stated that their 'controlled' prices for some agricultural products were hardly different from the 'free' prices in Nizhnii Novgorod: when asked why then they felt it necessary to control prices, they answered, 'Why not?'

In some areas, private farmers report constant harassment from tax inspectors, land-use controllers and quality controllers as well as continued attempts by Department of Agriculture officials to direct production. Demands for bribes are reported to be widespread, and harassment from illegal mafia-style groups is matched by harassment from corrupt officials.

The reform process presents a considerable threat to local-level officials: under the Soviet system, these officials were crucial links in the chain between the central planning authorities and local producers. According autonomy in terms of production and decision making to the new 'owners' of land and assets entails a loss of absolute power for local bureaucrats, who formerly mediated between Moscow and the local producers. As it was local-level bureaucrats from the Department of Agriculture who stood to lose most, their lack of enthusiasm for reforms, often reflected in performance of the bare minimum required of them by law, is not surprising.

It is impossible to overstate the importance of the role played by local bureaucrats in the direction and extent of rural development. Where the local administration refuses to take on responsibility for the social spheres, farms are placed in an impossible position. Either farm managers also refuse to continue supporting these services, alienating an already frustrated workforce and causing considerable social distress, or they continue to support them but fall further into debt. The fact that a significant majority of agricultural enterprises face bankruptcy in the near future indicates that the reforms may backfire before they really begin. Given that a significant proportion of the debts are owed to the state, bankruptcy could conceivably result in land and assets reverting to the state.

FARM MANAGERS, ADMINISTRATORS AND SPECIALISTS

Perhaps the most important individual in terms of farm reorganisation is the ex-state farm director or ex-collective farm chairperson. If she/he is categorically opposed to reform, it is extremely unlikely that the general meeting of the collective will vote for it. Similarly, a director who is enthusiastic about the opportunities presented by current reform options can inspire the workforce to truly original innovations.

Conservative farm directors can be further subdivided into those who see reforms as a threat to their own personal power base, and those who simply want things to stay as they were. The former often manage the farm in a dictatorial manner; often their skills lie in the web of connections they have built up over the years. Their unique position in this network of useful connections makes them almost indispensable to the management of the farm. However, they are more motivated by a desire to retain control of the farm's resources than to run the farm effectively.

Other conservative farm directors are less interested in maintaining their own position, but are primarily motivated by their responsibility to their members. These Soviet-style paternalistic farm directors often have no *a priori* political orientation about reform, but are simply ill-equipped to deal with the new opportunities. Relying on now defunct skills and methods, they often seem helpless in the face of worsening financial difficulties and breakdown of traditional support. Frequently, farm members note that they continue to elect the director 'because there is no one else who could manage the farm any better', or, 'because he is a good man, even though he is weak and useless as a director'.

On the other hand, more innovative farm directors may agree that reforms were necessary, but not that changing the ownership structure of the farms was the main priority. These attitudes reflect distinctive understandings of the problems which plagued pre-reform state and collective farms. Where some directors locate the causes of Soviet-era inefficiency outside the farms, in irrational directives from Moscow or in the absence of inter-enterprise market relations, others emphasise the internal farm structure and insuperable problems in motivating the labour force and maintaining labour discipline. These diverse assessments of the causes of Soviet-era inefficiency are reflected in the ways in which farm directors have implemented the reforms. Those who blamed outside forces often reacted by changing the farms' external relations while maintaining internal structures. Dictatorial in style, these farm directors are often scornful of the potential of reorganised ownership structures as they reign over thousands of hectares of landholdings held in 'collective' ownership.

Farm directors who recognised the internal problems of Soviet-era-style management, on the other hand, often adopted a more democratic approach to farm reorganisation. In an impressive example from Stavropol Krai, a young farm director had encouraged his members to set up individual peasant farms, with land shares demarcated and registered with the local land committee. He had then been instrumental in assisting them to set up associations of peasant farmers, ensuring that all members enjoyed an optimum mix of independence and autonomy while retaining the benefits of collective labour practices. This young director proudly announced that the old farm administration building had been turned into a secondary school and that he was gradually working himself out of a job.

Interestingly, in the short term at least, the more dictatorial approach of the market-oriented but traditionally well-connected farm managers seems to produce better economic results than the laissez-faire approach of the more democratic practitioners. Yet, to the extent that much depends on the personal skills and connections of the farm director, it is difficult to judge whether this style of reorganisation will continue to produce good results in the longer term.

Middle management and administrators on the farms often comprise one of the most conservative sectors of the farm population. Middle-level administrators recognise that restructuring is likely to be attended by a substantial decrease in their status and authority, at worst resulting in unemployment as the need for complex administration decreases. Because many mid-level administrators are women, the opposition of this sector to reorganisation is often downplayed. It is frequently the middle managers who have the education, skills and experience to provide leadership for new enterprises.[9] On the other hand, recognition of the very real problems facing the agricultural sector discourages many of them from embarking on entrepreneurial initiatives.

Zootechnicians, vets, agronomists, engineers and skilled mechanics are often among the most pro-reform representatives of the farm population. Enjoying considerable status and prestige under the former farm structure, their services continue to be in demand. As some of the most highly educated members of the rural population, these specialists very often provide the necessary leadership for new enterprises.

THE FARMWORKERS: CONSERVATIVES, CYNICAL PESSIMISTS AND LATENT ENTREPRENEURS

'Conservative' farm members simply want things to stay as they are, or, preferably, to return to the way they were in their recently regilded memories of the 1970s. As one woman noted cynically, 'We don't want to make decisions for ourselves. We've always been told what to do . . . we are like slaves . . . if you tell me to stand in the corner I will'. 'Conservatives' also refer frequently to Russian peasants' collective tendencies. Sentences start with 'we' and any proposals that may be associated with the emergence of novel distinctions between people are vehemently rejected. They see the worsening economic situation in agriculture as intimately linked with reform and reorganisation. 'Before', they received their wages on time and could afford to buy sausage; 'now', wages are months late and inadequate for the satisfaction of basic needs. This conservatism is wholly understandable; women are somewhat more prone to conservatism than men and there is a direct correlation between increasing age and increasing conservatism.

A second common attitude among agricultural workers is 'cynical pessimism', phrased in terms of resignation to the inevitable. Changes are always for the worse, generated from above by people who know little and care less about rural populations. Why else would rampant inflation in all sectors of the economy contrast with falling real prices for primary agricultural produce? Why else do other workers see their wages keep pace (more or less) with inflation while agricultural workers go for months without wages?[10] 'They know we can't go on strike, the cows have to be milked whether we get paid or not.' Cynical pessimists *know* that the overt intentions of policy makers are but a cover for their more covert agendas. The benefits of any new policy *always* end up in the pockets of the bureaucrats, be these at the level of the farm, raion or oblast. Frequently, they assert that 'there is no point in trying to improve things, we [the peasantry] will always come out the worse'. Needless to say, cynical pessimists are less than enthusiastic about the potential for further reforms; they have no confidence in their ability to exploit the opportunities presented by ownership of land and assets. This is partly based on a realistic assessment of their chances of success and partly based on *a priori* assumptions about natural injustices. Cynical pessimism is found among all categories of the rural population.

The third group of agricultural workers might be called 'latent entre-preneurs'. Young and more often male than female, these 'would like to take advantage of the novel opportunities presented by reorganisation', *but* fear reprisals. Frequently, they will say, 'I would love to set up on my own, but they [indicating farm administration building] would never let me . . . they would make my life impossible. I would get the worst land and machinery and equipment [if any]. They would sabotage my work, or get me for taxes or breaches of some regulation.'

Others are less worried about deliberate opposition from local adminis-tration than about their chances in the current economic climate. Many recognise that they should have set up a private peasant farm in 1991–92, when interest rates were low. They are clear that they will initiate some form of private enterprise, as soon as a realistic opportunity arises. They do, however, share some of the pessimistic cynicism noted above and are convinced that the odds are stacked against them. Access to credit, inputs, transport and markets are substantially influenced by patronage. Without powerful patrons, the single entrepreneur has but the weakest chance of survival.

Although it is the young men who may be most likely to benefit from reorganisation, pensioners have fared surprisingly well. On the one hand, even the smallest pension acquires extra value through being paid regularly, in contrast to reliance on irregular and unpredictable wages. Further, pensioners have been allocated equal land shares, but often have comparatively large property shares (due to the system whereby property shares are calculated on the basis of length of service and salary).[11] With fewer expenses than their younger counterparts, but equal access to individual subsidiary plots, pensioners are on their own admission faring less badly than others.

Those who have suffered most from the disastrous consequences of economic reform in the country as a whole are undoubtedly unskilled rural women with dependent children. Their standard of living has dropped over the last three years, and the threat of further deterioration in their situation is substantial. Rural unemployment disproportionately affects women, who are often occupied either in unskilled manual work or in low-grade administrative tasks. Any reduction in social sphere provisions, especially childcare, also exacerbates women's difficulties. As it is, many households survive by relying on produce from the family's individual subsidiary plot; the bulk of the labour is female labour. With some significant exceptions, the entrepreneurial leaders of new private peasant farms and other new enterprises are rarely women, although women have for many years been intimately involved in both management and specialist occupations. What is deeply worrying is the extent to which the burden of reform resting on women is not acknowledged by aid agencies, bureaucrats at any level, or by rural populations themselves.

CONCLUSION

Comparative research on the results of agricultural reorganisation reveals that there is no simple causal relationship between structural change and improved economic efficiency or standards of living. Two of the most efficiently run farms I visited had both 'retained the status of collective farm'. Both were run by 'Soviet-style' directors, who were both well connected to the traditional bureaucratic structures *and* progressive enough to try out new market-oriented strategies. They had changed production structures, improved labour management, implemented privatisation of some aspects of production and were exercising cautious financial control over their enterprises. On one of these farms, workers' incomes came almost equally from wages, bonus payments for improved productivity and dividends from investments in one of a number of 'private' on-farm enterprises (a beer factory, a brick factory and a seed-grading plant). In contrast, another 'successful' example was a substantially restructured farm where all land and assets had been distributed *in kind* to individual members. Some joined together to form associations of peasant farmers in order to reap the benefits of collective labour and reduced overheads while retaining the autonomy guaranteed by individual land and property holdings. In another case the members had also voted to distribute land and assets to individuals as 'private peasant farmers', and had then joined all their land and assets together to continue production on a collective basis. Members of this association of peasant farmers emphasised that they had voted to become individual peasant farmers so that they could guarantee the secure individual tenure of their collectively worked and managed lands. Structurally they had 'split up' but the intention was to enable them to 'stay together'.

Many examples of 'substantial reorganisation' according to aid-agency criteria are, however, multiple representations of old-style agricultural management. One badly run, large state or collective farm is 'reorganised' into a number of smaller, badly run partnerships, private peasant farms and joint stock companies. Very often 'substantial reorganisation' is a desperate, last-ditch attempt to stave off collapse, disintegration and/or bankruptcy. In terms of actual outcomes, many aid-agency representatives express a preference for the development of private peasant farms, possibly united in formal associations of peasant farmers. This preference is based on numerous examples throughout the former Soviet Union and on the basic resemblance between the private peasant farm and images familiar to western agriculturalists. Unfortunately, the transformation of a state or collective farm into individual 'private peasant farms' is understood by many Russian agriculturalists, from 'experts' to farmworkers, to be synonymous with 'collapse and disintegration'. The logistical difficulties of demarcating hundreds (sometimes more than a thousand) private plots and of fairly allocating land parcels combines with a preference for retaining existing economies of scale; this makes the adoption of widespread individualisation of ownership and production an unrealistic policy in practice.

In conclusion there are two major problems facing rural policy makers in the former Soviet Union. On a practical level there is a major distinction between emphasis on the internal structural causes of agricultural inefficiency and emphasis on the external contextual causes of financial difficulty. Where those who emphasise the former are concerned with overstaffing, poor labour discipline, inefficient production techniques, inappropriate accounting procedures and lack of market orientation, those who emphasise the latter are concerned with the unequal rates of inflation between agricultural and manufactured produce, taxation, corruption and the effects of off-farm policy decisions. Although each camp pays lip service to the other, it is the aid agencies which are largely associated with the former while agricultural producers are largely associated with the latter. Local bureaucrats similarly pay lip service to both positions, but are often more concerned to mask their own interests in pursuit of solutions.

On a more conceptual level, the criteria on which evaluation of reforms is to be assessed contain their own contradictions. In theory private ownership of the means of production should encourage both more rational and efficient economic behaviour as well as 'empowering' the rural proletariat, through the transformation of exploited, agricultural employees into enfranchised, land-owning shareholders. In practice, however, land reform has done little to 'empower' the rural proletariat, whose interests seem to them to be best defended by inertia or a reversal to past practices and certainties. In practice improvements in the status of farm members have been accompanied by a serious deterioration of their material welfare. To shift from small but reliable wages to neither wages nor dividends is not an empowering experience. Privatisation of the ownership of land and assets has neither improved economic efficiency nor unleashed a well-spring of frustrated entrepreneurialism in the countryside.[12] It seems fairly clear that the contradictions of 'transition' have roots both in political, social and economic structures inherited from the Soviet period (large scale, collective and bureaucratically controlled) and in the uneven progress of the reform process (disparity of prices, inflation, lack of liquidity). Most cogent, perhaps, is rural populations' experience of 'transition', where the 'increase in economic freedom and self-reliance' is associated with impoverishment and insecurity.

APPENDIX 1

Table 9.2 Wages and incomes in Nizhnii Novgorod, Voronezh and Belgorod oblasts (Data collected in May–June 1995)

Nizhnii Novgorod earnings in rubles/month	
Average income/worker	361,800
Industry	453,300
Construction	459,500
Transport	436,900
Agriculture	**156,100**
Social sphere	241,800
Credit, finance and insurance	930,300
Pensions	
Average	129,494
Minimum	73,865
Maximum	152,025

Earnings as percentage of minimum subsistence budget

Average	187
Industry	209
Construction	212
Transport	202
Agriculture	**83**
Social sphere	112
Credit, finance and insurance	430
Average pension	96

Voronezh minimum budgets (in rubles/month)

Minimum subsistence budget April 1995	164,218
Minimum consumer budget April 1995	217,000
Minimum medical budget[1] April 1995	340,000

Average monthly wages (in rubles/month)

1993	26,600
1994	139,500
Dec. 1994	233,000
April 1995	303,000

*Average wage in **agriculture** (in rubles/month; 23% of workforce)[2]*

1994	**99,000**
April 1995	**139,100**

Belgorod: comparison of minimum subsistence budget and agricultural wages

Minimum subsistence budget	150,000
Average agricultural wages	**130,000**

Notes:[1]The average minimum medical budget covers the costs of food, housing, utilities, transport and clothing, plus the cost for medicines and special dietary needs for the seriously ill.
[2]This average wage for agricultural workers masks wide differences between raions. In 1994, the average monthly wage in one raion was 93,200 rubles while it was 179,800 rubles in another. As can be seen from the tables, monthly agricultural wages are on average 25,118 rubles lower than the minimum subsistence budget.

NOTES

1 These include first-hand fieldwork in Belgorod, Nizhnii Novgorod, Stavropol, Tver and Voronezh and collaboration on research done in Krasnodar, Pskov, Rostov and Saratov oblasts.
2 Funding agencies include the UK Overseas Development Agency's Know How Fund, United States Agency for International Development (USAID), and the International Bank for Reconstruction and Development (the World Bank).
3 These were introduced in the late 1980s as a means of increasing productivity through incentives.
4 Interest rates of 8 per cent to 28 per cent were offered to aspiring private peasant farmers and guaranteed by the Association of Private Farmers and Cooperatives

(AKKOR) in 1991–92. These preferential interest rates were subsequently withdrawn, and by 1994 private peasant farmers could only acquire credit at commercial rates (of approximately 213 per cent).

5   This restructuring involves the following:

i   The setting up of an 'Intra-farm Privatisation Commission' chaired by the director/chairman and including representatives from the local village and/or raion administration, department of agriculture or land committee as well as members of the farm administration and representatives of the farmworkers. This commission was entrusted with the following tasks:

ii   Drawing up and confirming the official list of entitlement holders; according to Russian law all current farmworkers and all pensioners still resident on state or collective farm land who retired from the state or collective farm are entitled to both land and property shares. The position of 'social sphere workers' (workers in schools, health services, day nurseries, shops, canteens, etc.) was unclear from the start. On many farms the decision to allocate land and/or property shares to 'social sphere workers' was decided by a vote of the General Meeting of the Labour Collective. This uncertainty resulted in considerable differences between farms, confusion and bad feeling as many social sphere workers felt that they were being discriminated against. Resolution 708 of September 1992 clarified the position of social sphere workers, but by this time decisions had already been taken on most of the farms undergoing the reorganisation process. (Understandably, as they only had three months left in which to comply.) Some farms started the allocation process again from scratch in order to comply with Resolution 708, while others ignored it altogether. This kind of legal and administrative confusion is characteristic of the reorganisation process as a whole.

iii Mapping and surveying the landholdings of the state or collective farm.

iv   Conducting an inventory of all movable and immovable assets of the farm and evaluating them at book prices as of January 1992.

v   Dividing the sum of landholdings by the number of land entitlement holders in order to ascertain the legal entitlement of eligible farm members to land. Land is divided equally between all eligible farm members and the average land share is about 5 hectares per person.

vi   Allocating entitlement to the farm's assets to farm members on the basis of length of service and salary. In other words, although land is distributed in equal portions, assets are distributed unequally to reflect the different inputs of individual farm members.

6   This section is based on experience of working with the UK Know How Fund, USAID and the World Bank. Although there are differences in the approach and philosophy of the three institutions, these will not be addressed here. Consequently, I will present a composite picture which is based on the assumptions shared by all three agencies, rather than on the less significant differences between them.

7   The 'social sphere' refers to non-productive activities including the provision of housing, schools, kindergartens, health facilities, cultural amenities, shops and canteens.

8   This section is based on discussions with bureaucrats and officials from oblast and raion administrations, the Ministry of Agriculture, the State Land Committee, the State Property Committee, and with members of various

committees dedicated to the development of market-oriented economic policies.

9 This was evident from the pilot reorganisation project in Nizhnii Novgorod.

10 See Appendix 1 for wage comparisons.

11 This is only really relevant on farms where dividends are actually paid on the basis of differentiated property shares. On many farms pensioners continue to receive a variety of 'free' services (ploughing private plots, delivery of heating fuel, subsidised utilities), which have often been reconceptualised as 'dividends'.

12 However, beneath the surface of official statistics and explanations, there is evidence of an increase in self-reliance and diversification. One of the by-products of agricultural reform has been the recognition of the importance of individual subsidiary holdings (private plots), and in many cases, an increase in both the size and security of tenure of these small plots. As incomes from official labour become both lower and less reliable, rural populations are increasingly reliant on both food from their private plots and on incomes from the sale of surplus. Interestingly this income is sometimes 'reinvested' in more profitable activities such as trade. A home-reared pig is sold at market, and the cash used to buy alcohol or cigarettes, which are then resold at a profit. The emergence of this kind of unofficial entrepreneurialism is an unforeseen consequence of the reforms.

10 Playing the co-operation game

Strategies around international aid in post-socialist Russia

Marta Bruno

> All so-called progress is reaction,
> If it means the collapse of man.
>
> We are not to be bought by a foolish toy,
> by a clockwork nightingale!
> (Andrey Voznesensky)[1]

'Did you know that in England they have this machine, called a lawn-mower, which they use to *cut* the grass?!'
(Story told by painter Oleg Buryan to his friends in St Petersburg after returning from England in May 1992)

The process of 'getting to know each other' which is taking place between the West and Russia is currently well under way. It now extends from people's private lives through experiences of tourism, friendship and residence to the more public spheres of educational exchanges, business and economic co-operation. This newly found intimacy is on many levels very exciting, having reciprocally opened up entire new areas of interest to both western and Russian economic initiative and political and cultural imagery. At the same time it presents many problematic areas, where what should be arenas of exchange become instead ones for cultural colonialism and imbalanced power relations. As is the case for many other countries, the experience of 'benefiting' from western aid and technical assistance can be a very mixed one. While many of the critiques of development projects stemming from assessments of experiences in Third World countries are relevant to similar ones being carried out in the former Soviet Union, in this chapter I shall analyse traits specific to the interface between Russia and western organisations and attempt to decodify the gap between theory and practice, official versions and lived experiences present on both sides.

Many international organisations, especially the large government-funded ones, are in the business of the production of knowledge and transfer of 'know-how'. Very often they are more absorbed in trying to enlighten Russians with symbols of capitalism such as the market and privatisation than in attempting to understand and take on board the specific Russian cultural context. The result is that very often the outcome of projects, in terms of the targets that these same organisations have set for themselves, are not very successful. Even the organisations which place great emphasis on respect for cultural diversity and on political correctness often miss their mark because they implement their projects with excessive rigidity among recipient groups, the members of which may not share the same degree of open-mindedness to difference. On the whole, smaller, usually non-governmental organisations tend to obtain better results – that is, a more consistent process of cultural exchange – if they have a more flexible internal structure. Their better adaptive strategies may not always be voluntary; if they have limited budgets, instead of high-brow foreign consultants they may have to hire foreign students who have little relevant expertise but who speak Russian and want to live in Russia. The simple fact of having a foreigner who speaks the language has often proved more useful in involving recipients in the substance of the project and going beyond the *pro forma*. Furthermore, projects with small budgets are less interesting to local bureaucracies and elites who may let them pass by without wanting to be involved, making it easier to reach the target recipient.

On the other side of the fence, Russians are experiencing the construction of economic and political forms which are not – so far – endogenous to their culture and as recipients of international aid could be the designated victims of a whole array of western 'colonialist' experiments. But, I will argue in this chapter, this is usually not the case. Russians have accepted the 'given' of international aid and co-operation projects (whether wanted or not) and are weaving them into the complex system of patronage, social relations and survival strategies which are taking shape in post-socialist Russian reality. Many of the glass barriers and obstacles which international projects come up against, but fail to foresee and understand, arise from the fact that, as sources of income but also as loci of power, development projects and international co-operation have been engulfed in the realm of local social, economic and political relations and therefore follow a logic which is Russian more than western. With the demise of communism, western capitalist societies have had a tendency to think they have the monopoly on the definition of social reality (Verdery 1996). In the field of aid and development this attitude is being substantially challenged by the dual strategies of Russians who have learnt to play along the lines of international organisations but also use what is on offer in an entirely different logic.

This chapter is based on interviews with experts, fieldworkers and recipients and on participant observation conducted between 1991 and 1996.

While most of the material is from Russia and on gender- and employment-related projects, some observations come from research conducted in Uzbekistan and Kazakhstan as well as from various forms of interaction with international organisations in the West.

EXERCISES IN 'APPRECIATION OF DEMOCRACY'

In the period between 1991 to the present the volume and extent of international organisations' activities in the former Soviet Union has steadily grown. The days when it was possible to buy on the black market the *gumanitarnyi syr* ('humanitarian cheese') from food-aid packages from Germany are long gone. Now it is possible to go to the remotest town in eastern Siberia and find some valiant volunteer from the US Peace Corps or from the British Voluntary Service Overseas teaching English or some aspect of business at the local institute. Spreading in waves from west to east and from north to south all major western development agencies, large and small non-governmental organisations, charities and voluntary organisations have opened offices, sent long-term staff and initiated projects. Working in the East is the new sensuous experience of the 1990s in the field of development.

The impact of the opening up of eastern Europe and the former Soviet Union has been so great that western governments have set up entire new agencies or sub-agencies with ample financial capacities to foster the enormous potential for expanding in these areas. Tacis, Intas, Tempus, Know-How and USAID Programs are but some of the new government-funded initiatives entirely devoted to devising projects in the fields of education, social, economic and political democratic development on the other side of the old iron curtain. The general aim is to foster a 'healthy' construction of democratic, market-type institutions and societies in an area with enormous potential for western economic expansion. As is the case with government-led development agencies in other parts of the non-western world, much of the funding is ultimately destined to return to western subcontractors and 'consultants'; nevertheless, the spin-off from injecting consistent funds in the development circle has been to foster a huge increase of interest and a hunt for partners in the East on the part of western organisations, institutions and businesses. As a representative of a consultancy firm on a hunt for opportunities in Russia put it: 'We've got to move into the East. That's where the money is these days and will be for a while. All these other funds for western Europe and other parts of the world are drying up' (interview with O., UK, May 1996).

The more hidden, but by no means secondary aim behind western organisations' enthusiasm in expanding to the East is to reinforce the victory of capitalism over socialism. The prime battleground for this 'cultural colonialism' is the former Soviet Union, since its democratic identity and market credentials are much weaker than those of most eastern European countries. Russia has the added negative values both of having had superpower capacities, and of having been the heart of communist power. Therefore, efforts in proselytising must be concentrated in this country since it poses the biggest threat. Despite masquerading behind carefully worded politically correct intentions, western organisations are bearers of a 'fixed' identity (Verdery 1996) and perceive themselves as going into a country with a fluid, confused identity in need of shaping. Democracy, markets and private property are symbols and their meaning is often elusive except in relation to the fixed identity of the West.

The warring attitude of western international organisations is best exemplified by considering the general Tacis handbook on how to design a project. The aggressive, dynamic language full of catchphrases and Euro-jargon is reminiscent of a combat manual. Prospective European applicants should start off by proposing an 'identification mission'. A project should include a number of phases and elements listed in an index. These include: a 'Task manager', 'assessment of impact', 'inception report', 'country strategy and sectoral strategy', 'action programming', 'risk assumption and monitoring of relevant targets', 'flowchart of identification and formulation strategy'. Other essential requirements in project design include PEST and SWOT analyses. Fortunately, the anonymous authors also provide an explanation as to their meanings in a glossary. Thus, it is possible to discover that PEST is an 'analysis of the political, social and technological environment within which an organisation or project operates' and SWOT is an 'analysis of an organisation's strengths and weaknesses and the opportunities and threats it faces'. The glossary also provides a hint as to the use of SWOT by suggesting it is a 'tool used for appraising the partner institution during project planning'.

Tacis effectively requires that projects be designed by applicants along the suggested guidelines. By imposing such a specific and rather obscure language and a substantial degree of rigidity in project design and proposed implementation Tacis is effectively setting a constraining cultural context. To be successful in an application for funding, western partners not only have to write it in 'Tacis language' but need to ensure that their Russian partners do the same. The pledge to combine western experience with 'local knowledge and skills' (Tacis Conference on Employment, Brussels, 3–5 July 1995) becomes an attempt to reconfigure local knowledge into Eurocratic language, expressing a western view of the world. The unspoken rule is 'if you want our money you have to talk like us'.

In defining the logic behind the new Partnership and Co-operation

Agreements (PCAs) the 1995 Tacis Annual Report states: 'The concept of partnership embodies the shared principles and objectives which are the basis for the relationship: respect for the rule of law and human rights, the development of political freedoms including the establishment of a multi-party system with free and democratic elections, and the establishment of a functioning market economy'. By declaring that these principles and objectives are *shared*, Tacis is attributing a collective political identity to former Soviet states built to resemble that of the West. The image of shared values is furthermore an ideal one. By failing to define and spell out what 'a functioning market economy' or 'political freedoms' may be, other than through tautologies or by using analogous symbols, it is forcing post-socialist states and nations to identify with a platonic ideal of the perfect western system which in reality does not exist. In this respect the West is enforcing, by play-acting development games, the same ideology it openly promoted during the cold war.

Verdery suggests that the West is so absorbed in constructing its own role in the East, that it is often unable to see what lies behind it.

A number of the stories of post-socialism have the knights of Western know-how rushing in to rescue the distressed of Eastern Europe. These stories present socialism – quite contrary to its own evolutionist preten-sions – as not the endpoint of human social development but a dead end on the far more progressive road to capitalism, to which they must now be recalled. The rescue scenario has two common variants: 'shock therapy' and 'big bang'. The first compares the former socialist bloc with a person suffering from mental illness – that is, socialism drove them crazy, and our job is to restore their sanity. The second implies that *(pace* Fukuyama) history is only now beginning, that prior to 1989 the area was without form and void. While the image of 'shock therapy' represents Western advisers as doctors, the 'big bang' figures them as God.

(Verdery 1996: 204–5)

In order to begin to understand lived realities in the former Soviet Union it is necessary to refuse the evolutionary approach because, as Verdery suggests, 'with images like these guiding our approach to the transition, it would be surprising if we learned very much about what is happening in the former socialist world' (Verdery 1996: 205).

DEVELOPMENT AND FEUDALISM: THE FORMS OF A NEW SOCIAL CONTRACT?

In this section I analyse the (mis)construction of development projects on the part of international agencies and the ways in which they are experienced but also used by Russian recipients. Most evidence focuses on the specific sector of employment and training in both urban and rural settings.

In the opening address at the 1995 Tacis Conference on Employment the task manager for NIS employment projects outlined the common aims and activities of projects in this field.

> Essentially, they aim to reinforce and support the development of effective and efficient employment services, applying the transfer of know-how gained from both positive and negative experience in the EU – experience gained successes and lessons learnt from failures. As such, the projects are helping to set in place the necessary infrastructure for the matching of supply with demand on the labour market, which is essential to the adequate functioning of a market economy.
>
> (Report of the Tacis Conference on Employment: 8)

This statement presupposes a clear picture of what the patterns of demand and supply in the Russian labour market actually are, and that a homogeneous labour market actually exists in Russia. One response to this statement would be that overall comprehensive information on 'the labour market' is currently non-existent from either a quantitative or a qualitative perspective. Statistics on labour are still inadequate, a fact recognised by the task manager at a later stage in the report: 'the need to gather reliable statistics is increasingly recognised as key for good policy making and this has been included in the scope of some projects too' (Report of the Tacis Conference on Employment: 9). As I have argued elsewhere (Bruno 1996) this depends not only on the fact that adequate structures and systems for gathering data are not in place, but also on the more substantial issue of the cultural context within which data are collected. Initially, organisations such as the International Labour Organisation and the World Bank would use western frameworks to obtain statistics on unemployment; they would adopt as figures for total unemployment, numbers of those registered as unemployed with the Federal Employment Service which, on its own admission, fails to attract people out of work. Only recently have mechanisms such as hidden unemployment or downward redeployment started to be acknowledged by these agencies.

A major problem in designing effective labour market projects is that there is a wide gap between what western donor agencies define as labour market and what Russians' lived experiences and rationale of employment are. Most western consultants tend to read the labour market in Russia in terms of dualism between social partners, for example, between workers and employers.

Structures for social dialogue in many countries of the EU are established and function well. These are based on the conviction behind the so-called 'European Social Model' which holds that economic growth must go hand in hand with growth in social well-being. It is my belief that valuable experience could be transferred in this area. This could serve both to ensure consultation of the social partners in public policy formulation and indeed also at the level of the enterprises as regards collective agreements and the drawing up of social plans to accompany mass redundancies. In Europe we have undergone successive massive waves of redundancy in traditional industries such as coal and steel and have many tales to tell on how to do it and not to do it!

(Report of the Tacis Conference on Employment: 10)

This model of labour relations with employers on one side and workers on the other is not a very useful one for understanding what is happening in Russia in terms of employment. The legacy of the Soviet system, whether one subscribes to the 'social contract' theory or not, placed the state in opposition to the labour force in its entirety, with managers and directors on the same side as the workers. This informal division is evident in the fact that mass redundancies, which were expected to accompany the privat- isation of state enterprises, failed to occur. The nature of the Soviet firm was such that managers and workers needed to be allies to resist and subvert the demands of central planners. The relative isolation, in both geographical and managerial terms, of most large state enterprises made them into social, economic and political units unto themselves: communities that resembled mini-states within the state. As is well known, the quality of workers' private lives (in terms of housing, healthcare, education, recreational activities, holidays, consumption) was heavily dependent on the workplace. Given the structural labour shortage which plagued the Soviet system until its end, directors needed to attract workers, and persuade them to stay, by offering them the best possible trade-offs. Since offering higher wages was not an easy option, due to the façade of egalitarianism in Soviet ideology, this was done by offering workers a wide range of facilities and infrastructures as well as benefits in kind. It was of primary importance for a director to maintain the best possible network of social relations with the workers in order to maintain a solid power base within the firm. If a director was known to have a solid power base within the firm he could command respect and build his power outside as well. Social relations within the firm would usually follow a benevolent and paternalistic hierarchy and the workers would expect to be well looked after by management in exchange for providing a critical mass for the locus of power.

The ways in which the programme of privatisation was devised and implemented did little to upset this model of social relations within the enterprise. The issuing of vouchers to the workers coupled with a workers' buy-out option was a case of '*il faut que tout change pour que rien ne change*'. While the fact that the privatisation programme was seemingly going ahead kept the West and donor agencies more or less happy, Russian industry was getting itself in a Catch-22 situation. Directors and the higher echelons of management needed to appropriate their firms to maintain their power bases, but in order to own the firms they needed the workers to back them with their vouchers and votes. To ensure this support they had to be able to guarantee an extension of protection from the onslaught of economic reforms. Given the bad overall state of Russian industrial production, the pattern described above was hardly broken by the interference of outside bids. Most firms were valuable only to their directors and workers, and not for their economic potential but for their function as social and political entities. Even for those enterprises that were in viable economic sectors, the power relations within the firm were usually so tightly knit that control might be extended to members of the local bureaucracy or politicians who already had strong connections with it and could offer substantial trade-offs in terms of political protection. This pattern was even stronger in agricultural enterprises which had suffered from even greater isolation under the Soviet system and therefore had an even deeper feudal-type structure (see Perrotta, this volume).

Thus, the Russian post-socialist economic system is based on units made up of workers and their apparent 'employers'; so far this has represented a very strong internal cohesion. The duality in labour relations is still very much an external one, with the weak Russian state trying to implement reforms, often in response to threats of curtailment of funding on the part of western agencies. However, this 'soft' (Myrdal 1968) state is at present in no position to break this coalition within the labour market; if anything, it is more likely that structural causes of economic decline will bring about a gradual corrosion of this paternalistic system of reciprocal social and political cohesion. So far, and for the immediate foreseeable future, what Humphrey (1991) defines as 'suzerainties' are very much the dominant reality.

As long as donor agencies fail to recognise this fundamentally different pattern of social and economic relations they will make little headway in effectively tackling labour-market issues and problems. The first consideration they should reflect upon, in their obstinacy in talking about 'employers' in Russia, is a basic linguistic one. The Russian language has no term which precisely translates the notion of 'employer'. The terms currently used, *rabotodatel', nanimatel', shef* and *khoziain* have literal meanings which express notions which are subtly but fundamentally different to the dominant use of the term 'employer'. *Rabotodatel'* and *nanimatel'* express respectively concepts of 'giving' and 'taking/adopting' to work while *shef* means chief/boss and *khoziain* 'host'. The Collins English Dictionary defines the verb 'to employ' as 'to use the services of (a person) in return for money', a notion which expresses a different type of power relations between employer and worker.

Further contradictions surround the issue of the best attitudes to adopt in the face of the threat of mass open unemployment. While the majority of western experts express the opinion that enterprises will not reach economic viability unless they rid themselves of surplus, redundant labour, many of the Russians they work with tend to pursue, in actual practice if not in declaration of intent, protectionist policies. Western advisors, led by the shock-therapy ideologues, advocated 'mass privatisation which was expected to lead to enterprise restructuring and labour absorption by the growing private sector, and also to drive the management of restructured enterprises away from soft budget constraints' (Report of the Tacis Conference on Employment: 12).

The task manager for NIS employment projects expresses the basic dilemma as follows:

> What should policy be on managing hidden unemployment? Should it be forced out into the open? Or should it be tolerated, with action concentrated on formalising and supporting the informal activities which many workers concerned are undertaking already? A provocative question no doubt.
>
> (Report of the Tacis Conference on Unemployment: 9)

From the same Tacis conference it is possible to learn from the Russian deputy head of the Tacis-supported Federal Employment Service that in 1994, 'the forced redundancy of almost 500,000 workers was averted and 365,000 people received special state support to maintain their jobs' (Report of the Tacis Conference on Employment: 19). In this particular case, the Russian recipients seem already to have chosen an answer to the question put by the Tacis task manager.

What most large international donor agencies fail to realise is that their lack of substantial curiosity, beyond reports from fact-finding missions and 'experts'' reports, places them in a very weak position to obtain a more structural impact on their targets and be taken seriously, beyond acquiescent façades, by their recipients. What they should try harder to dispel is the image evoked by Shaban Kamberi, head of environmental protection for the city of Tirana who helped a group of western consultants with the 1993 World Bank environmental-strategy paper. 'Hundreds of thousands of dollars were spent to produce a document that told us nothing new. In fact, the information in the study was provided by [the Albanian side] from existing studies. The western consultants flew in, copied the information, and the Albanians received no payments at all. It's a pity because we really need new information' (interview quoted in Woodard 1996: 54). Discussing a similar situation, a Russian participant in a technical co-operation project spelled out a significant dividing line: 'If we, and our officials, get enough money out of the project, than we keep quiet and say what a good project it is. If we feel that your "experts" are getting all the money and our share is not big enough, then we might start pointing out how unrealistic and inappropriate most of these projects are' (interview with E., Russia, November 1995).

By providing money for projects which are apparently tailored to the Russian environment, but are in reality designed according to dominant western ideology, and having taught a select group of Russians how to apply for them, international donor agencies have inadvertently entered into the complicated network of feudal-type economic and social relations which are *chisto russkii* (strictly/exclusively/fundamentally Russian). The whole sector of foreign aid tends to be viewed as the new luxury end of the old system of state allocation and distribution which is largely still operational. Development projects are almost miniature versions of something similar to the old social contract. The Soviet catchphrase 'We pretend to work and they pretend to pay us' could be turned into 'They pretend to pay us for development projects and we pretend to do them.' 'Ordinary' Russians view their compatriots taking part in international co-operation projects with very much the same suspicion and scorn that they used to reserve for old Communist Party members benefiting from exclusive luxuries by virtue of their connections. Presumably involuntarily, donor agencies are offering, through development projects, new sources for reinforcing the elitist, feudal-type system of social stratification.

BUILDING A MARKET BETWEEN LOGICAL FRAMEWORKS AND PYRAMID DREAMS

In this section I analyse more closely some of the elements which have become common practices in many development programmes, and the ways in which they are produced at the western end and consumed or rejected on the Russian side.

Workshops

One of the common features of most development projects is the workshop, usually held at the inception and conclusion of a programme. These usually require the presence of one or more 'experts', who are flown in for the occasion. Workshops are seen by western agencies as one of the prime sites for completing and assessing the transfer of know-how. Further, they can be intended to bring together local recipients who did not know each other previously.

A Russian described such events as follows:

> 'Westerners just adore workshops. They fly some poor sod in who's never been to Russia before, doesn't speak the language and would not even be able to take the metro on their own, to teach us how to find a job, or build up our confidence. In the beginning we went out of interest, but after a few workshops the topics were so ridiculous, just ridiculous [*prosto smeishno*]! But we all need the money and the funding to continue so we all keep on attending and pretend we are "cascading" and "log-framing".'
>
> (interview with E., Russia, November 1995)

The increasing and widespread disillusionment on the part of Russians with the western consultants seriously undermines the potential usefulness of workshops as spaces for the exchange of ideas and constructive learning processes. As long as recipients see these occasions as a ritual lip-service or as 'tax' which they have to pay in order to obtain funding, they will simply reinforce the artificiality of development projects. Since workshops have the potential to be very useful sources of exchange, as the altogether different experiences of smaller NGOs or even of commercial foreign firms with a greater urgency to achieve tangible results demonstrate, it is up to the western partners to dispel the dominant opinion, voiced by a Slovak official, that 'the main beneficiaries of western assistance in our country are the five-star hotels' (interview quoted in Woodard: 54).

The practice of bringing together in a workshop different groups of recipients who do not know each other can also have a boomerang effect. Individuals in post-socialist societies still tend to privilege those social relations determined exclusively through personal connections. Strangers are to be trusted only if they are linked by a common acquaintance who is also trustworthy. This system operates as much in the public and work spheres as it does in the private one. Unless western project workers have good and close personal relations with the recipients and therefore can serve as a guarantee of trustworthiness, it can be counterproductive to bring together previously unacquainted recipients. Given the usually limited amount of resources of aid projects, other recipients are seen as undesirable competition and the dominant attitude is one of suspicion. Furthermore, intricate cultural attitudes stemming from ethnic, social and gender stratification may also come into play and reinforce negative reciprocal feelings. These frameworks of social relations usually escape Westerners' sensibilities, unless they are project workers with extensive knowledge of local cultures.

Study-tours

Study-tours are another frequent feature of develpment projects. Unlike workshops, they are viewed quite benevolently by recipients since they involve trips to the West to 'see' how things are done there in a comparable field. The person being sent on a study-tour could also be attending a specific course or be given training in a relevant area. The notion of 'development' through seeing how 'things are done in the West' is an ambiguous one, which could fall easily, albeit subtly, within the realm of 'cultural colonialism'. On the whole it is extremely difficult for the western hosts to strike a balance between overly idealising the 'West' and being too critical of it. Excessive criticism can provoke puzzlement, as expressed by a Russian who had been flown to the United States to view the American health system and had been shown all the negative and problematic aspects: 'I have almost started to think that our system is better. Even if our hospitals are not in very good shape at least they are free' (interview with S., Russia, December 1992). On the other hand, excessive idealised praise of how much better everything works in the West can easily bring out national pride in the 'visitors', a feat which curtails any constructive observation of different realities.

A further difficulty with study-tours is that they are viewed as a prerogative of senior bureaucrats who are usually not the most congenial recipients of training abroad. No self-respecting official would allow a junior person to go to the West first, unless they were a protégé . The hierarchy of invitations is usually part of the informal agreement between the western and the local partners in a project, and is used to strengthen the power of local bureaucrats *vis-à-vis* the network of social relations. Since the number of visits envisaged for each project is limited, the people ideally targeted for the study-visits are not usually the ones who go. The more geographically remote from the West the area of the project, the more this informal rule is enforced. In Kazakhstan and Uzbekistan it is significantly harder to side-step the local officials than in Moscow, where a visit to the West is no longer considered an exceptional event. The intrinsic value of a study-tour is inversely proportional to the degree of intimacy with the West. As an Uzbek woman remarked: 'It is almost impossible for a woman to go abroad on one of these visits. First the directors and all the people up there get to go. Then, when they get to the younger ones, usually the men who are friends with the the director go. If you are a woman you have all the problems about leaving your family and so on. The only ways of going abroad are if you are working on a women's project, like P., or if you are the director's wife!' (interview with A., 1996).

Bureaucracies

The inevitable and active presence of both foreign and former Soviet bureaucracies is a source of endless and disparate hindrances to development projects. The misdemeanours of either individual bureaucrats or of bureaucracies as systems were one of the recurrent themes that cropped up in the interviews. A western consultant adroitly summarised the issue: 'You would have to be a visionary to be able to imagine the type of obstacles that bureaucrats put in your way. I think the Uzbek and European bureaucracies are in a secret competition to outshine each other in creating problems for us' (interview with C., Uzbekistan, July 1996). Rather than try to list all the tales of bureaucratic woe collected in the course of my research I will give some examples which I believe to be representative of the presence of bureaucracies.

European bureaucracy is noted for its commitment to 'dis-adaptive' strategies. Until recently it would only refund accommodation expenses to Westerners upon presentation of receipts. While this practice is a good procedure in western countries, in the former Soviet Union it forced foreigners to reside in hotels in order to secure receipts, thereby ruling out the option to stay in rented accommodation which is considerably less expensive. Especially on projects with small budgets this means that a substantial proportion of available resources would be put aside for something relatively pointless.

Another example of inefficiencies generated by western procedure is that of an academic co-operation project in the field of science. The project was supposed to fund a fieldwork season for Russian scientists in an area with very harsh climatic conditions in the winter. Scientists could only go into the field between June and September but the money for the project could, for bureaucratic reasons, only be paid to them in October. By the time the next fieldwork season arrived most of the money had been spent by the scientists on survival, especially since they had not received local wages for several months. Similarly, a project which proposed to bring to the UK a group of unemployed women for a pilot training course could not proceed after the women were refused travel visas on the ground that they were unemployed. Ironically, two bureaucratic branches of the same state had funded the project and then made it unmanageable.

On their side, former Soviet bureaucracies tend to produce obstacles more in the logic of self-interest and gain or loss of power than for reasons of administrative rigidity *per se*. As analysed above, many aspects of development and co-operation projects are subsumed into the realm of insider power relations. Bureaucrats, who out of the former Soviet elites are the ones most at risk of losing their former status, often view international aid projects as their new sphere and source of influence. Especially for projects which would ideally target recipients at the grass-roots level, local bureaucracies present often insurmountable barriers. A meaningful example is that of the 'business-plan circle' which I first encountered in Kazakhstan but have since learnt to be common across the region. In micro-lending programmes in rural areas, western donor agencies require the recipients to produce business plans for their prospective activities. In order to gain access to recipients at the grass-roots level, foreign project workers have to go through the local bureaucrats who, as a bonus, are trained to extend teaching of business-plan design. Local bureaucrats, having learned what type of business plan is likely to obtain funding, strike deals with potential applicants for the loans. They will write them successful business plans if the beneficiaries of the micro-loans agree to give them a cut.

The value of information

Another area in which post-socialist and western cultures manifest their differences is that of information. The production, management and consumption of information crystallise many of the incompatibilities between contemporary forms of western thinking on capitalism and post-socialism. The West sees information as one of the key elements for the healthy development of market-type democratic systems; it is making a great show, albeit nominal and ineffective, of getting and producing a lot of information on all the countries of eastern Europe and the former Soviet Union. Exchange of information figures high on the list of priorities of donor agencies and is addressed constantly in projects and publications. An open attitude to information is the key to capitalist practices such as efficiency, innovation, saving time and therefore increasing productivity. The market is impersonal and therefore a free flow of information is needed to gain access to it. For Russians, on the contrary, information which is public and easily accessible loses its value. Verdery talks about 'the secretive flows of information (except for rumours!)' (Verdery 1996: 34) that characterised socialist management of reality. A free flow of information was something that terrified the Soviet leaders, who saw it as politically destabilising and dangerous and always tried to clamp down on it. For individuals, informa-tion, procured secretively and at great peril from networks of friends and acquaintances, was something that ensured both material and spiritual survival but which should only be circulated with extreme circumspection. Information was power but could also lead to ruin. The legacy of this system is that the post-socialist society is an 'insider' society. Individuals are striving hard to defend the personal dimension of existence against the impersonality of the market because networks and connections are still the only strategy for survival. Information is a good source of barter, exchange of favours and procurement, but its value rests in its secrecy and exclusiveness. There seems to be a fundamental incompatibility in the logic of the ways the two systems manage reality.

SURVIVING WITH THE TRICKLE FROM THE GRAVY TRAIN: GENESIS OF A NEW SOCIAL GROUP

The enormous volume of activity on the part of western donor agencies has led to the appearance of a new social/economic group in the former Soviet Union: that of individuals who survive on funding from aid and co-operation projects. In the absence of systematic evidence on the recipient population of international aid I shall tentatively suggest characteristics on the basis of qualitative research in the area. First, there is a geographical pattern; despite great talk of targeting grass-roots recipients, most western governmental agencies tend to locate their projects (even rural development ones) in capital cities or major urban centres for reasons of convenience and because of difficulties of access to more remote areas. Local bureaucracies further ensure that access to more remote areas occurs only through them. This is a vital practice, especially for middle bureaucrats, since with the changes in the political system, their sources of power and therefore of livelihood have been severely undermined. The control of development money allows them to replace their former status with a new, somewhat diminished, but sufficiently effective one.

A further geographical stratification is determined by the way western countries implement bilateral programmes without much exchange of information and co-ordination. Rival local bodies and organisations will try to forge preferential and exclusive links with a western nation and maintain a monopoly over it. As one official declared, 'We have Canadian money here. When the X [rival] Institute found out, they tried to approach them with a different project. But we told the Canadians they had to choose and since they had worked with us before, they stuck with us . . . now it is going very well' (interview with R., Russia, November 1995). Local recipients also strongly resist attempts to duplicate successful projects in different regions and try instead to divert funds by proposing new, or follow-up projects, maintaining the same partnership. This is reasonably easy if the projects are seen to be successful, since most governmental agencies prefer to work with 'safe' partners whom they already know. This practice has created significant divisions in access to international aid funding. Former Soviet organisations and groups with no track record of previous projects will usually be cut out unless they find a western partner with good links to funding bodies who will pull them into the mechanism. Active, almost manic networking with western organisations has thus become a fundamental element of survival strategies in this sector.

The most coveted types of project are those that make provisions for local wages for NIS partners. This enables many people to avoid the otherwise widespread processes of de-skilling or of holding multiple jobs in order to survive. One of the drawbacks of these types of wage is that they only cover the duration of the project, usually an average of one to three years. This factor reinforces the necessity to forge exclusive links with donor agencies and to discourage project enlargement to other groups and institutions. The majority of people who receive these wages tend to come from the technical and academic intelligentsia, the former middle-layer elite. The short-term nature of foreign funding often makes them question their decision to stick to these projects instead of looking for more commercial jobs. The main positive aspect of surviving from co-operation projects is that usually this enables people to stay in the professional field in which they worked under the Soviet system; this factor is viewed, especially by academics, as extremely desirable. 'Sometimes I think it would be so much easier to work in business. I could stop worrying about getting another project and what will happen if I don't. Then I think I've studied such a long time to do what I'm doing. I defended my doctoral dissertation. Most of my colleagues have left the institute because we didn't get paid. At least I can do what I really like doing' (interview with S., Russia, July 1996).

The wages paid by donor agencies are usually characterised by the same spirit of cultural colonialism. Foreign partners expect a whole range of behaviours which are linked to Western notions, such as productivity or time-management, which do not always correspond to local frameworks. For example, a Russian participant in a project, upon being confronted by suggestions that he had 'drunk' part of the budget, commented, 'At least I drink cheap Russian vodka. Foreign consultants drink just as much as me but they go to all the expensive foreign bars and they charge it in the project!' (interview with F., Russia, November 1995).

Local partners are confronted by foreigners' mistrust in a number of aspects of both work and private life. Striking a balance between meeting foreigners' expectations and managing daily survival can prove difficult, especially for women. One woman respondent, in a fit of considerable frustration, thus described her situation: 'Foreigners just think that Russians are not very reliable. Most of them don't understand the realities of daily life. Surviving is not easy. It wasn't easy before and it hasn't become any better, maybe harder. I understand they are trying to help and so they want us to listen to them, but maybe they should learn how to listen to us a bit more also' (interview with T., Russia, 1996).

What is emerging is a social group of well-educated, broadly 'middle-class' (for want of better definitions) individuals who have acquired a 'know-how' of the workings and thinking of foreign donor agencies and who are actively using this to procure their livelihood. As mentioned above the dominant attitude of this group tends to be one of exclusion of newcomers. Despite this, selective entry is allowed through connections and networks which operate still in a very 'Soviet' fashion. People may live market realities through their networks of personal relations, or else they may dream of pyramid schemes, like Mavrodi's MMM in Russia or Caritas in Romania (Verdery 1996; Stewart, this volume) to remove them from the harsh realities of surviving the 'transition' period. For some, one effective economic strategy is to play the co-operation game with the West.

ACKNOWLEDGEMENTS

I would like to thank a number of people who have given me ideas, material and help, and with whom I've had invaluable 'chats'. Among these, special thanks to Aviana Bulgarelli, Carol McCusker, Elena Fadeeva, Sean Smith, Neil Malcolm, Ros Shreeves, Silke Machold, Michael Brockert and Clive Oppenheimer. Thanks also to Chiara Busca for being there and to Filippo Mercurelli for being such a good combination of encouragement to, and distraction from, my work.

NOTE

1   From 'Oza', in A. Voznesensky (1968) *Antiworlds and the Fifth Ace*, translated by W.H. Auden and others, London: Oxford University Press, p.238.

REFERENCES

Bruno, M. (1996) 'Employment strategies and the formation of new identities in the service sector in Moscow', in *Gender, Generation and Identity in Contemporary Russia*, edited by Hilary Pilkington, London: Routledge.

Humphrey, C. (1991) '"Icebergs", barter and the mafia in provincial Russia', *Anthropology Today*, 7.

Myrdal, G. (1968) *Asian Drama: An Enquiry into the Poverty of Nations*, vols I–III, Harmondsworth: Penguin.

Tacis (1996) *Report of the Tacis Conference on Employment, Brussels, 3–5 July 1995*, European Commission.

—— (1995) *Annual Report 1995*, European Commission.

—— *Handbook on How to Design a Proposal*, European Commission.
Verdery, K. (1996) *What Was Socialism and What Comes Next?*, Princeton: Princeton University Press.
Woodard, C. (1996) 'The Western aid cavalry isn't coming', *Transition*, 2, 15.

11 Survival strategies in an industrial town in east Ukraine

Michael Walker

Ukraine – the only country in the world where the rouble is hard currency.

(Joke circulating in Lugansk, 1994)

The people of east Ukraine are facing both the collapse of the old economy, with its accompanying rising unemployment, and the effects of rapid monetary inflation eroding the purchasing power of their frequently unreliable incomes. They are responding to these pressures with a wide range of survival strategies, from growing vegetables in their garden plots to running market stalls or other, bigger businesses, from manufacturing security doors to putting dogs to stud. Some of their stories are tragic, particularly those from the elderly, with very little by way of strategy and much bewilderment at what is happening to them. Others, who are younger, exhibit amusing chutzpah, and still others show signs of becoming the wealthy class of the future. The overriding point is that everyone needs at least two sources of income; for many, three or four sources are needed to try to maintain a viable living standard in the medium run. For those who are unable, for various reasons, to achieve multiple sources of income, life is bleak and survival in more than the short term dubious.

In the town of Lugansk, where this research was undertaken, there have been a number of initiatives both from the city and oblast (county) authorities, and from Lugansk's twin cities in France and South Wales, from religious organisations, from exiled Ukrainian communities in Canada, and from farmers in the USA. These initiatives, in various ways, have attempted to assist the people and to ease the transition towards the private-enterprise market economy which is widely assumed to be the end point of the process. Thus, this chapter looks at both the survival strategies of individuals and strategies organised on a wider regional and international scale. As far as individuals are concerned, I will look at the strategies of people from various former manual and non-manual occupational groups, men and women, young, middle aged and old, as they try to live from day to day. These strategies are developed against a background of rapid socio-economic change, a distant government in Kiev which produces frequent changes in laws and taxation rules, rapid and unpredictable inflation and the inversion of many of the values by which people lived in the past.

Lugansk is an industrial town with a population of about half a million on the edge of the Donbass area of east Ukraine, a major coalmining, steel-producing and heavy-industrial area of the former Soviet economy. The town celebrated its two hundredth anniversary in 1995. It is only about thirty-five kilometres from the Russian border at the closest point and the population is fairly mixed ethnically, with Russian as the main everyday language.

The attempt, under the 'guidance' of western economic experts, to make a rapid transition from state socialism and central planning in the running of the economy to market capitalism in a few years was, in retrospect, clearly a severely flawed policy: it involved a drastic underestimation of how different the ideas of people were in the former Soviet system, and of how long it would take before people became familiar with the immense amount of knowledge of the market economy which people in the west pick up as they grow up. Thus the concept of 'transition' is subject to criticism later in this chapter, when more details of life in east Ukraine have been explained. In any event, in Ukraine the policy of privatisation has been subject to many, at least temporary, massive modifications. As a western-educated Ukrainian economist, running Enterprise Lugansk, an institute dedicated to training people in business practice, put it:

> 'We cannot run things like you do in the West. Take, for example, the 'X' works. In western terms it is totally bankrupt and should be closed down. Yet if we close it down we put 25,000 people out of work. That is impossible. So it is funded to continue working three days a week while we encourage workers to think of alternative products which can be made with the machines and equipment of the present enterprise. We have to find a way of integrating western business methods with our own culture.'

This attitude contrasts strongly with that of recent western managerial theories which would have suggested an urgent 'downsizing' plan for plant 'X'. The 1994 general election in Ukraine put a large block of communists into the parliament who, while not totally opposing privatisation, had serious concerns about the ways in which the workers are treated and how their pay and terms and conditions of employment are handled in the privatisation process. This is an issue which has led them, on more than one occasion, to block moves to privatise put forward by President Kuchma (who was elected as president in 1994 following on from President Kravchuk, the first president of Ukraine after independence). In east Ukraine Kuchma was strongly supported as someone more likely to take economics seriously as the former head of a large Soviet industrial enterprise, while Kravchuk was seen by many as more influenced by Ukrainian nationalism and less interested in economic issues.

REGIONAL AND CITY-WIDE STRATEGIES

At the city-wide level a number of initiatives have been developed. One of the most important was the establishment of the organisation called 'Enterprise Lugansk'. The origins of this organisation began in 1991, before the final break-up of the Soviet Union. The chair of the Lugansk City Soviet, anticipating the way things would go, visited both Cardiff and St Etienne, Lugansk's two twinned cities in the west, to try to establish connections between western and Lugansk-area enterprises, to bring western know-how and business ideas into these enterprises, and so forth. At this level his visit, accompanied by several enterprise directors, was not *prima facie* successful. However, by a lucky confluence of circumstances, including a British government decision to open up 'Know How' funding to the former Soviet Union, ideas developed which ended up with the establishment of Enterprise Lugansk in mid-1993, financed mainly from Cardiff's 'Know-How' funding. It was headed by an economist seconded from the University of East Ukraine who had spent several months in south Wales in 1992, supported by Cardiff City Council, studying business practice and business training methods. Built up by her initiative and drive as well as support from the city and county authorities of Cardiff, Enterprise Lugansk developed a range of courses in private business practice, trying to mesh together western ideas on business with ideas in line with the values and culture of east Ukraine. Such courses were available to all those who took over small and medium-sized enterprises when they were auctioned by the city authorities and have undoubtedly helped some of these small businesses to keep afloat and to expand. More recently the twin town of St Etienne in France has allocated funds to assist the work of Enterprise Lugansk, funded some young businessmen from St Etienne to assist in the work and also paid for some new buses for the local transport authorities. The head of Enterprise Lugansk has many ideas for the establishment of new businesses. She has also acted as an adviser on business affairs to the local city council. Unfortunately, at the time of writing (mid-1996) the funding source appears to have dried up; thus the Cardiff initiative is in abeyance while an enterprise developed from St Etienne has gone out of business following the economic failure of a major customer.

Canadian Ukrainian communities have banded together to establish in the centre of town a library, with books in English, Ukrainian and French, with a very pleasant reading room, computer equipment and other facilities. Perhaps unfortunately, the strong Ukrainian nationalism which is prominent in this centre limits its attractions in an area where the level of Ukrainian nationalist support is very low indeed. Something like 94 per cent of those who voted in the 1994 elections to the Ukrainian parliament voted Communist; the majority of those I interviewed were in favour of inter-nationalism and the use of both Russian and Ukrainian. Any use of Russian when speaking to the library staff is frowned on severely.

Several American religious organisations have funded pastors and church organisations which offer not only alternative religious services to the standard Russian/Ukrainian Orthodox services in the area, but a moderate degree of social support and assistance to pensioners in need. However, again, most of the pensioners I interviewed pointed out that they did not use such facilities because they were atheists and the evangelical and funda-mentalist attitudes behind such centres were unacceptable. Thus the American religious and Ukrainian/Canadian nationalist initiatives, despite their undoubted good intentions and western funding, appeared to have too strong an ideological bias to be widely acceptable in such a setting.

Much of the Lugansk Oblast is rural. One of the farmers I interviewed had been involved in an initiative to invite an American farming team which included experts in growing and storing grain, meat production, specialists in setting up cooperative organisations and in management of such organisations, plus several others. Their training programme had helped the development of a successful cooperative farm with thirty-five people working in it and more than thirty units of machinery by the summer of 1994, all built up on money earned from previous harvests. This enterprising cooperative was also in the process of setting up a business to import and trade new and second-hand farm machinery with other countries, as they felt that there were few machines produced in Ukraine which were useful for their farm. In the summer of 1994 the manager of the farm reckoned they were earning a total of around 20,000 dollars a year, much of which was being ploughed back into building, buying machinery and paying salaries.

Another farmer I interviewed referred to the help he was getting from the Regional Farming Management Centre, housed in the offices of the former Regional Communist Party in the town centre. He was a retired military officer aged 44 who had only recently gone into farming. He claimed that the Ukrainian government had passed a law to give farmers money on credit to buy machinery and to support them until harvest time, but that this law had not been put into practice. Interest rates on loans from banks were impossibly high, as they had to be in a situation of high inflation. However, he had a friend in the Regional Farming Centre who was helping him to obtain the necessary credits to try to build up his farm; he had come in to see the friend on the day I was conducting interviews in the centre. As far as I could establish it was personal contact with someone with influence with local banking officials that provided the essence of his chances of survival as a farmer. He quoted Stolypin's pre-1917 agricultural reforms rather bitterly as far better than the policies of the current Ukrainian government; he had voted for a businessman in the recent parliamentary election in the hope of a sympathetic attitude towards farming business.

Beyond these elements I did not find further regional, local or international assistance operating at the business level. One further cultural link was developed by the deputy head of a south Wales primary school with an English-language school in Lugansk. With funding from various sources including the Cardiff/Lugansk Twinning Association, she had developed teacher exchanges and a scheme whereby children under eleven in both schools were studying *Peter and the Wolf* as a play and musical and exchanging letters, videos and ideas. This was an imaginative project designed to emphasise common cultural heritage. To date it has been a great success. By comparison with the resources of the Welsh school the school in Lugansk is poorly equipped. None the less, the Lugansk teachers were delighted with the enthusiasm of the children for the project both in Lugansk and south Wales. Funding for the project, however, which has involved several teacher exchanges, has been difficult and time-consuming for the Welsh teacher centrally involved, and the continuance of it for further age groups of children is currently in some doubt.

PERSONAL STRATEGIES

At the personal level I found a range of survival strategies. Probably the most common one, well known in Russia and other former Soviet republics, is that of using gardens, land around dachas, and any other available land to grow food to supplement the family budget (Lane 1995: 204–5). Many of the professionals – doctors, university lecturers, schoolteachers and so on – had access to such land and were spending a lot of their spare time cultivating a range of vegetables and fruit which they all regarded as a vitally important addition to what they could afford to buy. In many cases, living in the city, they had to travel substantial distances to their plots. In one case a retired miner and his wife had bought their land in the 1980s; now it was on the far side of the new, international border, near Rostov-on-Don in Russia. Thus they had to go through *two* customs inspections each time they went back and forth, greasing the palms of the customs inspectors each time.

However, since the wife was about to be forced, against her will, to take early retirement from her job in a trading enterprise they were thinking of improving the house on the garden plot and moving in, while retaining a pied-à-terre with her older sister in her flat in central Lugansk (see Walker 1996: 45–7).

Businesses of various sorts were another means by which people were surviving, in some cases, but by no means all, better than they had in the former Soviet period. Ivan, for example (all names quoted are pseudonyms), had turned his former hobby – hiking from camp to camp in the mountains with a group of friends – into a small travel business. However, he felt highly restricted by the independence of Ukraine. This meant that only a small part of the Carpathian Mountains in the extreme west of Ukraine were now available for mountain holidays without visas and money exchanges. The Caucasus, where he and his friends had enjoyed many holidays, was now in a foreign country and only the Crimean coast and Odessa area were still available for seaside holidays. Given political uncertainties about the future of Crimea, even this was of limited availability. At 40, he felt he was too old to try to branch out into international travel. Most of his business was with trade union organisations, since very few private individuals had sufficient funds to travel on their own. Wealthier people expected much better facilities and wider destinations than he was able to provide. Also, since the Ukrainian currency was at that time inflating faster than the Russian rouble, and he did not appear to have the personal connections necessary to convert the Ukrainian karbovanets into roubles, dollars or deutschmarks, he had the problem that next summer his prices would appear to have doubled. In the summer season of 1993 Ivan had a good business season and had thought at the end of the summer that he had earned and saved enough money to support his family, wife and two children, until the spring. However, inflation accelerated in the early autumn and the money only lasted for six weeks. He then had to try to drum up winter travel business. He also used his telephone for trying to buy and sell products to supplement the travel earnings and, like so many others, relied upon his garden and orchard as a complete source of vegetables and fruit during the summer. Thus Ivan survived, managing to maintain an income which allowed for occasionally being able to buy some new clothes for the family, still entertain a few friends, '*but our table is not as rich as it used to be*', and indulge in a little travel in the restricted area of Ukraine. He noted that he was earning substantially more than his former colleagues still working in the University of East Ukraine.

However, while some businesses were able to benefit from inflation if they were lucky enough to buy at one price and then sell on, maybe after processing, at a much higher price, one problem which could have disastrous consequences was that credit became almost impossible to obtain. Business expansion had to be funded by ploughing back profits. One business, for example, had been initiated during the later 1980s. It was set up to provide a showroom and exhibition centre for the best products of the area and was given a former cinema building to convert into the showroom. During the early part of 1991 it was able to obtain credit to fund the conversion at 2 per cent per annum, while the rate obtainable for savings was 5.5 per cent. However, by the end of 1991 the rate for credit was 200 per cent and that for savings 50 per cent. In 1993 the rate for credit reached 400 per cent a year. Thus by 1994 the conversion of the cinema was unfinished and the enterprise was bankrupt. The premises could not be sold as they had been allocated in the Soviet period. However, by some means the enterprise managed to remain in business with little prospect of recovery unless inflation and the interest rate for credit were to be massively reduced (Draper 1994).

An amusing and serendipitous piece of business survival was produced in the case of twin sisters, Inna and Irina, aged 28, who had both been history teachers in local high schools. Inna had been made redundant in 1993 when her school was changed into a specialist mathematical institute. She had spent an unhappy and poverty-stricken year trying to get unemployment benefit, being sent to unsuitable jobs by the 'employment centre' and finally obtaining the lowest possible unemployment benefit as the education department refused to send the employment centre details of her former salary. However, she happened to own a fine young pedigree dog. One day, out of the blue, someone had offered her a substantial sum if she would allow the dog to mate with their pedigree female. She agreed and was pleasantly surprised by the amount of money received, equivalent to many months' unemployment benefit. The benefit was due to run out soon anyway. By the summer of 1995 she had five dogs and was making a comfortable living taking them to dog shows and getting mating agreements.

Her sister Irina had continued to teach for several months after Inna was made redundant but then resigned because the private bus fare to take her across town became equivalent to about half her salary. She took lessons in dog trimming and grooming and had built up a substantial clientele. Thus, through a stroke of luck, after the misery of Inna's experience of un-employment, the two sisters were now enjoying life, travelling to dog shows, buying in dog equipment of various sorts, and building up a substantial business. They had two fears for the future but these did not seem to bother them much. The first was what they would do with their charges for stud activities and grooming if/when the tax authorities caught up with them. The second was the possible onset of what they called 'total poverty', that is, that the 5 to 10 per cent of the population who could afford the luxury of pedigree dog ownership – almost all in private business – might disappear. Meanwhile, the sisters had just solved a major problem – how to go away on holiday. Their father was prepared to look after the dogs for a day or so when they were away at dog shows but not for a whole holiday. Now their income was sufficient to fund an apartment on the Black Sea coast for a month, where there was room for the dogs as well. These two young women were delighted with their good fortune and amazed at how they and their new friends, all business people who also officially 'were not working' (that is, had no work recorded in their workbooks) had the time and money to socialise, travel, buy clothes and enjoy life.

However, it was very apparent that many people, especially older former professionals, had a substantial mental block against getting into any trading activity. For example Akulina, a retired university teacher aged 59 interviewed in early 1995, having recounted the problems of living on a small pension, said:

'I cannot overcome the psychological barrier and start some business trading. I feel ashamed at the thought of doing it; I consider it to be some sort of speculation, making money out of people like myself. It may be, if the situation becomes unbearable, I may have to start trading, but not yet. I have received offers to sell things, to become a trader of goods, but I cannot step over my internal barrier.'

Akulina felt that there was no point in starting to think of setting up a pensioners association. She pointed out that the government was besieged by special interest groups and did nothing for any of them. She had been watching the debates in the parliament and noted that, when a deputy had suggested that his fellow deputies should try living on the pension for a few weeks, there was commotion in the debating chamber and the Speaker told him to stop telling jokes and speak to the point. Her only other income came from working in children's summer camps, something she had been doing for years and felt was worthwhile. Her interview ended with a poignant comment:

'My only hopes now lie with my daughter. In future, if this life continues I shall have to go and live with them, to work about their house, to work for a piece of bread, to overcome my own pride and dignity, otherwise I do not know what to do or how to survive.'

Serafina, aged 59, and her husband were both retired. She had been a plant engineer, and her husband an army officer. Both had received higher education and enjoyed a good income in the past. In the winter of 1993/4 they had tried to live on their two pensions: '*It was not a life; it was bare existence.*' In the summer of 1994, overcoming their professional reluctance, they had taken unskilled jobs in a children's summer camp, she cleaning and washing and he looking after the equipment. They had put the money they earned into a bank which had promised them 25 per cent interest a month, but they only got 10 per cent which meant that their savings were eroded by inflation. Finally, with initial support from a friend, they had started selling cigarettes near a bus stop. Serafina said they had to sell for a week to earn enough for a kilo of butter, and maybe a lemon or two. The pension did not allow them to buy such luxuries. Again the interview ended with a poignant comment:

> 'I worked for thirty-seven years; and I hoped that when I retired I would have been able to lie on a sofa like a pretty she-cat and watch TV, having a well-deserved rest and walking about the flat in warm slippers. Now we have to stand out here in the cold wind by the fence and sell cigarettes to provide for our minimum requirements.'

Neonilla, aged 43, explained how and why she had gone into the trading business. She had been a construction engineer since graduation and towards the end of more than twenty years' service she was effectively deputy-head of her department. Then, a few years after the independence of Ukraine, pay in the plant became irregular. Neonilla and her husband, who worked in the same plant, had two dependent daughters, both students in higher education. Neonilla had needed more money to help the daughters so she left the construction department and got a job as a lecturer in the Higher Aviation School. Then one of her daughters broke a leg and Neonilla, taking, as she thought, leave to look after her, found herself dismissed. Her husband's mother, a pensioner, also lived with the family and needed financial support.

After a month, experiencing severe depression at the loss of her prestigious profession, she went in desperation to a friend who finally persuaded her that trading was the only way that she could obtain another income. The friend lent her money, bought goods to sell and showed her how to sell at a location near the town centre: 'When my husband saw the head of his department he hid behind me. A horrible thing!' Shortly thereafter she said her reluctance to sell changed. Things went on this way for a month or so, with the friend's help. Then one of her elderly neighbours asked her to look after her kiosk. Neonilla explained that at first she was upset in the kiosk when customers addressed her as 'mother' or 'young girl' (*devushka*). But she got used to it. However, although she was earning a moderate living and found the selling, accounting and stock control interesting at first, she now found that the work, by comparison with her previous job, was both boring and involved much longer hours to earn the same amount. With two daughters and the grandmother all needing support, Neonilla had been forced to overcome her professional resistance to trading and had resigned herself to continuing as the only available means of survival.

At the opposite end of the survival scale were a number of other pensioners. Several, with their earlier savings wiped out by inflation, had no apparent survival strategy other than living from day to day as best they could. For example, Kseniia, a former manual worker with a wide range of previous jobs but no garden plot or gardening knowledge, predicted that she would soon have to go around naked when her limited stock of existing clothes fell to pieces. Her pension was totally inadequate to contemplate buying clothes. She could not even afford to have her winter boots repaired. New boots would have cost more than ten years' total pension. A younger neighbour appeared to be giving her some help, but for Kseniia, aged fifty-nine, who had worked in manual jobs all her life and protested that she did not understand what was happening, why the karbovanets was not the same as the rouble – '*surely money is money*' – the future looked bleak indeed. She was born in 1935, lived through the Great Patriotic War as a child, through the post-war reconstruction problems under Stalin and the relatively advanced economy of the later Soviet system. She, and many other pensioners, some of whom either fought in the war or suffered in Nazi concentration camps, faced either a very bleak and restricted life on a pension, or, as illustrated above, the prospect of long and boring hours on market stalls, the poorest of which consist of little more than a small piece of cloth at the roadside bearing a few trinkets or a handful of carrots.

A recent article (Brezhinski 1996) confirms the above argument. He points out that the real income of pensioners in Ukraine has fallen to a quarter of its value before independence, despite many rises in the level of monetary payment. Thus pensions, which were not particularly generous before the break up of the former Soviet Union, are now certainly below any reasonable subsistence level on their own. Brezhinski quotes a French economist who points out that the Ukrainian government, aware of the problem, reacts by imposing higher retirement contributions on employers. This encourages employers to move into the underground economy to survive, and, in any case, could not assist the present generation of pensioners, who presumably have to die out before any successful transition to company pensions can take place. Since large numbers of people are still working in publicly funded jobs – universities, schools, hospitals and so on – they could be heading, particularly the older professionals, for a fate similar to that of the pensioners, as virtually every publicly funded source of employment is deeply in debt and unable fully to fund their current wage and salary bills.

Several other pensioners had gone back to work in order to make ends meet. Ella, aged 75, who had started work on a collective farm in the 1930s and survived the war, was working part time as a school cleaner to supplement her meagre pension. Her pension was about 50 per cent of the inadequate pensions of the retired professionals. She had used some of her peasant skills, for example to buy jars of tomatoes and sacks of flour when they were at their cheapest, and to make her own bread. In order to have something to give to her grandchildren, she saved any sweets or chocolates she was given so that she could pass them on. Her main worry was whether her relatives would be able to afford a proper funeral for her when her time came. She had her coffin stored already in the loft but there were a lot of other expenses for a proper funeral, including a good feast after the ceremony. One of her friends who had died recently had been buried in a plastic bag with minimum ceremony and with no food provided for the mourners. Ella feared this would be her fate too, with only the proper coffin as the difference. Thus survival of the passage to the grave was her main problem, although she had others more immediate as well. Her son had been made redundant and was currently in a rather insecure job driving for a construction enterprise, with insufficient regular wages to support his wife and daughter. Her skills in producing food cheaply for the whole family were highly significant.

Elizaveta was, when interviewed, in a precarious position. She is a highly skilled watch and clock repairer, who had worked for many years in a kiosk near the central market area of Lugansk. During the approximately fifty minutes of the interview, in her kiosk on a busy weekday mid-morning, not a single customer approached the kiosk. The only visitor was a dealer in spare parts from Russia. However, the real precariousness of her position was the result of a recent decision by the city council to auction off the kiosk site early in 1995. She and her partner, who dealt with electronic watches and clocks, needed 2 million karbovanets (about $37) to make a bid for the kiosk and its site. However, as Elizaveta ruefully commented, when people are living on the bread line a watch is an unnecessary luxury. People could always ask someone else the time. Thus, the income to the kiosk was now barely enough to fulfil the quota to the employing organisation let alone sufficient to accumulate the necessary funds for the purchase. She gave herself until the end of 1994 in her job but feared what would follow. The employing organisation was the former public organisation responsible for repairs to a wide range of consumer durables, of which the watch repair kiosk was a subsection. In 1994 the organisation was deeply in debt and the council was trying to sell off its various special units such as watch repair sites to cover the debt. Elizaveta and her husband were the only two people in their household of six adults who were employed and in receipt of significant incomes, so the survival here of six people was in jeopardy.

Many younger people, however, seemed to have accepted the new situation. Some had funded purchases of household equipment and clothes by short-term marketing operations during the early years of independence when the border controls were relatively loose. Marfa had been buying bread sticks in Ukraine and selling them in Russia. However, the car she had been using had broken down and now the cupboards in her apartment were full of boxes of bread sticks. In late 1995 she obtained a work visa for Canada and a job looking after an elderly widow. Sergei, a doctor in his late twenties, had been selling cups and saucers in Russia to fund a washing-machine, audio equipment and clothes for his family. Now the customs officers were too alert to allow any profit in this. A number of younger people who were fluent in English had found part- or full-time jobs as translators, for example to businessmen importing products from the Arab Emirates, India and so on, or to American evangelists. One 55-year-old engineering professor said he was being supported by his two children, both with well-paid jobs in private enterprises, based on their language skills.

THE CONCEPT OF 'TRANSITION' AS APPLIED TO EAST UKRAINE

A number of journalists and other commentators on the post-Soviet societies apply the concept of 'transition' to their present state, apparently applying this as a blanket term for all of these societies. Lane, in his introduction (Lane 1995: xiv) points out that the term 'transition' cannot be taken to mean that one outcome is clear. He points to ambiguities in the policy of the Yeltsin government and the possibility that it will not achieve its intended outcomes. Sidenko makes a similar point in a collection of papers based on a conference held in Kiev in 1994 on 'Trends, Concepts and Forecasts for the Post-Communist World' (Sidenko 1994: 170–6).

Writing, as I am, about Ukraine where the government's moves towards privatisation have been much more tentative than those in Russia, I have to criticise severely the application of this concept in this context. 'Transition' is defined in the Oxford English Dictionary as 'a passage . . . from one condition . . . to another'. Now there can be no doubt that life, the economy and society in Ukraine are passing from one condition, although that condition in the later Soviet period was a much more complex condition than many western commentators assumed. The question is *who* or *what* is passing to *what* other condition? From the interviews I conducted, and articles in the local press pointing to the rising death rate, I would say that the answer to this question certainly has to take a number of forms: that is, that people's lives are in transit from their previous condition to a significant range of other conditions, and for most of them what they are in transit to is both somewhat unknown and not likely to be pleasant.

Even this statement becomes inaccurate on closer analysis. For a significant minority of the population, those women and men who have managed to get in at the start of various new private business enterprises as senior managers, or in some cases as assistants or translators, a transition has probably taken place and is already completed. Many of them are already in a position to enjoy a higher quality of life and activity than they had in the previous system, and to take advantage of a range of western goods available to those with the spare cash to buy them. They have to battle with a range of taxes and duties, as indicated above, but most seem to have devised methods of coping with them. However, there is no doubt that these people form a relatively small minority of the population. Some people from this sector can buy expensive foreign cars. They are able to have large modern houses built, paying in cash for each stage of the construction. The results of this are highly visible and also audible; most of the gardens of such houses I observed contained at least one large and noisy guard dog.

However, in contrast, most of the rest of the population is, if anything, at present in transit in the opposite direction. Their standards of living are continuing to fall. To what end points, particularly for the older members of the population, I shudder to speculate. The rate of inflation had, by 1996, slowed down somewhat. However, the rapid inflation of the earlier period has wiped out completely any savings that people had in the former system, when many of them had substantial sums, or could, if young, see their way to accumulating such sums. Inflation has created, for the vast majority who do not have access to instant karbovanets/dollar conversion, a society in which people spend their wages, salaries or pensions as soon as they receive them, in order not to see them lose value as the month goes on.

To make the point even more strongly, I shall illustrate it with the position of schoolteachers in Lugansk. During the summer of 1994 I observed a degree of anxiety as the monthly pay day approached. Would the pay be there on time? However, on each occasion the word went round very quickly; the pay was there and the staff hurried to collect it. Later, in the summer of 1996, the teachers had not received any pay for three months. Thus, in late July the last monthly pay they had received was at the end of March. Even if they were to receive their April pay in August, its purchasing power would have already been eroded by inflation. Those who did not have substantial kitchen garden facilities available to them were virtually reduced to begging in order to acquire sufficient food to keep body and soul together. The position of the schoolteachers is replicated in the cases of tens of thousands of public employees, although the miners and those in one or two other essential manual occupations still retain enough unity to strike when things get too bad. Thus, despite the optimism that many of the people I interviewed in 1994 expressed, that things had to get better soon, things continued, for the majority, to get worse.

The city authorities were pleased to have managed to sell by auction almost all of the smaller shops and enterprises which were theirs to sell. Most of them were running with a deficit previously, and as accountancy became more important than human relationships the case for selling them off became that much the stronger. But what happened to their staff can be illustrated with the case of Raisa, a hairdresser in her late twenties with a degree in economics and business. She had been the manager of a hairdressing establishment with sixteen employees in a suburban region of Lugansk since the late 1980s. In the previous society she had planned, by saving hard for three years, to accumulate a sufficient sum to buy herself a good flat. However, she and all the staff were made redundant when the premises were sold by the city. The new owners turned it into a fairly successful 'night' shop. By staying open for substantially longer hours than the municipal food store next door they had built up a profitable business. Raisa and one or two of the others managed to get jobs in a hairdressing establishment in a neighbouring quarter of the town, but the majority of the staff was still redundant in late 1994. Raisa's new job was as a hairdresser, not a manager, and her pay could now buy much less than her previous salary. Her job was still insecure as the new establishment was also on the city's list for privatisation. Many people, including a number of school-teachers and a university lecturers' cooperative in the University of East Ukraine, had gone into do-it-yourself hairdressing (Walker 1995: 100) so the demand was falling rapidly and a further reduction in the number of hairdressing establishments was likely to be necessary.

Thus, for possibly 80 per cent of the population, the transit is in a negative direction for individuals and families. The proportion may well be some-what lower for the younger age groups but many of them, as in the case of Raisa, are in much the same position as their older compatriots. Sidenko, in his review of economic strategies, suggested that the transition to the market economy would take 'at least fifteen to twenty years' if the state went for an independent economic strategy and at least ten years if the radical economic efficiency reforms were undertaken (Sidenko 1994: 170–6). However, he qualified the latter by pointing out that it would also lead to rising unemployment, 'further intensification of work in industry without adequate wage compensation', a shortage of personnel skilled in market operations, a lack of adequate information systems leading to economic irrationality, and a major lack of ideological support.

Thus, if we take Sidenko's ideas as the basis for our conclusion, it must be that the so-called transition will take probably twenty years or more. What the end will be even the experts can honestly only guess at. In the meantime a government short of revenues (since the tax base is declining except in the small and slowly growing private sector) is unlikely ever to be able to refund the lost savings of the pensioners, or to create a system in which middle-aged people can save for their old age in a meaningful and secure way. Those who have garden plots will be able to survive, using the age-old system of small-scale agricultural production with all its inefficiencies, as long as they are fit enough to do so. Many others will die in poverty: life expectancy is likely to fall for some years. Brezhinski quotes a recent United Nations publication indicating a six-year fall in life expectancy in Ukraine as a whole since 1991 (Brezhinski 1996). The latest figures I have from the Lugansk region indicate similar statistical support – a falling birth rate, a rising infant-mortality rate, and a falling life expectancy (Walker 1995: 116).

The problem is that the rising death rate is the product of many individual cases, none of which rate as news value. There is no massacre taking place, but a lot of formerly very solid Soviet citizens are nonetheless going to their somewhat premature demise quietly, victims of the illusion that the transition to a mature market economy could take place in a relatively short period of time. Currently in east Ukraine there are two societies: rich and poor.

REFERENCES

Brezhinski, M. (1996) 'Back to work for old in Ukraine', *Guardian*, 13 May.

Draper, Nigel (1994) *Policy Advice on the Development of Small Business in Ukraine*, Cardiff and Vale Enterprise International.

Lane, David (ed.) (1995) *Russia in Transition*, London: Longman.

Sidenko, Volodymyr (1994) 'Economic independence or economic efficiency: foreign economic strategies in the economy of the transitional period', *Political Thought: Post-communist World: Trends, Concepts, Forecast (Politichskaia Micl')*, 2, Kiev.

Walker, W. Michael (1995) 'Changing lives: social change and women's lives in East Ukraine', in S. Bridger (ed.) *Women in Post-communist Russia*, special issue of *Interface: Bradford Studies in Language, Culture and Society*, 94–116.

—— (1996) 'Ukraine: an emotionally charged research environment', in K. Carter and S. Delamont (eds) *Qualitative Research: The Emotional Dimension*, Aldershot: Avebury, 42–55.

12 Tackling the market

The experience of three Moscow women's organisations

Sue Bridger

'It's hard to imagine now what we're capable of. We sit here and we don't know what will become of us in the next two to three years. We don't know where to turn.'

(Unemployed engineer)

'Life today is making women think, change jobs, change their way of life. If women's organisations could be set up they would get women together and give them some temporary support.'

(Unemployed economist)

From the mid-1980s, the reform process which gave rise to open discussion of social problems in the USSR also permitted the development of autonomous non-governmental organisations for the first time since the imposition of Communist Party control. Among the mass of charities and campaigning organisations springing up by the end of the decade, however, relatively few women's organisations were to be found. In part, this reflected the Party's attempt to revitalise the official women's organisations, the *zhensovety*, under the aegis of a more radical Soviet Women's Committee. More significantly, it could be interpreted as a by-product of the USSR's own particular brand of women's 'emancipation' and the habitual denigration of what was termed 'bourgeois feminism' which accompanied it. By the time of the USSR's demise, very few women's organisations which could be described as feminist in the western sense had emerged: those which had were overwhelmingly the province of women academics and professionals and functioned primarily as discussion and consciousness-raising groups for the like-minded.

As the economic situation deteriorated, however, and it became apparent that the introduction of market mechanisms was immediately and adversely affecting women's position in the labour force, a greater diversity of organisations aimed at practical action came into being. Some of these stemmed directly from the academic and professional women's groups, some became identified only gradually as women's organisations, while others which had no brief to cater for women especially found themselves in the circumstances with a predominantly female clientele. As a result, the term 'women's organisation' came to embrace an enormous diversity of groups and establishments with widely varying attitudes both to western-style feminism and to the emerging Russian women's movement itself. Nevertheless, these new 'women's organisations' almost all had a commitment to assisting women in developing strategies to cope with an unprecedented and highly complex situation.

This chapter is based on research carried out in Moscow between May 1993 and April 1994. It focuses on three organisations which by then were already well developed and apparently well established, having been set up prior to the demise of the USSR. Although very different in both their aims and approaches, all three were united in a common concern to tackle directly the impact of unemployment and the development of a labour market which was becoming openly hostile to women.[1] The choice of Moscow was not accidental: contrary to expectation, it was the relatively well-educated women of the capital who were hit first and hardest by post-Soviet unemployment. The closure of the USSR Ministries, together with cutbacks in the many research institutes and defence establishments of the capital and its satellite towns had immediately put many women scientists, technicians, engineers and economists out of work. As a result, organisations aimed at alleviating their situation had sprung up very quickly in Moscow in the period immediately before and after the USSR's demise. This article looks at the nature of the organisations in question, their aims and achievements and the problems they ran into during these early years of market reform.

On the basis of these case studies, the article then considers some of the issues raised by the development of non-governmental organisations – above all, the question of their viability – in a situation where state and other forms of partnership funding were not forthcoming. In a hostile economic environment, organisations developed to assist their customers in surviving the new demands of the market were, paradoxically, faced very rapidly with the issue of their own survival. The extent to which securing their own position might mean compromising their effectiveness from the point of view of their customers became a central issue in the development plans of the organisations themselves.

THREE ORGANISATIONS: AIMS AND APPROACHES

Missiya (Mission) was set up in 1989 by Tatiana Luk'ianenko from the USSR Council of Ministers Committee on Women's Affairs and the

Protection of Motherhood and Childhood and by Irina Savel'eva, a former Aeroflot employee and Communist Party member. Tatiana Luk'ianenko had become interested in western feminism while studying economics at Moscow University and, in founding Missiya, was seeking a way of disseminating in Russia information about the international women's movement and the UN Convention on the Elimination of all Forms of Discrimination against Women. Another major objective in developing Missiya was to assist in promoting women to decision-making levels in the political, economic and cultural life of the country. Outside the remit of Missiya, its two founders were themselves highly active: by 1993, Luk'ianenko was on the political council of the Economic Freedom Party founded by Konstantin Borovoi and Irina Khakamada, while Savel'eva had just graduated as one of Russia's first trained social workers. Missiya, then, was an exclusively women's organisation with an explicitly feminist position.

At the other end of the scale was Guildia (Guild), or the Guildia Small Business Development Centre, to give it its full title. The Centre was set up in 1991 by Irina Razumnova, economist and senior researcher at the Academy of Sciences USA and Canada Institute, together with a group of fellow researchers. Drawing on Razumnova's expertise as a specialist on western small businesses, the centre set out to offer information and advice both to people considering business start-ups and those seeking to develop business skills, especially in the areas of accounting and management. This commitment to small-business development and the creation in Russia of what Razumnova described as 'the new middle class, the third estate' was central to all of Guildia's activities. In practical terms, this meant a desire to develop Guildia into a Russian version of the US Small Business Administration, rather than any kind of women's organisation.

This long-term goal primarily reflected Razumnova's own negativity about the state of the Russian women's movement at the time and her professed anti-feminism, as reflected in statements such as this:

> 'I don't like this division of people into women and men because, in this country, the men are probably in a worse state than the women. They are weaker: all the best men were destroyed in our country and the women have turned out to have more zest for life and a greater capacity for business.'

> (Razumnova 1993)

A logical extension of this position, however, was that Guildia's staff were, from the first, exclusively female; they, moreover, expressed the view that men were not recruited because they would be unable to cope with the hard work required. More importantly, as a result both of the economic situation and of Guildia's recruitment methods, four-fifths of its customers were female. As interviews with some of them revealed, their experience of the humanity and concern which characterised Guildia's approach far out-weighed the apparent harshness of its business rhetoric. Guildia might therefore be characterised as avowedly anti-feminist but, in practical terms, strongly pro-women.

Finally, and in ethos somewhere between the two, was the Image Centre, founded in 1989 by the fashion designer, Elena Evseeva. The centre was set up initially to meet the new demand for trained fashion models to work in advertising and for image consultancy, especially from politicians. Whilst the demand for both individual and corporate image consultancy grew as the market in Russia developed, the centre also moved into areas far from its original remit. Observing the conditions in Russia's developing labour market, Evseeva herself became increasingly concerned to provide advice and information to enable women to cope with its demands.

The Image Centre's programme was designed to attract young women in particular through its classes on beauty and fashion; behind all of this, however, lay Evseeva's central preoccupation with personal development. The centre's slogan, 'Our information – your choice', encapsulated her concern to provide young women with the knowledge they needed to deal with an increasingly sexualised labour market. Evseeva's openly expressed objections to the tidal wave of glossy images portraying women as 'nothing more than objects of sexual desire' led her to produce a programme aimed at increasing self-confidence and reducing women's vulnerability to ex-ploitation (Staroi 1993). While there may be no reliable data on the prevalence of sexual harassment in Russia, Evseeva's view was that the anecdotal evidence was persuasive enough of the need for information which would give women at least some idea of what they might be walking into.

Image, like Guildia, was therefore not exclusively a women's organ-isation and yet the promotion of women's interests was central to its *raison d'être*. In the light of this, and particularly in view of the carefully non-threatening language Evseeva was using in interviews with the media, the Image Centre could perhaps be described as a covertly feminist organisation. While these three organisations, then, had very different approaches to feminism and to the women's movement, they were all concerned to offer women something of value in dealing with a changing situation. Moreover, in a climate in which so many appeared to be out to make a killing, they were determined not to exploit those who sought their help.

BUSINESS OR CHARITY?: ORGANISATIONAL SURVIVAL AND THE QUESTION OF FAIR RATES

The initial method of funding for each of these organisations closely reflected the style of activity each was involved in. As a project with an international and feminist perspective, Missiya was the only one of the three to receive pump-priming money from a western funding agency, namely the Global Fund for Women. Guildia, meanwhile, was concentrating its efforts on attempts to gain funding from first the Soviet and, later, the Russian government. Fresh from a visit to America in 1989 as a guest of the US Small Business Administration, Razumnova was seeking to establish a similar organisation in Moscow. Only the municipal authorities in Moscow, however, offered some degree of support and even this was nothing like enough for the kind of agency she had in mind. Of the three organisations, only Image, which began as a business first and foremost, had a financial base which avoided the dispiriting process of constantly writing grant applications and canvassing for commercial sponsorship.

It was this issue which soon led the other two organisations to follow a similar path. Relatively meagre returns on all the time and effort involved in trying to secure continuous funding produced a radical change of emphasis for Missiya in particular. By late 1991, the question of what could be done about female unemployment was very much on the agenda for an organisation concerned with discrimination. Temporary or permanent layoffs were hitting increasing numbers of women in Moscow's research institutes, defence establishments and government bodies. In the absence of a social security safety net, Missiya's organisers were concerned that well-qualified women would have no breathing space in which to look for other suitable professional work; they would simply be forced into whatever jobs were available and their skills would be lost. In an attempt to counteract this situation they set about creating their own company, Litt, to offer home-working to women as a form of temporary financial support.

While at first glance an improbable choice for an avowedly feminist organisation, a homeworking operation had major advantages: low initial capital costs, modest overheads, high flexibility and a ready market for the small, everyday items it produced. Litt concentrated on cheap, high-volume, easily assembled articles mostly of haberdashery and clothing. As none of them were complicated to make, women could start earning from day one, while Litt's pricing policies ensured quick sales and a high turnover. An efficient system of pick-up and delivery for the homeworkers and the relatively low costs involved in maintaining their central stores soon secured a satisfactory profit for the organisation and allowed Litt to offer work to more newly unemployed women.

Guildia, meanwhile, having failed to become effectively an arm of government promoting small-business start-ups, registered as a small business itself. One of the results of their constant canvassing had been to secure sponsorship from Avon Beauty Products. The choice of Avon was not as unlikely as it might at first seem: through her earlier work, Razumnova was familiar with the programme Avon runs through the US Small Business Administration to encourage women entrepreneurs, most visibly with its 'Women of Enterprise' Awards. Asking Avon for a partnership deal was, therefore, a logical step: for Avon, it offered the prospect of assistance in breaking into the potentially enormous Russian market; for Guildia, the Avon sponsorship helped with capital costs and essential overheads such as repairs to their premises, help with the lease and the cost of the indispensable security guard. In addition to the Avon deal, office equipment was provided through direct funding from the Canadian government; thereafter they were on their own as a company offering training courses, consultancy and business information packs. Ironically, the team offering business advice to the newly unemployed survived for the first six months simply by not paying themselves a wage.

If becoming a business appeared to be the only way forward in the absence of significant outside funding, it did not immediately have an adverse effect on either the aims of these organisations or on their attitudes towards those they had been seeking to assist. In Missiya's case, their role as a social organisation could continue to be fulfilled not merely by providing employment but by developing an explicitly non-exploitative policy on pay. Homeworkers were not put under any pressure to meet stringent targets, as was often the case in other similar operations, and were asked simply to indicate how much they felt they could do. Aiming to offer a comparable wage to what might be available in a state institution, Litt set its piecework rates accordingly. In August 1993, for example, rates were calculated to allow the average employee to earn 1,500 roubles for a full day's work, that is, around 30,000 roubles per month, roughly the same as a teacher's or researcher's wage. Whilst this wage level was by no means overgenerous at the time, it did at least have the compensation of appearing to be fair by comparison with some other forms of employment and was certainly a far cry from the very poor rates on offer when this form of work had been organised for women in the former USSR. Although most of the home-workers, in practice, put in only a three- to five-hour day, the fair rates were undoubtedly a source of attraction, as the increasing numbers of enquiries to the firm testified.

Guildia's financial situation remained rather more complicated. They offered a range of courses but concentrated on basic start-up and accounts training. By definition, therefore, the majority of potential customers were likely to be people who were trying to organise something for themselves and were not in receipt of funding for training either from their enterprise or from an established commercial business. Despite the obvious dis-advantages to Guildia as a small business itself, the organisation continued to operate on the principle of maximum accessibility. For this reason the courses were deliberately kept cheap and, in addition, offered free or at reduced rates to customers who were disabled, unemployed or had large families: almost a fifth of their customers fell into these categories. The result was a constant need to keep on seeking outside funding or contracts which allowed them to make some money. From 1993, for example, Guildia began to provide bespoke courses funded entirely by regional employment centres for local unemployed women. Initiatives such as these, however, while very welcome, usually took the form of one-day seminars and could not in themselves resolve Guildia's permanent cash-flow crisis.

The position of the Image Centre was very different. It was only through the development of the business that a distinct social role had emerged; as Evseeva became more involved in working with would-be models, she became increasingly aware of the vulnerability of young women in the commercial free-for-all of the time. From an established basis as a fashion designer, trainer of models and image consultant, therefore, she was well able to afford the luxury of providing programmes which reflected her own concerns. Charging full commercial rates for individual and corporate image consultancy, in particular, allowed her to place hefty subsidies on her courses for women. By 1993, a course costing 50,000 roubles for a hundred hours of tuition was being offered at 3,500 roubles to the women who signed up for it. In her own words, 'People who come from firms pay a lot, people who walk in off the street pay peanuts' (Evseeva 1993).

Whatever the immediate financial situation of their organisation, therefore, all their founders were anxious to continue offering a service which would be accessible to as many as possible. All saw themselves as having something distinctive to offer to help people, not necessarily only women, to cope with an unprecedented situation. All were expressing concern about aspects of the 'transition' as it directly affected women's livelihoods – unemployment, the lack of business skills, the risk of sexual exploitation – and were convinced that, if they could maintain and develop their organisations, they could be part of the answer. With two or three years' experience behind them, some of them had very big plans indeed.

GOING TOO FAR? ORGANISATIONAL DEVELOPMENT AND THE IMPACT OF MARKET FORCES

By the summer of 1993, the achievements of these three organisations were substantial. Missiya had set up a thriving Moscow-based small business employing some 200 women at any one time and had organised subsidiaries of Litt in Tver', Riazan and the neighbouring republic of Belarus. Guildia's group of between five and eight employees had put over a thousand people through its business training courses and a further 300 through its extramural programme. Elena Evseeva's one-woman show at Image, meanwhile, while far less precise about figures, had provided programmes and advice for several hundred women, quite apart from the aspiring models and image-conscious politicians and businessmen.

On this basis, Evseeva then branched into radio phone-in advice programmes and launched a new series of free weekly drop-in sessions for women over the autumn and winter of 1993–4. At Guildia, expansion plans included the addition of higher-level courses to their range. In the summer of 1993, for example, they offered for the first time the University of Western Ontario School of Business Administration's 'Leader' programme which had already run successfully in eastern Europe. There were, furthermore, plans to set up a business club which would be able to give long-term support and advice to people who had been on their courses as well as a business consultancy for established businesses. Most of all, they were looking to set up a series of centres in other cities to train teachers of business skills and develop start-up courses right across Russia.

It was at Missiya, however, that plans were most ambitious. On the assumption that the market for the kinds of goods they were producing was wide open, they were convinced that the basic pattern of the firm could be reproduced across the country. Missiya was, therefore, planning to set up several new branches of Litt over the autumn and winter of 1993–94. Still more impressive was their scheme for an investment fund for women. As investment funds to soak up the Russian people's privatisation vouchers were springing up like weeds, Missiya's founders saw the opportunity to extend their work of creating employment and developing production. The idea was attractively simple: people would place their privatisation vouchers with Missiya's fund which would then invest in small or medium-sized companies in predominantly light industries employing large numbers of women. This investment would help these firms avoid redundancies and even, it was hoped, create new jobs. Because the firms were producing essential consumer goods, it was believed that they were assured of a market while investors in Missiya's fund would get a steady, reliable return on their money. In addition, attracting women as shareholders would mean that, in due course, they could influence the range and quality of products being made by the firms. Finally, investors could expect future benefits in kind, such as preferential rates and treatment in the repair of domestic appliances. Everyone, in a word, would be a winner. In September 1993, therefore, Lukan'ienko and Savel'eva held a press conference to launch the 'Missiya First Women's Specialised Investment Fund for Social Protection' with the warm support of several high-profile speakers. They were expecting to report major progress with the fund's development within six months.

These substantial achievements and impressive development plans had, however, been made in the face of increasing economic insecurity. All three organisations were operating in an environment which was constantly changing and presenting them with unexpected problems. They could not, after all, expect to remain immune from the forces of inflation which were ravaging incomes at virtually every level. Indeed, by the summer of 1993 considerable concern was being expressed, at Missiya and Guildia at least, about the unpredictable nature of their overheads; with a buoyant demand for their products, however, they clearly hoped to keep ahead of the game.

Only the Image Centre was managing to avoid the worst effects of price increases by keeping overheads to an absolute minimum. An initial series of problems over premises had meant that the use of the word 'Centre' in the organisation's title was subsequently somewhat misleading. Forced into making *ad hoc* arrangements over space with other institutions, Evseeva eventually came to make a virtue of necessity. If the centre, therefore, only existed wherever she happened to be based at the time, there were clear advantages to be gained by not 'paying a bribe for every fireman', as she described it. Guildia and Missiya, on the other hand, with their apparently modest overheads, began to look remarkably exposed as the climate grew harsher.

By the spring of 1994, concern over the effects of inflation had developed into an unavoidable need for action. Missiya's reliance on maintaining their own transport to service the homeworking operation meant that they were constantly having to absorb price rises on fuel: as time passed, this was becoming ever harder to achieve when accompanied by increases in the cost of raw materials and both central and local government's punishing approach to business taxation. Problems over premises were also creating a headache as demands for higher rent were becoming increasingly unpredictable: in one month alone in 1993 their rent had been raised four times, while in early 1994 they were threatened with a fourteen-fold increase on the rent on their stores' premises. Guildia were similarly plagued by difficulties with their premises: by the spring of 1994 their rent had gone up eighty-seven times and, in addition, they were being threatened with eviction so that the church which owned the site could sell it off to a commercial institution. They were also concerned over the size of the bills they had just paid for a new telephone line and for water charges, while, at the same time, still trying to keep their course fees low.

While all of these questions of cost were potentially disastrous in themselves, it was the issue of the changing market in Russia which finally tipped the scales and forced a change in the organisations' approaches. For Guildia, the change first made itself felt over the Avon partnership. Despite Russia's apparently open doors for foreign firms, Avon had failed to make any significant headway in the Russian market and, blaming both this and what they regarded as political instability in the wake of the 1993 elections, had reduced their sponsorship of Guildia. The team at Guildia could not be accused of reneging on their side of the deal: not only had Avon constantly received free publicity, but the Guildia staff had even tried selling the cosmetics themselves. The problem, as Guildia saw it, appeared to be the particular niche Avon fitted into in the beauty market: in Russian conditions women who might be expected to like their approach would almost certainly not have enough money for regular purchases, while those with spare cash were likely to be looking for more up-market designer labels. Nevertheless, Guildia had responded to this blow by making greater efforts to sell information packs and individually tailored business advice. They had also become involved in work for the BBC, notably in its Russian radio series, *In Business*.

The most significant change, however, directly concerned their training courses. Increasing overheads and reduced sponsorship meant that the price of their courses inevitably had to rise. Whilst increases had been kept to a minimum and the courses still looked extraordinarily good value by comparison with other commercial training companies, the fact remained that far fewer people could afford the fees when living standards had been hit so hard. More damaging still was the disappearance of post-Soviet euphoria. By the spring of 1994, the degree of optimism which was still being expressed only six months earlier appeared to have evaporated almost entirely. In its place was a widespread perception that anyone who was not already in business had effectively missed the boat, and that government demands and restrictions were so punitive that official business start-ups were best avoided. When money was scarce, spending it on a business start-up course was therefore likely to seem pointless. In this climate, Guildia's customer base was drying up while the organisation lacked the funds for an advertising campaign which might stop the rot.

The result was a major retrenchment and rethink for Razumnova and her colleagues. Their expansion plans for centres in the provinces had effectively been abandoned and the business club for former trainees could not be set up. They were still attempting to reply to all the letters they received but no one could be spared to do this full time or to offer the necessary on-going support to the new businesses which their courses had spawned. Trying to think up new ways to keep the show on the road was clearly taking its toll, as Razumnova remarked, 'I'm not optimistic any more. Everything's falling apart. We keep writing letters asking for help because we keep thinking that people will get fed up of us in the end and pay us to go away' (Razumnova 1994).

Over at Missiya, meanwhile, the impact of market forces had produced a more startling set of changes. When Litt had been established, the USSR with its empty shelves and its shoddy consumer goods still existed. In a country which attempted to be self-sufficient in the production of everyday items and expected its citizens to put up with the consequent shortcomings, it was natural to assume that the market was wide open. Litt's lines in attractive hairbands, amusing soft toys and comfy slippers found customers ready and waiting in the revamped department stores and the street kiosks of the new Russia. Within a couple of years, however, the picture started to look very different, as cheap imports began to flood on to the Russian market. For Missiya's founders, matters came to a head on a trip to Bahrain in the winter of 1993–94 where they came face to face both with the intensiveness of work outside Russia and with the alarming discovery that migrant workers in the Middle East were paid even less than people in Russia. As a result of this eye-opening trip they had been forced to conclude that cheap, home-produced consumer goods would not be able to compete much longer in Russia with similar items from countries where no one was interested in non-exploitative pay policies. At the same time, moving up-market into quality goods seemed to Missiya to be unlikely to succeed given the inauspicious nature of Russian traditions and attitudes in the workplace.

These deliberations had significant implications both for Litt and for the long-term future of an investment fund based on the anticipated success of light industries. In the post-election climate of early 1994, however, additional anxieties over the future of privatisation led Luk'ianenko and Savel'eva to take the decision to suspend the fund as they now felt that investments could not be guaranteed. At the same time, Litt was being broken up into a series of smaller companies with very different profiles. Homeworking was being transferred out of Moscow altogether in order to cut costs, while the team which had run the operation had been disbanded, leaving only the two founders in place. Missiya had effectively become a series of small, professional firms offering design consultancy, accountancy and even political lobbying. The fate of Missiya, while in some respects an extreme example, inevitably raises questions about such issues as the interconnection between non-governmental organisations and business, or between personal survival and social action. On the basis of developments in all of these three organisations, it is possible to draw some preliminary conclusions about the position faced by would-be non-governmental organisations in the wake of Russia's market reforms.

SURVIVING THE MARKET: THE PROBLEM OF THE BOTTOM LINE

First and foremost, it would be no exaggeration to conclude that the development of all three of these organisations represented a remarkable example of the art of the possible. Each of them had achieved an immense amount in highly inauspicious circumstances through ingenuity, vision and sheer hard work. Nevertheless, their major strength – the commitment and determination of their founders – was also their greatest potential weakness. To a western observer, the total reliance of these organisations on the continuing efforts and enthusiasm of one or two individuals was perhaps their most striking feature. For these were not grass-roots movements with a broad base of support; they had no management committees or steering groups to spread the load of responsibility their founders were shouldering. Rather, the situation in all three cases reflected the legal and financial status they had taken on: whether willingly or unwillingly, all three were primarily functioning as small businesses.

In the case of Image the significance of this was not perhaps so obvious at first glance; the aims of the Image Centre as a social organisation had, after all, developed directly from its operation as a company. In the case of Missiya and Guildia, however, organisations set up with the rationale of meeting a specific social need found themselves obliged to take the route into business in the absence of sufficient funding to attain their goals. Once installed as the owners of registered companies, they became subject to all the financial implications and pressures which this entailed. In Guildia's case, as an organisation dispensing business advice, this could be seen as either deeply ironic or singularly appropriate, depending on one's point of view. Whatever the specific situation of each organisation, then, this dependence on the continuing energy, motivation, goodwill and acumen of their founder-owners was common to all.

As circumstances became more difficult, this factor came to be of increasing importance. Given their responsibilities it would have been understandable for any of them to feel that they had had enough. Yet the fact of business ownership undoubtedly complicated the question of finding others who would take over the reins: the demands involved made the matter of succession a far cry from simply appointing new workers responsible to a council of management, for example, as might happen in an outwardly similar organisation in Great Britain. Ultimately, the situation in which they found themselves inevitably raised questions about their own personal survival as against that of the original conception of their aims. As business owners there was, of course, nothing to stop them following any path of development they saw fit; in a situation of continuing economic and political uncertainty it would be understandable if they came to feel that the 'big idea' had to be sacrificed to keep the business – and themselves – afloat. In the light of the immense pressures under which they were operating it should perhaps be more surprising that these organisations stuck to their original aims as long as they did.

What all three organisations had wanted to do was provide services or opportunities for women who could not afford to pay the hefty sums mainstream commercial outfits were charging. In the case of Missiya, their business with a social mission meant paying well above the market rate for the work their women employees did. All of these, while admirable goals in themselves, were expensive luxuries for small businesses to afford. As a result, survival depended ultimately on the success of other forms of income generation and the control of overheads. In an environment of high inflation, however, this was extremely difficult to achieve. By the spring of 1994, only one organisation – Image – was operating as before. That this was so reflects its solid foundation in a business for which there was growing demand. No less important were its minimal overheads and maximum flexibility; the initial handicap of a lack of premises and permanent staff was beginning to look like a major advantage. Nevertheless, however successful, the Image Centre was just one small Moscow-based agency offering courses for a relatively modest number of women each year. In Russian terms it remained a drop in the ocean given the scale of the problems women faced. And, given that Image was so much the product of one individual and her particular talents, the prospects for the development of additional agencies of this type and on this model appeared to be limited.

In terms of its commitments, Missiya was by far the most extended of the three organisations; its retrenchment, in turn, was the most dramatic. In the process of restructuring not only the Moscow-based homeworking operation but the fundamental ethos of the company as a business for women was lost completely. The new homeworking company, based outside Moscow, was to employ primarily disabled workers, which would make it eligible for tax exemptions. In the other new Missiya spin-offs most of the employees would still be women but three of the new managers were men because, 'our problem has been finding people who can take responsibility, independent people'. This transformation of a feminist social organisation into a collection of mainstream commercial companies had been directly facilitated by the creation of Litt as a business. In the process many of the women who had seen Missiya as a means of securing their own survival were laid off, leaving the two founders in sole control of the new organisational structure.

By early 1994 there had been no redundancies in the Guildia team but they were actively seeking other avenues of income generation due to the falling demand for their courses. Their situation was highly paradoxical: although users of their start-up courses were beginning to find it virtually impossible to set up a business of their own, this did not mean that the service Guildia provided was either pointless or ineffective. By the spring of 1994, the women who had been on the full-length business start-up course at Guildia were the only ones of the unemployed women interviewed who had found alternative work in a very different form of professional employment. All spontaneously ascribed this to the knowledge and confidence gained on the course; without it, they would not, they felt, have realised that they were capable of a radical change of direction. What the Guildia course was doing, therefore, was making women aware of the relevance of the experience they already had. As such, it was one of the very few organisations in Russia to be promoting the transferable skills women already possessed, rather than pushing them into inappropriate forms of retraining. It was, therefore, a great pity that this resource was effectively hidden in a course which women were beginning to identify as unattractive or pointless.

This issue of the effectiveness of non-governmental organisations is a crucial one. Whilst none of these three organisations had gained substantial, on-going funding from either Russian or foreign sources, this is not to say that such funds have not existed. In the case of western governments, international aid programmes and charitable trusts, considerable sums have been made available for the development of non-governmental organisations, some of which has gone to women's projects. In looking at projects which have or have not been funded, the question of effectiveness cannot be divorced from the issue of the acceptability of organisations to western sources of funding.

As organisations working for women, all three of these bodies were unorthodox by most western, and certainly by feminist, standards. Organising beauty courses, employing homeworkers or promoting Avon cosmetics and taking a dim view of the women's movement, are not positions with which many women's organisations in the West would feel naturally at home. Yet the pragmatism which led these Russian organisations down these routes proved highly effective in a complex and very specific set of circumstances. The unthreatening and non-politicised approach of offering beauty courses attracted women who would never have considered attending a programme on sexual harassment. Money from Avon cosmetics allowed Guildia to offer free training to women on low incomes, while Missiya's homeworking rapidly provided essential earnings for women who had no access to state benefits. Women who used the services of these organisations often saw them as providing something unique and extremely valuable, as the following characteristic comments illustrate:

'It's necessary information for Russian young women. No one else tells them about this.'

(Final year student on the Image programme)

'I dread to think what would have happened if I'd been made redundant and this firm hadn't existed. Where would I have gone? No one would have been interested in me at my age.'

(Redundant computer programmer at Missiya)

'I'm very glad I went to the course at Guildia, it helped me a lot . . . It helped me understand my own abilities.'

(Unemployed doctor, now business manager)

Organisations which, at first sight, might appear to espouse unpromising attitudes were clearly highly effective in providing something women felt they needed, even if this turned out to be something different from what they were expecting.

This question of expectations is important, not only for users of services in Russia, but also for potential partners in the West. The widespread assumption that Russia was embarking on a process of reform which would rapidly transform the country into a market-based liberal democracy undoubtedly led to the funding of many ill-conceived, 'quick-fix' schemes. The sheer speed with which bids have been expected to be put together and funding decisions made by western agencies has inevitably militated against proper research and evaluation either of the cultural context or of the effectiveness of prospective Russian partners. In addition, the frameworks of the funding process itself may have been set up to serve agendas quite different from that of assisting development in Russia. The insistence in some EU initiatives that bids be put together by partner agencies in two member states as well as with Russian partners is a case in point; it is a factor which undoubtedly increases complexity and inhibits flexibility in getting projects under way. Finally, the introduction of competitive tendering, especially when it is dominated by prominent commercial interests, may further cloud the picture.[2] When both bidding and decision making involves agencies with limited experience of the field in which they are operating, the easy option is to find Russian partners who 'speak your language' – literally, in some cases – irrespective of whether they can actually deliver. All of this underpins a system in which all too often ready-made western models have been imported for immediate application irrespective of their appropriateness in local conditions. Applied to the case of women's organisations, this may go some way to explain the plethora of western-funded feminist data bases and information networks and, simultaneously, a relative lack of western interest in local initiatives with a track record of service provision.

Finally, the problems experienced in keeping organisations afloat, such as those described in this chapter, stem most obviously from the lack of a tradition of service-provision by non-governmental organisations. Not only has the political and legal framework been lacking but, most importantly, there has been no history of channelling public funding through such projects. Those, like the founders of these three organisations, who were quick to see a niche for NGOs in the changing political and economic climate were often met with either incomprehension or the ethics of the closed shop on the part of those within Russia whom they approached for support. As an established tradition of fundraising has also been absent, organisations such as these have been obliged to take a very different course from the one they at first envisaged. In the chequered progress of 'transition' the demise of large-scale organisations such as those described in this chapter may go largely unremarked, yet, in current conditions, they will not be easily replaced; without them, women have been left just a little more out in the cold than before.

NOTES

1 The research on which this chapter is based was generously funded by the Leverhulme Trust. A more detailed description of both the research itself and the three organisations discussed here can be found in Bridger, Kay and Pinnick (1996). The English spellings of the organisations' names are those which they themselves preferred.
2 For an interesting discussion of this process from the perspective of the British division of an international NGO, see David Wright (1995).

REFERENCES

Bridger, S., Kay, R. and Pinnick, K. (1996) *No More Heroines? Russia, Women and the Market*, London: Routledge.
Evseeva, E. (1993) Personal interview, 9 June.
Razumnova, I. (1993) Personal interview, 4 June.
—— (1994) Personal interview, 24 March.
Staroi, V. (1993) 'Zhdite siurprizov', *Klubok* 1.
Wright, D. (1995) 'The role of international NGOs in assisting the realisation of children's rights', Paper presented at the Vth World Congress of Central and East European Studies, Warsaw.

Index